DATE DUE

Civil Wrongs

A Publication of the Center for Self-Governance

CIVIL WRONGS

WHAT WENT WRONG
WITH AFFIRMATIVE ACTION

Steven Yates

ICS PRESS
Institute for Contemporary Studies
San Francisco, CA

This book is a publication of the Center for Self-Governance, dedicated to the study of self-governing institutions. The Center is affiliated with the Institute for Contemporary Studies, a nonpartisan, nonprofit, public policy research organization. The analyses, conclusions, and opinions expressed in ICS Press publications are those of the authors and not necessarily those of the Institute or of its officers, its directors, or others associated with, or funding, its work.

Inquiries, book orders, and catalog requests should be addressed to ICS Press, 720 Market Street, San Francisco, CA 94102. (415) 981-5353. Fax (415) 986-4878. To order, call toll free in the contiguous United States: (800) 326-0263.

5 4 3 2 1

Library of Congress Cataloging-in-Publication Data

Yates, Steven.
    Civil wrongs : what went wrong with affirmative action/Steven Yates.
        p.   cm.
    Includes bibliographical references and index.
    ISBN 1-55815-292-X
    1. Affirmative action programs—United States.
2. Minorities—Employment—Government policy—United
States.   3. Multiculturalism—United States.   I. Title.
HF5549.5.A34Y38   1994
323.1'73—dc20   94-21400
                                                            CIP

To TIBOR R. MACHAN
for igniting the spark

Table of Contents

A Note from the Publisher

Civil Wrongs is an important book that will advance and deepen our political discussion regarding how we as individuals and communities in America relate to one another. In examining affirmative action, Steven Yates takes on a key legal and social institution, one whose structure can significantly influence our modes of association and affect how we as a people are able to create social, economic, and political wealth.

Part of the problem in the debate about affirmative action is that the dialogue takes place within a distorted set of assumptions about democracy and the nation state, assumptions underpinned by a very weak notion of citizenship and by confusion about how strong and productive people develop. The American experiment in self-governance began with a different set of ideas—a more vigorous philosophy of citizenship and of confidence in the capacities of men and women to act on their own behalf. How to build and sustain the habits of reflection and choice essential to self-governance is a critical question: If men and women are to govern the institutions that affect their lives, the issue at hand becomes how to protect access to the decision-making process, rather than how to impose reparations.

Despite its noble goal of producing an integrationist society, affirmative action fails because it ultimately reflects the mindset it nominally seeks to destroy. Racial entitlement in no way promotes racial advancement. Racial advancement can only occur through the self-governing habits of the individuals who make up that race.

One of the moral imperatives of a self-governing system is a set of institutions and organizations that assists in the development of each person's capacity to be self-governing in all spheres of life. The cardinal principle of such a system is that individuals are the primary producers of most of the goods that benefit themselves and their families, businesses, and communities. To develop these capacities requires great reflection and effort that can only be productive when based on what is genuine and fundamental. To rob individuals of these experiences is to rob them of the very stuff from which true and growth-inducing experiences come.

The fact that most of the conflict about affirmative action surfaces in our universities and in the job market is symptomatic of a much greater problem. We are moving toward a centralization of American life where children grow up in large bureaucratic systems without seeing their parents govern their own lives. Consequently, active participation in the fundamental decisions that affect our communities, schools, and local governments will continue to decline. Ultimately, confronting the grave moral damage visited upon our society will require rebuilding the fabric of our civil institutions so they are once again conducive to the advancement of self-governing individuals.

ROBERT B. HAWKINS, JR.
President
Institute for Contemporary Studies

Foreword

There can never be too much intellectual ammunition in the defense of individual liberty, economic freedom, voluntary pluralism and social civility against collectivistic programs like affirmative action. This contribution by Professor Steven Yates is a welcomed addition.

As Professor Yates documents throughout this very insightful and carefully analyzed work, the list of indictments against affirmative action is a long one. It has not benefitted those for whom it was intended. It compromises standards of excellence throughout the economy and the educational system. It undermines the reliance on merit as the standard for college admission, hiring and promoting employees, and awarding contracts. It contributes to the creation of a culture of mediocrity in which efforts by individual minority group members to succeed on their own merits are penalized. It reinforces the stereotype of minority group members as people unable to make it on their own. It adds fuel to racial tensions by incurring the resentment of those not in protected groups. It corrupts the language of public discourse by politicizing such terms as minority, equal opportunity, discrimination, racism, sexism, so that they mean whatever anybody wants them to mean. Its set-aside programs for business enterprises run by minorities, women and the disabled are rife with corruption and fraud. It fosters anti-intellectual scholarship that rejects standards of objectivity, dispassionate analysis, analytical clarity, and the search for universal intellectual and moral truths. Indeed it relies on such scholarship to promote its ideological rationalization.

To focus on what went wrong with affirmative action is to focus on such dysfunctional consequences as those just mentioned. This is the approach that many of its critics take. Were Professor Yates's analysis limited to documenting the dysfunctions of affirmative action it would not add much to what has already been noted by numerous critics. What distinguishes his effort is that he shows not only what went wrong with affirmative action, but also why it could not and never can go right. His thesis is that affirmative action is dysfunctional because it is wrong, and it is wrong because it rests on false premises. It is also wrong because it is unjust: it violates the equal protection clause of the Fourteenth Amendment of the Constitution; it violates the basic right of individuals to their own lives and the products of their labor.

To understand *why* affirmative action's quest for equality of condition was doomed to fail, Yates uncovers the mistaken premises that are its philosophical underpinnings: collectivism, sociocultural determinism, the psychology of victimization, intergroup egalitarianism, and elitism. Together these perspectives constitute what he calls "the philosophy of social engineering." Affirmative action is an expression of that philosophy's "fatal conceit" that any one person or committee of persons or government can know what is good for an entire society. The social engineering approach assumes that injustice can be remedied by large-scale social planning. But, as Yates points out, it results in the concentration of power of the state, the discouragement of achievement, a dysfunctional educational system and economy, increased intergroup conflict, declining standard of living, and a culture of dependence. However, such consequences are not what makes social engineering wrong; it is wrong because its deterministic view of human nature, its organicist view of society, and its positivistic approach to science have no basis in fact.

Professor Yates's answer to the philosophy of social engineering is "the philosophy of social spontaneity." He draws this perspective from a synthesis of ideas developed by conservative, libertarian, and individualist scholars who have demonstrated the invalidity of the premises of social engineering and provided empirical evidence of its threat to individual liberty and the improved life chances of minorities. The philosophy of social spontaneity consists of individualism, the conception of individuals as autonomous acting agents, individual liberty, limited government, reliance on voluntary associations and private organizations for the amelioration of social problems, and the reassertion of the concept of property rights. The philosophy of social spontaneity is the only rational and just alternative to the philosophy of social engineering; it is the only perspective that can adequately challenge the false premises of policies like affirmative action.

Many critics of affirmative action develop analyses in answer to the question, *Cui bono?*—who benefits? It is a useful question when unanchored in notions of Marxian material determinism. Much can be learned by relating a given policy to a group's material purposes of social action—i.e., its interests. Identifying whose interests are served by a given policy can tell us much about the measure's potential sources of legitimacy—that is, who is likely to view it as reasonable—but we cannot deduce from that information whether the policy is valid or not. Some examinations of affirmative action ask whether its benefits outweigh its social costs. But such cost-benefit analyses are inadequate responses to affirmative action's erosion of our intellectual, political and economic freedom.

Critics who merely observe that more is lost by affirmative action than gained are ill-equipped to answer proponents who justify it in terms of how many beneficiaries it can claim. The number of beneficiaries a policy can claim neither validates nor justifies it. Critics of affirmative action must do more than show that it harms more people than it helps. They must evaluate its correspondence with reality and scrutinize its moral justification, as Steven Yates does.

In the face of egalitarianism's massive onslaught on free speech, dispassionate inquiry, and scholarly merit, political scientist Aaron Wildavsky recently wrote in *The Rise of Radical Egalitarianism* that the only appropriate role for scholars is opposition. By "opposition," he meant: "You must say it is wrong. It's not that you can't do it; it's that you ought not do it. It is fundamentally wrong to have quotas. Positive discrimination is fundamentally wrong." That is the message of *Civil Wrongs*. In stating that affirmative action is wrong and showing why it is wrong, Steven Yates's analysis certainly exemplifies the serious opposition to affirmative action that no scholar of integrity should want to avoid. But he does more than oppose; he also makes a significant contribution to the philosophical defense of individual liberty, individual achievement, and individual responsibility, and he shows why only the institutionalization of these principles can check the spread of social engineering, save our civilization, and justly improve the life chances of us all.

ANNE WORTHAM
Normal, Illinois

Associate Professor of Sociology, Illinois State University, and continuing visiting scholar, Hoover Institution, Stanford University

Acknowledgments

This book went through a number of stages and owes a great deal to many individuals and institutions. The earliest essay that eventually evolved into a precursor of *Civil Wrongs* was supported by an F. Leroy Hill Summer Fellowship from the Institute for Humane Studies at George Mason University. I am grateful to Tibor Machan, Bob Andelsen, and Scott Kleiner for their original support for my first venture into what was then virtually terra incognita. I would also like to thank Christine Blundell of the Institute for her support and assistance throughout the term of that fellowship.

Two essays written for different purposes came to be different steps along the path that led to *Civil Wrongs.* The first was "Affirmative Action: The New Road to Serfdom," which appeared in the Foundation of Economic Education's journal *The Freeman* when it was edited by Brian Summers (December 1990). Discussions with him and Beth Hoffman greatly improved this article.

"New Road" then came to the attention of Diane Carol Bast of the Heartland Institute, and the result was a policy study, *Beyond Affirmative Action* (September 1991), where my earliest version of the contrast between the Philosophies of Social Engineering and Social Spontaneity was cashed out. I am extremely grateful to Diane Bast for the detailed information about the effects of set-asides on the construction industry and for numerous suggestions of one sort or another she has provided along the way. Her final remarks greatly improved Chapter 1.

Grateful acknowledgment is also due the CBS news magazine *60 Minutes* for their kind permission to reprint crucial passages from the reprint of their segment "The Numbers Game," first broadcast March 24, 1991.

I would also like to thank the following either for criticisms of earlier work or for assistance of one form or another that contributed to bringing about a better *Civil Wrongs:* Ellen Frankel Paul (who commented on an early version), Frederick R. Lynch (who read the entire manuscript of another version and offered useful suggestions), and Glenn Ricketts (for information about the Madison Plan and similar items); also Ken Masugi, Greg Johnson, Tom Shull, William Hunter, Steven Horowitz, Ray Barker, David Osterfeld, Walter Williams, Anne Wortham, Dinesh D'Souza, Daniel Garcia-Diaz, and M. Vali Raza for conversations, correspondence, criticisms, suggestions, and bits of crucial information supplied along the way.

I am extremely grateful to Gus di Zerega, former Resident Scholar at the Institute for Contemporary Studies, and now Senior Research Associate, Foundation for Research on Economics and the Environment, for his detailed comments on an earlier draft of this manuscript. Acquisitions Editor Anne Wollaeger of ICS Press made numerous substantive and stylistic suggestions, which took the manuscript in the direction it needed to go. Finally, I am grateful to Patricia Summerside, Michael Kloess, and Jan Ponyicsanyi for their editing, which greatly improved the clarity and accessibility of this work.

Lastly, I wish to thank my parents, William C. Yates, Jr., and Alice Yates, for their continued support and encouragement (and sometimes necessary prodding) during what often seemed a dreary and thankless task.

It goes without saying that the conclusions reached and arguments presented, including any remaining errors, excesses, or inaccuracies, are solely my own responsibility, and not that of any individual or institution named above, nor any university or philosophy department with which I have been affiliated during the three years it took to write and revise *Civil Wrongs.*

—S. Y.

The Long Road to a
Colorblind Legal System

In 1776 Thomas Jefferson wrote in the Declaration of Independence, "We hold these truths to be self-evident, that all men are created equal, that they are endowed by their Creator with certain unalienable rights, and that among these are life, liberty, and the pursuit of happiness."

These ideals, the touchstone of American freedom and political democracy, have proved difficult to practice consistently. Before the Civil War, the generally accepted status of black Americans was that of slaves, a fundamentally inferior kind of human being. Women, too, were regarded as intellectually inferior to men and denied the right to vote. In 1857, the U.S. Supreme Court's decision in *Dred Scott v. Samford* established the inferiority of blacks to whites in legal precedent.

After the abolition of slavery, laws were passed whose effect was to keep the majority of blacks in a permanent lower-caste status. In 1896, *Plessy v. Ferguson* called for "separate but equal" facilities, opening the floodgates to government-sanctioned segregation.

Gradually during the 1950s and 1960s our nation attempted to repudiate this past. *Brown v. Board of Education of Topeka, Kansas* was decided in 1956; the Civil Rights Act of 1964 and the Voting

Rights Act of 1965 were signed; President Lyndon Johnson's 1965 Executive Order 11246 extended the Civil Rights Act's provisions. The feminist movement opened up new opportunities for women by vigorously promoting the view that within limits, "anything a man can do, a woman can do." Nondiscrimination on the basis of involuntary group characteristics became a widely accepted social goal.

Unfortunately, this goal was soon sabotaged by court interpretations and administrative policies that did the exact opposite. Instead of being replaced by genuinely colorblind and genderblind practices, legally sanctioned discrimination against blacks, other minorities, and women came to be replaced by legally sanctioned discrimination against white men.

The first use of "affirmative action" in civil rights legislation occurred in John F. Kennedy's Executive Order 10925, which ordered "affirmative action to ensure that applicants are employed, and that employees are treated during employment, without regard to their race, creed, color, or national origin."[1] The better-known EO 11246 repeated much of this verbatim ("creed" became "religion," and "sex" was added as a new category). Next, the Civil Rights Act of 1964 mandated that the courts may "order such affirmative action as may be appropriate" to deal with discriminatory practices.[2] It appears that no specific policy was meant, merely a range of loosely described activities designed to remedy demonstrable cases of bias in hiring and promotion.

The term stuck. Over the next several years affirmative action programs appeared everywhere, and problems quickly emerged. The Civil Rights Act of 1964 explicitly disavowed preferential treatment to achieve a preset ratio or correct a perceived imbalance:

> Nothing contained in this title shall be interpreted to require any employer, employment agency, labor organization, or joint labor-management committee subject to this title to grant preferential treatment to any individual or to any group because of the race, color, religion, sex, or national origin of such individual or group on account of an imbalance which may exist with respect to the total number or percentage of persons of any race, color, religion, sex, or national origin employed by any employer, referred or classified for employment by any employment agency or labor organization, admitted

to membership or classified by any labor organization, or admitted to, or employed in, any apprenticeship or other training program, in comparison with the total number or percentage of persons of such race, color, religion, sex, or national origin in any community, State, section, or other area, or in the available work force in any community, State, section, or other area.[3]

This section of the Civil Rights Act has been, and continues to be, massively violated—in the name of civil rights.

The Short Life of a Colorblind Legal System

New interpretations of the Civil Rights Act emphasized the supposed *spirit* rather than the *letter* of the law. In practice, such interpretations required taking group membership into account as a positive factor (the antipreferential clause in the Civil Rights Act notwithstanding). According to advocates, race-conscious or preferential policies had to be adopted to counteract both the effects of past discrimination and the remaining tendencies by white male employers to discriminate in "subtle" ways. Some advocates of preferential policies frankly admit that they constitute reverse discrimination, but maintain that this is justified because white men have long had advantages and privileges; thus, mere nondiscrimination is inadequate to "balance the books."

In the late 1960s, a formal rationale for "positive discrimination" emerged in the doctrine of "disparate impact." By 1969, quotas were established in the construction industry by the Department of Labor's revised Philadelphia Plan. This plan introduced "goals" and "timetables" for achieving greater representation of minorities "under-utilized" in various job categories. (It was assumed that any statistical disparity between minority employment in these categories and their overall percentage of the population represented "under-utilization.")

In 1970, the Office of Federal Contract Compliance issued Order No. 4 extending similar provisions to other occupations. As a result, the operative meaning of the term *discrimination* expanded until it simply designated a lack of government-approved statistical parity.

In 1971, the Supreme Court gave the "disparate impact" doctrine legal sanction in *Griggs v. Duke Power Co.* This decision required that employers prove the "business necessity" of employment tests that resulted in statistical disparity. The crucial passage was the following:

> What is required by Congress is the removal of artificial, arbitrary, and unnecessary barriers to employment when the barriers operate invidiously to discriminate on the basis of racial or other impermissible classification.
>
> Congress has now provided that tests or criteria for employment or promotion may not provide equality of opportunity merely in the sense of the fabled offer of milk to the stork and the fox. On the contrary, Congress has now required that *the posture and condition of the job-seeker be taken into account.* It has—to resort again to the fable—*provided that the vessel in which the milk is proffered be one all seekers can use. The [Civil Rights Act of 1964] proscribes not only overt discrimination but also practices that are fair in form but discriminatory in operation. The touchstone is business necessity. If an employment practice which operates to exclude Negroes cannot be shown to be related to job performance, the practice is prohibited.*[4]

Here we see how the term *discrimination* had shifted in meaning. Not only persons but also employment literacy tests and other such practices could discriminate if they resulted in something other than politically approved parity.

Many employers were therefore faced with a choice between: illegal "covert discrimination"; racenorming (different standards for different races); or an across-the-board lowering of standards. The antipreferential clause in the Civil Rights Act of 1964 was effectively rendered null and void without being openly repealed. An era of Orwellian evasion and doublespeak began.

In 1972, the Department of Health, Education, and Welfare (HEW) issued a set of guidelines for universities, instructing them that to comply with nondiscrimination legislation they must make "efforts to recruit, employ and promote members of groups formerly excluded, *even if that exclusion cannot be traced to particular discriminatory actions on the part of the employer.*" (Emphasis added.)[5]

Though the legislation carefully refrained from explicitly mandating quotas, it in effect required "an extensive effort to record the race, color, and (some) national origins of just about every student and employee and recipient of government benefits or services in the nation,"[6] ostensibly to prevent discrimination on these very grounds. When the gathering and analysis of racial data was combined with specified goals and timetables, no reasonable observer could avoid concluding that the government's denial of preferential requirements was verbal hocus pocus.

White men began bringing Title VII lawsuits of their own, charging institutions with reverse discrimination. The most famous case was *Bakke v. University of California at Davis Medical School* (1976). The confusing final decision seemed to repudiate racial ratios, but stated that race could be a factor in college admissions. The ambiguities and inconsistencies have been with us ever since in decision after decision, mandate after mandate.

I will not try to untangle affirmative action legislation here. Rather, I will conduct a review of its actual consequences. Though preferential policies may have begun with the best of intentions, they clearly have gone off course and taken on a strange and diffuse life of their own. How has this happened? And why? And what can we do about it?

The Philosophical Foundations of "Benign" Discrimination

As a philosopher, I believe that affirmative action and kindred policies cannot be understood apart from their philosophical and ideological roots. After years of studying the problem, I have concluded that affirmative action is the product of a widely disseminated ideology I call the Philosophy of Social Engineering, a body of thought with Continental European rather than Anglo-Saxon foundations, and deeply antagonistic to the principles on which the United States was founded.

Rather than surveying human history as accurately and comprehensively as possible to draw reasonable conclusions about the political principles and arrangements that have the best track records of sustaining prosperous, free, and secure societies, the Philosophy of Social Engineering implicitly imagines an absolutely ideal society, or utopia. It then observes that a given society fails to meet its criteria for morality and justice and sets about redesigning that society from the top down to bring it into alignment with the utopian ideal.

In our society, this ideal has taken the form of a race and gender utopia—one in which ethnic groups practice widely divergent cultures and yet are statistically indistinguishable; in which the disparate behavioral and emotional tendencies of male and female children are permitted to have no social effects or social recognition—an oddly neovictorian regime of taboos and "no nos" repressing every sexual manifestation except copulation.

There is a catch, though. If the conception of human nature and institutions implicit in the Philosophy of Social Engineering is false, its ideals are unrealizable. Instead of utopia, they will lead to tragic results ranging from intergroup violence to political totalitarianism.

The results of preferential policies to date are suggestive. They have fueled a balkanization of the body politic into militant factions. They have led to mounted attacks on the principles of free speech and academic freedom, and on the ideals of objective research and reasoned discourse. The Philosophy of Social Engineering shares considerable conceptual terrain with other totalitarian ideologies that have spawned misery around the globe. If its track record so far gives us any clues, social engineering is the greatest threat to freedom in this country's history.

If there existed strong evidence that the positive effects of preferential policies outweigh the negative effects, we would all be familiar with that evidence: It would be widely disseminated by a highly supportive media corps. Instead, a veil of silence surrounds the actual methods and actual effects of affirmative action. This veil is a tacit admission that these methods and results will not bear close examination.

To forestall such examination, several strategies are employed. One is the old ad hominem argument: All who criticize preferential policies do so from dishonorable (that is, racist) motives, so their logic and evidence need not be honestly tested against the logic and evidence on the other side.

To this, one can reasonably ask: Should debates on public issues be reduced to a moralistic competition regarding who has the purest motives? History provides ample evidence that noble motives can produce human tragedy on a massive scale. Attempts to stigmatize all critics of a policy (as racist) and to chill debate on the issue (as divisive) do no credit to the policy in question.

A closely related but more subtle strategy is to focus attention exclusively on the putative goals rather than the actual results of preferential policies. Again, I can only say that when a policy's advocates discourage examination of basic policy questions (such as unintended side effects and relationships between means and ends), they do the policy no credit.

Affirmative action is one of several policies in contemporary American society that are pursued zealously in the face of growing evidence of many negative—and few positive—results. This degree of denial would seem to indicate a dominant ideology combining strong emotional appeal with serious defects in its capacity to comprehend reality deeply or to predict outcomes accurately.

So in the final analysis, this book is a philosophical work, though not in the narrow, academic sense. I will argue that the central problems surrounding affirmative action and its kin are philosophical. Ideas are *important*. They are the prime movers that direct historical, sociological, and economic currents, and hence shapers of the development of cultures.

Bodies of ideas, accepted for a time by populations, have offered answers to perennial questions such as what kind of world this is, how we fit into it, and how our communities should be organized. If the ideas peoples accept are mostly true—that is, if they more or less correspond to reality—their cultures will grow, flourish, and nurture strong economies and political systems.

For a while, we had such a body of ideas. It proved its worth to generations and can be credited for some of our highest achievements. It created a society that many people willingly risked their lives to become part of and to preserve.

But no body of ideas is self-sustaining. If it is systematically abandoned, the advancement of the culture will gradually halt. All this is embodied in Richard Weaver's famous pronouncement that *ideas have consequences*. They are not mere epiphenomena buffeted about on a sea of blind historical and socioeconomic forces, as a Marxist would have it. Thus, although the ideas we will confront in examining affirmative action are complex, we have no alternative but to tackle them. A flight from ideas right now is absolutely the last thing we need.

The idea to be examined here can be posed as a question: Has social engineering succeeded in resolving the dilemmas of racial, ethnic, gender, and class discrimination in American society? I believe that it has not: On the contrary, since it is based on a body of ideas that can be shown to be false, it takes us in the opposite direction.

The Structure of Our Critique

Here, then, is a brief outline of the critique to follow: In the first chapter, I show that—whether understood as government demands for specific statistical outcomes or as "voluntary" adoptions by organizations to avoid litigation—quotas are real and not figments of right-wing imagination. In fact, the legislation that mandates quotas in the construction industry can be found in any library with a good government documents room. We will see that such quotas have devastated the careers and lives of many people and their families. They bring harm to innocent third parties while failing to achieve any useful social goal.

The second chapter documents that preferential policies in higher education have:

- increased the volume of racial incidents on campuses

- discriminated against groups who had no role in the original mistreatment of blacks (Asians, for example)

- fueled irresponsible demands and unattainable goals

The second chapter also examines the relationship between affirmative action and the "political correctness" epidemic. A large and growing body of evidence indicates that an intolerant ideology, sometimes called the New McCarthyism, has insinuated itself into campus life, in which an atmosphere of near-censorship pervades campus "discussion" of race and gender. Serious repercussions follow violation of the new speech and thought codes. These codes, whose existence and effects are now well documented, exist primarily to protect preferential policies from serious criticism in the academy.

The official policy of higher education is now multiculturalism:

Support for the multicultural agenda is built into the very job descriptions of many top administrative posts. Even accrediting agencies have gotten into the act by threatening to withdraw accreditation from colleges and universities that have not done enough to increase the diversity of their faculties and student bodies.

Chapter 3 probes more deeply the intellectual defenses of the multicultural university, showing that group-based preferences have seriously compromised intellectual standards. The affirmative action era has produced an avalanche of what I call *antischolarship*.

Scholarship is motivated primarily by intellectual curiosity and the desire to produce lasting contributions to human thought. In contrast, antischolarship rejects the ideals of objectivity, neutrality, clarity of analysis, and the search for enduring intellectual and moral truths. Antischolarship takes the view that since all discourse is inherently and equally political, its value can be judged by a single, supreme criterion—whose political interests are being furthered.

The two relevant categories of political interest are said to be white heterosexual men on one side, and everyone else on the other side. Multiculturalism claims to represent everyone else and thus, being on the side of the angels, is free to disregard or even attack standards of reasoned discourse.

Support for multiculturalism is now a stated or unstated litmus test for permanent faculty and administrative appointments at most colleges and universities. Support for free speech and genuine ideological diversity, on the other hand, is a serious handicap on the academic racetrack.

Chapter 4 will turn to the Philosophy of Social Engineering—the intellectual bulwark of preferential policies, multiculturalism, and antischolarship. This pivotal chapter will show that tacit commitment to social engineering underlies race and gender preferences as well as the various forms of antischolarship. The Philosophy of Social Engineering has five basic components:

1. collectivism as opposed to individualism, with the rights of the group elevated over those of the individual
2. sociocultural determinism as opposed to the idea that human beings are free, moral agents
3. a psychology of victimization, as part of a social metaphysic that dichotomizes society into victims and oppressors

4. intergroup egalitarianism as an ideal, any departure from which is attributed to oppression
5. elitism, the view that social engineers comprise a special group with the knowledge and moral insight to rectify historical injustices through large-scale social planning

This body of ideas is fatally flawed. It is internally inconsistent, empirically unvalidated, and socially suicidal.

In Chapter 5, I chronicle the damage that social engineering is wreaking on our society. The theme will recur throughout this book that no one can legislate motivation, talent, qualifications, and abilities into existence ex nihilo, nor can they be redistributed by legislative or bureaucratic fiat. As a result, preferential admissions either place—for example—black students in situations for which they are unprepared (thus impeding rather than advancing their chance of success, while offending white students); or they lower standards for everyone—black and white.

The more recent application of social engineering ideology to the military poses the same dilemma by placing women in combat. There are strong arguments from on-the-ground military experience why women should not be placed in combat situations. The effort to do so has resulted in a gendernorming that threatens to compromise the integrity of the armed services—perhaps, in a quite literal sense, fatally.

By looking at some occupations in which no one can reasonably deny that there are objective criteria for what counts as a successful performance, we will be able to see the dangers of lowered standards not just to select institutions and occupations, but to everyone if preferential policies are ever implemented in a consistent way.

A Viable Alternative to Social Engineering

That being the case, where do we go from here? Criticism of affirmative action is likely to fall on deaf ears unless the critic can provide an alternative. Chapter 6 responds to this concern. In it I introduce the Philosophy of Social Spontaneity, a viable alternative to the Philosophy of Social Engineering.

The Philosophy of Social Spontaneity advocates:

- individualism

- the concept of individuals as autonomous, acting agents

- maximal individual liberty for all citizens

- reduction of the role of the government to the protection of individual liberty and the punishment of those who forcibly interfere with the liberties of others

- reliance on voluntary associations and private organizations for the amelioration of social problems

- reassertion of the Lockean concept of property rights

This last is the most important idea of all. It asserts one's right to one's life and the fruits of one's labor, including one's property. From this it follows that no governmental agency has a moral justification for telling any entrepreneur to hire any specific individuals. In a free society, entrepreneurs have the right to hire whomever they see fit, according to criteria decided by themselves.

A state powerful enough to implement social engineering is a state so powerful that its power will inevitably be misused. Lord Acton's aphorism holds true: "Power corrupts, and absolute power corrupts absolutely." Where does this leave women and minorities?

Slavery and segregation required government enforcement and protection against the corrosive influence of the free market in order to survive. Economist Walter Williams in *The State against Blacks*[7] has shown that many laws have impeded or discouraged efforts by blacks to advance economically, usually by favoring insiders (for example, those established in various occupations) against outsiders (newcomers who pose competitive threats to the status quo), or by encouraging dependence.

Affirmative action has done little for most black Americans. It helps those blacks least in need of it—the already well situated, socially and economically.

Thus it is not surprising that a growing number of black intellectuals have expressed doubt whether the advanced welfare state is a reliable friend to black interests; Thomas Sowell, Walter Williams, and Glenn Loury have been making such observations for years. In recent years, they have been joined by Shelby Steele,

Stephen J. Carter, Clarence Thomas, and others who have taken issue with the "civil rights" establishment.[8]

What does social spontaneity offer those who have suffered from discrimination? What it offers, I will argue, is genuine *freedom of opportunity*—the freedom of all individuals of all races to advance by their own merits unimpeded by government restrictions. It offers dignity rather than dependence.

For those interested in examples of black individuals who have risen from poverty to affluence without "benefit" of affirmative action, we note several. Anyone, black or white, can learn a great deal from the lives and writings of these outstanding individuals.

Preferential policies can be tolerated only by a society that has lost sight of some basic principles:

1. Rights are fundamental guarantors of human dignity and opportunity, not culturally relative ephemera.
2. Rights inhere in individuals, not in groups.
3. Individuals are moral agents, not mere respondents to environmental stimuli or deep drives (such as sexual or economic).
4. The role of government is to protect individual liberties and property rights, not to provide entitlements or to guarantee outcomes.

The systematic abandonment of the first of each of the above pairs coupled with adoption of the second has left our leading minds open to what Raymond Aron calls The Totalitarian Temptation—the view that injustices can be rectified by large-scale social planning. Our institutions' largely passive acceptance of affirmative action, militant feminism, and radical homosexual movements is sad proof that our political system long ago ceased to be an instrument for the protection of equal rights for all citizens under the law; and we have lost our awareness of what government should be.

During the past quarter century we have seen more and more power concentrated in the hands of the state, with individuals having less and less power to control their own lives, businesses, and associations. We have seen an evolution from a genuine concern for civil *rights* into the practice of manifest civil *wrongs* that systematically discourage achievement, and hence the genuine advancement of women and minorities. The consequences have come to include a dysfunctional educational system, increasingly unstable economy, escalating intergroup conflict, and a declining standard of living for everyone—especially those least plugged in to sources of power.

Although I follow no one author or school on every point, the ideas expressed here (particularly the Philosophy of Social Spontaneity developed in Chapter 6) owe much to twentieth-century exponents of the Austrian and other free-market schools in economics including Ludwig von Mises, Friedrich A. Hayek, Henry Hazlitt, and Thomas Sowell, along with libertarian theorists such as Robert Nozick, Tibor Machan, and John Hospers (the latter two came under the influence of the late philosopher-novelist Ayn Rand).

In different ways, all these individuals foresaw the growth and spread of collectivist and statist ideologies in our century and wrote extensively of their dangers. The choice is ours: We repudiate social engineering in all its forms, including affirmative action, or more and more of our freedoms—indeed, the very future of our nation—stand in jeopardy.

Set-Asides and Quotas:
Fiction or Fact?

The Debate over Quotas

Affirmative action and related policies have been a source of growing discontent and division in our society for over two decades now.
Arrayed on one side of the debate are those who begin by observing
that this country's past treatment of its racial and ethnic minorities
and of women is a blight on its history. Advocates of this position
maintain that justice requires some kind of systematic policy aimed
at remedying the effects of long-standing discrimination against
blacks, other minorities, and women. A long struggle led from *Dred
Scott* and *Plessy v. Ferguson* to *Brown v. Board of Education*, and
to the Civil Rights Act of 1964 and the Voting Rights Act of 1965.

But, say affirmative action advocates, full repair of the damage
done in the past requires that women and members of minority
groups have equal employment opportunities in the present and
future. The Civil Rights and Voting Rights Acts did not eradicate
patterns of discrimination that still concentrate power and influence in the hands of white men of European descent. Thus a long
period of sustained government action is needed to counteract these
patterns by mandating and enforcing affirmative action.

On the other side are those who contend that affirmative action has replaced discrimination against women and minorities with discrimination against white men—reverse discrimination. Critics of affirmative action argue that while such ideals as equal employment opportunity sound good in principle, in practice they have come to conceal equally unjust, equally harmful, and probably unconstitutional practices that give preference to some at the expense of others.

These practices, critics add, have replaced individual rights with group entitlements, and the concept of equal opportunity with demands for equal outcomes, which in turn have produced quotas in workplace hiring and promoting, in government subcontracting, and in college admissions and faculty hiring. The result has been compromised standards throughout the economy and the educational system. These policies have undermined the long-standing ideal of admitting students to college, hiring and promoting employees, and awarding contracts on the basis of merit rather than politics.

By creating a climate of dependence—which actually penalizes efforts by individual members of minorities to succeed on their own merits—affirmative action has reinforced the worst stereotypes of members of "protected groups" as consisting of people unable to "make it on their own." Preferential policies have added fuel to racial tensions by incurring the resentment of those not in protected groups, those who are expected to pay the costs of reparation despite never having engaged in discriminatory practices themselves.

Finally, continue critics, the affirmative action agenda has corrupted the language of the discussion and created a semantic wonderland that would have shocked even Orwell. Crucial terms such as *minority, equal opportunity, discrimination, racism, sexism*, and even the term *affirmative action* itself, have never been given unambiguous definitions. In practice, they have come to mean whatever politicians, federal judges, compliance officers, and other bureaucrats want them to mean.

Affirmative action's advocates have used morally loaded terms such as *social justice* without being required to supply any analysis of them. The abuse of language has concealed the fact that the affirmative action agenda, as it is being practiced, is fundamentally at odds with the basic principles on which this country was founded. These principles are:

- Rights and responsibilities inhere in individuals, not groups.

- Associations should be voluntary, not coerced.

- Individuals are presumed innocent until proven guilty.

- Government should be restricted to the protection of individual rights and the punishment of those who have been shown to have infringed on the rights of others.

Affirmative action has been instrumental in bringing about the most massive increase in American history in the power of government to interfere with once-private transactions. Thus there is more to this issue than race or gender. Affirmative action and other race-conscious preferences have accordingly been criticized not just by whites but by black intellectuals such as Thomas Sowell, Walter Williams, Glenn Loury, Anne Wortham, William Julius Wilson, Shelby Steele, and Clarence Thomas. Some of their criticisms have been as severe as anything ever produced by a white man. Even some who believe that race-conscious policies were once needed now contend that their day has passed—Stephen J. Carter is an example.[1]

Backers of affirmative action nonetheless contend that terms like *reverse discrimination* and *quotas* are red herrings concocted by white men who fear losing their long-established privileges. To the extent preferential treatment does occur, they maintain, it is justified by the fact that because of past discrimination most women and minorities are too far behind economically to compete effectively. The claim that they can be expected to "play catch up" by their own efforts alone is said to be naive, since it ignores long-standing patterns of discrimination that remain prevalent despite decades of counter-efforts. As for the objection that affirmative action "lowers standards," have these standards not always been set by white men? As for hiring on the basis of merit, does anyone really believe we have ever had a genuine meritocracy in this country?

These two camps have been at loggerheads now for twenty years, and many have despaired of ever reaching a rational resolution. Reasonable people can and do disagree, particularly when their disagreements stem from fundamentally different moral and philosophical convictions. And it has not always been clear what principles we should appeal to when attempting to resolve disputes such as this. But some opinions are nevertheless superior to others, since they are better supported with reasons and available evidence. This is my most basic assumption—indeed, without it further inquiry would be pointless.

I have found that there are good reasons why the critics of affirmative action and kindred policies now have the better of the argument. As we look past the arguments presented by the believers to the realities of implementation, the picture that emerges shows the critics to be essentially correct. Thus continued efforts to implement race-conscious policies by force should be disturbing to every American—of whatever racial or ethnic background—who wants to live in a free society.

To use the term "quotas" raises the hackles of affirmative action advocates, who claim that quotas are figments of right-wing imagination. Talk of quotas, they say, merely plays to our worst racial fears and hostilities. However, we can cut through at least some of the semantics by considering the existence of quotas as a question that can be investigated empirically like any other empirical question.

I have concluded that quotas do exist. They are real and have devastated the lives and careers of many people without significantly helping those in targeted groups. The Supreme Court decision *Griggs* (1971) seems to have completed the transformation of civil rights legislation from mandating nondiscrimination to mandating preferences. Before *Griggs,* discrimination meant *an action taken by some individual or organization of individuals against another individual, e.g., refusal to hire for a desirable position, based on a group characteristic.* After *Griggs*, it came to mean simply *lack of a politically acceptable statistical percentage.* (What determined *political acceptability* was usually the percentage of members of targeted groups in the local or regional population.)

Thus we came to hear expressions such as *covert discrimination,* which could be traced to no actions on the part of anyone but which nonetheless was assumed to be responsible for any statistical disparity between groups. Attempting to rectify covert discrimination by legislative and judicial force throughout institution after institution has produced what sociologist Frederick R. Lynch recently compared to a steamroller, flattening everything in its path.[2]

A Quota Law: the Surface Transportation Assistance Act of 1982

A recent policy study by the Chicago-based Heartland Institute uses the term *set-aside* to mean "a wide range of programs that may involve goals, earmarked funds, preferences, sheltered markets, quotas, and other variations."[3] Set-asides in public works projects first got off the ground with then president Richard Nixon's Executive Order 11458 in 1969. By 1989, thirty-six states and 190 local governments had adopted set-asides of one kind or another, earmarking a percentage of funds (the percentage varied) for business endeavors that came to be labeled Disadvantaged Business Enterprises (DBEs), Minority Business Enterprises (MBEs), or Women Business Enterprises (WBEs).[4] The federal Surface Transportation Assistance Act (STAA), which went into effect in 1983, provides ample illustration of the effects of these set-asides.

Aside from user fees, construction in the United States of public facilities such as highways, bridges, dams, sewage treatment plants, schools, and hospitals is financed by taxpayers through federal, state, and local governments. Basically, the industry works as follows: Government agencies issue bid requests (or requests for proposals) to which a number of private firms wishing to act as prime contractor respond competitively. Prime contractors, which tend to be heavy equipment-oriented firms, oversee the project and produce one or more of the services required by the contract. These firms subcontract the specialty jobs that require less capital investment.

Normally, construction firms must bid competitively for contracts by offering to build the project to specification for the amount of money stated in their bid. These bids are then evaluated openly, and the project—such as a new highway or bridge or hospital—is awarded to the lowest responsible bidder; that is, to the bidder who offers to do the best job for the least cost. This ensures quality work at a reasonable price while precluding favoritism and exemplifies how a free market is supposed to work.[5] Gerald Buesing of the Buesing Corporation based in Long Lake, Minnesota, a $10 million firm contracting in highway construction as well as hauling and trucking, calls this the "merit shop" philosophy.[6]

In 1982 Congress passed and then president Ronald Reagan

signed Public Law 97–424, known as the Highway Improvement Act of 1982 or the STAA. Section 105(f) reads:

> Except to the extent that the Secretary determines otherwise, not less than 10 percentum of the amounts authorized to be appropriated under this Act shall be expended with small business concerns owned and controlled by socially and economically disadvantaged individuals as defined by section 8(d) of the Small Business Act (15 U.S.C. section 637(d)) and relevant subcontracting regulations promulgated pursuant thereto.[7]

An additional U.S. Department of Transportation regulation mandated that 3.2 percent of highway contracts be awarded to WBEs. In 1987, the two were combined in Section 106(c) of the Surface Transportation and Uniform Relocation Assistance Act of 1987, offering MBE and WBE firms a combined goal of 10 percent.[8] Subcontractors must apply for the status of DBE, MBE, or WBE and become certified with federal, state, and local government agencies and bureaus.

Given any reasonable definition of quotas as mandated statistical outcomes, these laws clearly establish quotas. They require that prime contractors subcontract a minimum of 10 percent of their work to firms designated as DBEs, MBEs, or WBEs. Their plain language refutes decisively the claim that no laws set quotas.

Section 105(f) had the result that awards of subcontracts no longer could be made to the lowest bidder on the basis of ability to do the best work for the best price. Instead, it brought about reverse discrimination throughout the construction industry. Less qualified and less experienced DBE firms would be awarded subcontracts over more qualified and more experienced companies owned by white men, unless the latter teamed up with one of the former as a means of survival. This brought about lower efficiency and higher costs. Citizens and taxpayers of both genders and all races would pay the higher costs.

Under most circumstances, just under ninety percent of the work on a highway project is done by the prime contractor's own workforce. Only the remaining 10 percent or so—often landscaping, site safety, and similar light work—is available for subcontracting. The basic problem stems from the fact that, according to the most reliable information available, nearly all minority-owned and women-owned firms involved in highway construction are sub-contractors, not primes. So if a project is governed by a 10 percent set-aside requirement, then fully 100 percent of the subcontract work must be offered to DBEs, MBEs, and WBEs! Under such circumstances, Section 105(f) would exclude altogether the bids of subcontractors who are not in government-designated protected groups. Thus it does not merely discriminate against them—it threatens to destroy them, to wipe out their businesses.

Many individuals involved in the construction industry have testified to the problems created by Section 105(f) of the STAA. These problems include:

- business- and career-destroying discrimination against white male subcontractors

- the encouragement of corruption and fraud in the industry

- the failure to provide genuine assistance to the vast majority of those designated as minorities

The Harm Done by a Quota Law to Non-DBEs

A number of individuals who work as subcontractors have offered testimony before congressional committees on the harm done by Section 105(f) to their organizations. Their testimony also provides first hand insights into why quotas fail to help those in favored groups. A number of exceptionally clear and convincing statements have been presented by prime contractors and subcontractors in the construction industry to major U.S. Senate committees and sub-committees such as the Committee on Public Works and the Sub-committee on Transportation. We begin with the testimony of John C. Vande Velde, vice president of Warning Lites of Illinois, presi-dent of the United Subcontractors of Illinois, and vice chairman of the Statewide Transportation Alliance of Associations.

On behalf of a variety of small firms involved with the road construction industry in Illinois, Vande Velde testified to the false assumptions of Section 105(f). The 10 percent quota exceeded not just the percentage of members of minority groups qualified to do the work, but in some regions exceeded the entire minority population itself. "In fact, when the bill was introduced, there were less than three percent minority highway subcontractors nation-wide."[9] The effects on non-DBE firms such as Warning Lites have been devastating.

> On the average, during 1984, our bid prices were seven percent lower than the DBE's. However, the low bidder was not awarded the contract in most of the instances. Every contract where both Warning Lites and the DBE bid, Warning Lites was low. In 1984, we bid $8,000,000 of a possible $30,000,000 of work. Historically, we received forty to fifty percent of the contracts we bid. But in 1984, we received only $350,000 or four percent. And, in every case, we were low. We learned we could no longer compete equally. We had the best prices for reputable service. Yet we could not work. And 1985 has only proven worse.[10]

Vande Velde noted "a ninety percent decrease in state and city contract work . . . suffered during 1985" as a direct consequence of the quota law.

Donald Leslie of Johnson Electrical Corporation, based in Hauppauge, New York, offered similar observations. Johnson Electrical is "a specialty contractor in the basic electrical construc-tion industry, in addition to doing highway traffic signals and high-way lighting work."[11] Leslie observed that

> minority firms are nonexistent in the technical ends of the industry. When I say nonexistent, [I mean] not totally nonexis-tent, but for the terms of this program, they certainly are. We find it very difficult to find anyone even willing to bid on the work. In addition to that, we have various state agencies that have different compliance officers with all sorts of different rules and regulations and all sorts of different criteria as to who is and who is not a minority.
>
> So you can see now it is getting a little complicated in that we really have a lot of difficulty just sorting out what the rules of the game are, just by what agency we happen to be working for at the time. I might point out that we work for all munici-pal agencies, including school districts, fire districts, the de-partment of transportation, and so forth.[12]

Leslie described the harm to his firm:

> The losses occur . . . when we are unable to attain the goal for the various agencies and are unable to bid the project because we know we would be held responsible for meeting those goals or quotas. Just recently, in 1985, my firm has been unable to bid two projects—one was for a traffic signal reconstruction job for $1.8 million, and the other was a highway lighting job for $2.7 million—because we were unable to obtain any response whatsoever from qualified minority contractors to do any subcontract-type work.
>
> That is where my firm is being hurt, sir. It is being denied the right to bid the work unless we utilize some devious method of getting around the regulations, which we have been very reluctant to do.[13]

A major source of the difficulty, Leslie had earlier observed, was a factor entirely ignored in the strange universe of affirmative action: qualifications and technical competence, which cannot be created ex nihilo by legislative fiat. Leslie described the ensuing dilemma:

> The industry is a very technical one. It is one that you just cannot legislate into existence contractors who are qualified to do the work. At the same time, we are a public works contractor. We are under bond to perform. We are in a hard-money bidding process where we bid a firm contract price for a particular project, and we must perform within the guidelines of the specifications.[14]

This explains the relative nonexistence of qualified DBEs with which to subcontract. And since legislation cannot create qualifications by fiat:

> It takes some eight or nine years to develop into a contractor in my field that is viable in the industry, and that has the expertise to know what to bid, how to bid it, how to proceed with the project, how to conduct their business, and so forth— how to perform for the bonding companies and secure the

bonds, how to get the financing. There are all sorts of areas that you just can't take somebody off the street and say, "You are now an electrical contractor," any more than you could do it in the law field or the medical profession or anywhere else.[15]

Leslie's conclusion was that legislation alone had not helped minorities significantly, apart from giving them a "crutch."

This perhaps explains the experience of Gerald Buesing, who testified that he was unable to find a sufficient number of DBE firms for highway work in Minnesota. In attempting to locate DBE firms, he discovered:

The state listed 138 certified minority contractors. Forty-two of them did not even do highway work; eight on the list could not be located or their phones were disconnected; twelve were suppliers which we couldn't use; four told us they couldn't perform work in the magnitude needed; nine sent letters back saying they weren't quoting; thirty-one were contacted by phone and they said they weren't quoting. Twenty-seven DBEs were contacted and never returned our calls. That totals 133 out of the state listing of 138 certified DBEs. The remaining five DBEs did quote us. Of those five that quoted—one quoted on unrelated work, one was a supplier, which we couldn't use, and in the end we did receive three usable quotes—two on trucking and one on landscaping.

On that specific job the requirement for DBE was ten percent with a four percent requirement for WBE. I was not awarded the job. It is frustrating to go through the entire process of contacting 138 DBEs only to find three quotes that are usable. I want you to know, however, that this is not an exceptional case. This is a typical experience for highway contractors.[16]

Leslie described a similar experience and the hardship it created:

I had one particular instance where the minority firm that I had bid the job with was disqualified after the bid for a legal reason, and the State of New York Department of Transportation would not allow me to use them. At this point in time, I had to go back out onto the street and publicly look for additional minority participation, and at that point in time, there wasn't any available because of the workload in the area. It doesn't take much of a workload to fill up the capacity of those firms that are working in the minority business enterprise program.

So by the time all of this came about and developed into all the good-faith efforts that I had to go to prove to somebody that was 300 miles away there was no one else to take the place of that previously disqualified minority subcontract, some seven or eight months went by. This was on a highway project that had approximately a twelve-month completion date.

By the time I got a waiver, we were into December. The project was delayed up until that time, and we could not resume work until spring. My completion date was in March.

I am now working into the March-April-May area, completing the work with another subcontractor, along with my field forces, and I have been at this point subjected to liquidated damages for engineering charges on that additional time overrun, and no appeal was even heard of that issue. They just deducted it from my payment and sent me my final payment. That was it, take it or leave it.[17]

These are not isolated horror stories, but examples of a pervasive pattern. A survey conducted by the Associated General Contractors of America revealed that many in the construction industry said they had suffered enormous hardship as a result of the quota law. From Littleton, Colorado, Richard Randall of Randall and Burke reported:

We do highway seeding and landscaping work and our work is mandated to being subbed to minorities or if it is a prime contract, it is set aside for minorities. Our volume has decreased from approximately $1,000,000 in state work to $250,000 in an increasing market. We are told we are low [bidder] but they can't use us because of the ten percent goal.[18]

Ronald H. Lee of Lee Brothers, Inc., in Albion, Maine, wrote:

We are being forced out of the highway program by the ten percent minority clause. Our opinion of the minority quotas as set up in this state is that they are helping a handful of minorities with no visible effect on the others. We feel that the taxpayers of the State of Maine and of the United States are paying dearly for a pittance of benefits.[19]

Jan M. Livesay of Livesay Traffic Maintenance in Great Falls, Montana, noted:

> For the past two years, we have been competitive in our painting and signing prices. However, the prime contractors, needing to meet their goal requirements, have had to award this portion of the contract to a DBE/WBE. . . . Prime contractors have been outspoken to us on this matter—they chose the minorities and women businesses over us to guarantee award of the contract, even though we were low.[20]

Ernest Demetriades of Elderlee, Inc., Oaks Corners, New York, added:

> We lose approximately 45 percent of the projects we quote on because contractors are intimidated and coerced by the New York DOT Affirmative Action personnel into awarding the work to a minority firm at a higher price in order to meet the contract goals.[21]

Randy T. Rogers of Rogers and Clark, Inc., based in Garland, Texas, got specific on how the quota law drove up costs, which were then passed on to taxpayers:

> Texas DOT—Collin County; December 1984 letting—prime contractor was forced to use a DBE price on sewer that was $50,000 higher in order to meet DBE goals.
>
> Texas DOT—Grayson County; December 1984 letting—prime was forced to use a DBE price $180,000 higher to meet the goals.
>
> We were the losing subcontractor in each case.[22]

Many more specialized subcontractors have been especially hard hit by the quota law. Don Carlson of Border States Paving, Inc., based in Fargo, North Dakota, observed that:

> Many firms that are in the specialty items are being hurt by the minority firms because this is an area that is easy to get into and one area that is usually easy to get a minority quote. Many firms do not even quote any more because they know the minorities will get the work.[23]

Examples of such specialties include guardrail and seeding contractors. Jean P. Perry of Cumberland Paving Company, based in Fayetteville, North Carolina, reported:

> Guardrail and seeding contractors who existed prior to 105(f) have either disappeared or merged with minorities. They are a direct victim of discrimination. This is a program of reparation, not minority realization.[24]

John W. Minor of the Coral Construction Company in Wilsonville, Oregon, described his firm's situation:

> Our major line of work has been as a specialty subcontractor in the area of guardrail, barrier, and permanent signing. As a direct result of the 1982 STAA setting DBE goals, our company, as a non-DBE, has been adversely impacted economically. My partners and myself are seriously questioning our ability to survive any longer in this type of market.[25]

For some, it is already too late. Bob Fetting of Tri State Construction Company, based in Nelson, Wisconsin, recounted:

> [A certain nonminority firm] was the finest landscaper and most reasonable in the State of Wisconsin. He was in business for approximately 35 years and forced out of operation due to the minority requirements.[26]

Others are close to going under financially. Lee Middleton of Energy Electric Company in Sundance, Wyoming, testified:

> We have not yet been forced out of business, but our volume is reduced greatly because of minority business enterprise goals. We have stopped building snow fence, signing, guardrail, and many concrete items because general contractors must use minority prices even if we are low bidder.[27]

Fred Hobbs of Acme Concrete in Spokane, Washington, explained:

> [A certain nonminority company] was one of the leading signing and guardrail contractors. As a result of DBE/MBE requirements, their business has diminished considerably. They are not out of business, but they have a very difficult time obtaining subcontracts for signing and guardrail, even though they are usually very competitive. We receive many lower quotations from non-DBE/MBE subcontractors for signing and guardrail work that we must ignore in favor of higher DBE/MBE firms in order to meet these "goals."[28]

Gale Rewa of Milbocker and Sons, Inc., based in Allegan, Michigan, added:

> Some of the best and most reliable companies in the guardrail and restoration business have disappeared because of MBE quotas. Also, companies doing concrete curb, gutter, and sidewalk work have suffered.[29]

Thomas J. Hug of Hug Concrete Paving, Inc., of Norwalk, Ohio, offered a eulogy to the days before the civil rights movement was transformed into demands for guaranteed statistical outcomes:

> Our firm specialized in concrete curb, curb and gutter, sidewalk, median barrier, and pavement markings. What has been the detrimental impact of the DBE, MBE, and WBE set-aside program on our corporation? It has reduced the volume of

our work from just over $12,000,000 in 1980 to just over $4,000,000 in 1984, and as of December 1, 1984, we have ceased bidding.

We have sold some of our equipment to a minority firm and presently are leasing the rest to the same firm. If this firm continues to be successful, we hope to sell them the remainder of our equipment. This minority firm is also absorbing a large number of our employees—some of whom have been with us for over thirty years. It is quite a sad event to see that which took thirty-three years to build and which you expected to see your family continue suddenly dissolved, not because of anyone's deficiency but simply because of the color of their skin and federal and state Legislation.[30]

In short, the quota law penalized, to the point of destroying businesses and careers, non-DBE subcontractors without regard to whether they had ever discriminated against anyone. Vande Velde concluded:

The [DBE] program has eliminated free enterprise! In essence, nonminorities are being punished, punished for the societal discrimination that has for centuries plagued the racial minority members. We have not, however, been found guilty of such discrimination. There has been no due process of law. We have been sentenced, yet we were never tried. And according to Congressman James Moody, of the fifth district of Wisconsin, in a September 30, 1985, letter to the executive director of the Wisconsin Road Builders Association . . . ". . . *discrimination against nonminority contractors . . . is exactly what was intended [by the DBE program.]*." Need I say more?[31]

Corruption and Fraud Associated with the DBE Program

One of the most serious problems with implementation of the DBE program was the appearance of fraudulent DBEs and the difficulty faced by prime contractors and government agencies trying to distinguish between legitimate DBEs and fraudulent ones. Vande Velde discussed the growth of fraud and deception both as a means of survival by non-DBE/MBE/WBE firms and as indicative of the opportunism of relatively well-off members of minorities who were able to further enrich themselves by taking advantage of these firms' plight. He observed that people in the industry would be forced to bend the rules in order to survive.

The quota law, he said, had already encouraged the formation of "illegal shams and front operations" established for the sole purpose of filling quotas. These "brokerage-type firms . . . receive the contract award but serve no commercially useful function. Non-minority firms are forced to perform the work for the shams or perform no work at all."[32]

Many of these brokerage firms are owned by minority-group members who are relatively well off economically (in accordance with Thomas Sowell's observation that those who reap most of the benefits of preferential policies are typically among the most well off, and hence presumably the least harmed by past discrimination).[33] As Vande Velde put it:

> There are a few minorities who have benefited by the program. We do not refute that. Judging from the line of minorities camped at Warning Lites' door proposing we use them to set up a front, some people undoubtedly have become wealthy using this program. In fact, individuals from four states, three racial minority groups and all walks of life, have asked the question of Warning Lites. . . . In every case, the DBE entrepreneur requested five to ten percent of the gross as their "fee." Also in every case, Warning Lites, of course, would perform the work, using all of their own equipment, and paying all the bills. Yes, some have benefited![34]

Donald Leslie noted one of the reasons these methods for bending the rules get established:

> . . . State agencies [other than the department of transportation] and villages and counties and towns will allow you to utilize minorities that are off the general Commerce Department list, and basically, *the minority does not have to show that they are an ongoing viable firm in the business that they choose to bid for work in.* Those areas have been the areas where the

five percenters come into play, where you cover whatever minority goal there is just by contracting with whoever it is that you have in mind at the time to develop that goal for you, and you pay them five percent of that program for the right to utilize their name as a minority.[35]

The Heartland Institute policy study cites a number of cases of corruption and fraud in set-aside programs across the country, documenting their role in undermining respect for law. Some examples (condensed from this study):

- In December 1983 and June 1985, Wedtech Corporation, a New York defense contractor, obtained $135 million in contracts to build pontoons for the Navy under a minority set-aside program, despite repeated complaints about late deliveries and shoddy work. The company went public with a $30 million stock offering, yet was permitted to retain its favored status as a disadvantaged minority-owned firm. At one time 95 percent of Wedtech's business came from set-asides. Wedtech prospered, prosecutors say, as a result of promiscuous bribery of city, state, and federal officials and a conspiracy to win government contracts by fraudulently depicting itself as a minority-owned business.

- In June 1988, Illinois Attorney General Neil Hartigan brought a civil action against fourteen corporations and their officers, seeking $7 million in restitution for allegedly funneling phony bills through dummy minority contracting firms. It was, according to Mr. Hartigan, "just the corner" of the corruption involving public works projects and minority set-aside programs.

- Also in June 1988, evidence of fraud was presented at a hearing regarding a lawsuit against Precision Contractors Inc., a construction firm owned by Chicago businessman Noah Robinson. Over the last decade, Robinson has been awarded state and city set-aside contracts worth several millions of dollars. Robinson's testimony indicated that he has at times obtained government contracts through the set-aside programs and then hired white-owned firms to do the work.

- In November 1988, Howard Medley, a member of the board of the Chicago Transit Authority, remained under investigation by federal prosecutors on charges that he lied during an investigation into the business practices of Metropolitan Petroleum Company, which has been charged with using a phony minority contractor as part of its $38 million diesel fuel contract with the CTA.

- During investigations of graft and corruption in federal programs aimed at helping American Indians, a special panel of the Senate Select Committee on Indian Affairs heard non-Indian contractors testify that they had paid thousands of dollars in bribes to Shawnee, Chickasaw, and Navajo officials. Others told of set-aside abuses by contractors using Indians as fronts in minority construction companies.

- In "Opportunities Denied: An Examination of Minority and Women Business Enterprise Programs in Chicago," the Better Government Association summarized the findings of a lengthy investigation into the city's set-aside program. BGA investigators concluded that "in numerous instances, prime contractors have subverted the system with the result that millions of dollars intended for legitimate minority and women-owned businesses went to majority contractors instead."[36]

The widespread presence of fraud cast doubt on genuine efforts to aid the development of new minority-led firms. Warning Lites had such a close call not long after it began assisting a DBE firm in late 1982 in what Vande Velde described as a "mentor-protege" association:

Our representative taught the DBE owner the bidding process. We made our equipment available to him. Our employees became his employees. His accounting and tax records were maintained using our computer equipment and personnel. And, we turned over our customers to this competitor. What would undoubtedly have amounted to $3,500,000 in contracts in 1984 to Warning Lites if there was no DBE program, was awarded to "our DBE." We survived because the equipment the DBE used in contract performance was leased from us. And then, again, the crisis came. A state investigation was performed covering our relationship. Fraudulent activities with sham fronts were prevalent nationwide. And although we were found guilty of no wrong doing by the state and were legally advised that we were well within the federal guidelines, we felt the risk too great. It was not worth hurting our reputation or, even worse, losing our business. So our association was terminated. The result on Warning Lites: a ninety percent decrease in state and city contract work since 1985.[37]

Tom Stewart of Frank Gurney, Inc., based in Spokane, Washington, reported a similar experience:

In the latter part of September [of 1983] we just felt, out of fear for our own survival, that we had better commence a business work activity with minority companies. We did so in the latter part of 1983, and in 1984 we did work with minorities.

On December 20, 1984, one of the minorities that we had worked with had a compliance review with the State of Washington Contract Compliance Bureau. The contract compliance officer expressed a verbal disfavor with his association with our company, and at this time there hadn't been a formal written compliance status of that particular minority company. However, after deliberating the outcome of that and taking notice of the more stringent rules regarding working with minorities, as of January 1, 1985, we halted any work or bidding activity with minority companies. Since then we have been on our own.[38]

Companies that have shied away from manipulating the system have found themselves unable to obtain work. Ralph Stout, Jr., of Southern Seeding Services, based in Greensboro, North Carolina, reported:

We know we've lost jobs. At one time we tried to create a relationship with what I would call a legitimate minority contractor, a contractor who had been in business prior to the days of set-asides and goal programs, and who was in an allied business—he was a grading contractor. And through a discussion with our attorney and their research, we were encouraged to believe that we might effect a relationship where we could, in turn, get some work through these people.

We bid some jobs with the understanding to the primes that if this worked out we would in fact be doing the work as a sub-sub.

As it turned out, after meeting with the highway people, going over the contract that we had put together where we guaranteed to bond the job; we guaranteed to finance them; we guaranteed to pay this party a fee in order to help them in that way—it came to be that it was just not something that was going to work.

We ended up losing about four jobs in this particular instance, one of which the general contractor subsequently subcontracted to a minority firm from Virginia, who called me on two different occasions and asked me to subcontract the work from him, and I told him, "We can't legally do this." He asked me to put my people on his payroll and to lease the equipment to him, and I told him no, we weren't interested in doing business that way, so we didn't get the job. We bid it and were supposed to have gotten the job and we didn't, and we were just going to stay away from it.[39]

What is interesting is the near-absence of acrimony toward women and minorities from contractors hurt by affirmative action. Several praise the minority-owned firms they have worked with. Tom Stewart testified:

In our own experience, we have found that there are varying levels of bona fideness in minority companies. Some are really great. They don't need any help from anybody. They beat us at the bidding table. They don't need any help from anybody to complete their work. They are good; they are efficient.[40]

Jan M. Livesay added:

It is important for you to know some additional thoughts on this matter. We are not opposed to women in business. We are not opposed to Indians, Blacks, Hispanics, etc., in business. On the contrary, we welcome competitive bidding in our business. That is what free enterprise is all about to us. We are opposed to the control over the awarding of these contracts. This whole Surface Transportation [Assistance] Act belies the initial conception of its beginning, i.e., to avoid discrimination against any one individual(s). We have become the minority; we are being discriminated against.[41]

Those who have testified on behalf of the construction industry against quota legislation emphasize that most of those in its targeted groups are not helped by it. Vande Velde reported that as a consequence of his losses he had to lay off employees, many of them members of minority groups, because he could no longer afford to keep them on his workforce. "Warning Lites lives by the Equal Employment Opportunity mandate required," he reported.

Of approximately sixty employees during our peak season, forty-two percent are minorities. . . . Now, however, some of our minority employees have had to be laid off. They are still not working, let alone in the construction industry for a DBE. If the intent of Section 105(f) was to provide work for more minorities, as was stated by supporters of the bill, then the program has failed. In our experience it has provided fewer.[42]

Legitimate DBEs are often at a disadvantage relative to the front operations; the latter have the resources of larger, nonminority companies and thus can easily underbid them.[43]

The DBE program is sometimes explicitly rejected by those in its targeted groups who would prefer instead to compete in a free market. Consider the following from Elizabeth K. Powell of the Paul D. Powell Construction Firm in Larnard, Kansas:

We are WBE contractors. We feel that we are gradually being pushed out of business because of the goals of Section 105(f). . . . I feel that this is one of the most unfair pieces of legislation there is. Since when is it right to DICTATE that one business should get a job because they are a minority or woman? Even though we are a WBE, I would rather actively compete because I had the best price and did the best job.[44]

Ralph Stout explained why the quota law cannot really be expected to accomplish much more than what we have seen. When asked whether the set-aside program in his area helped women and minority entrepreneurs enter and succeed in the construction industry, he said:

> I don't think it has, and I'll answer that this way: I see two types of contractors. I see a minority disadvantaged or women contractor who is going to be in business, period. . . . There is one who is going to be in business whether there's a goal program, set-aside program, or not. Then I see contractors who are in business because of the goal program.[45]

Of these latter, Gerald Buesing offered reasons for doubting that government programs are going to help them:

> We believe that the DBE Program is a reactionary, short-term, stopgap measure addressing *not* the problems but only the symptoms of the DBE firms. We have poured money into a program which only assists minority firms in the short run rather than investing that money in a program that will give those firms the long-term capabilities they need for competing in the real world without any special preferential treatment. Forced requirements for bringing in DBE firms have not made them competent, competitive enterprises.
>
> Many DBEs have problems with the following: the costs of business, sound business practices, lack of supervisory personnel able to run the projects properly, and lack of good qualified craftsmen on their jobs. We know of no ABC contractor that will not accept the low bid from a competitive subcontractor who is capable, regardless of the minority status. The main requirement is that the subcontractor can deliver his services at the price he bid, within the time constraints of the contract and with the quality level expected by the owner . . . which in the case of highway construction is the American taxpayer.
>
> With this in mind, we feel that we should not be placing money in set-aside programs but rather going to the root of the problem and invest[ing] in the future of DBEs by making their firms skilled on both the craft and management levels, thereby

making them competitive without the need for special bid treatment.[46]

The Strange Case of Daniel Lamp

In 1989, a number of now-infamous Supreme Court decisions began to question the constitutionality of quotas. The rulings in *City of Richmond v. J. A. Croson* and *Wards Cove Packing v. Atonio* struck down some particularly stringent set-aside laws. In *Croson,* the mandated quota was *30 percent*. In *Wards Cove Packing v. Atonio,* the Court shifted the burden of proof in discrimination cases from the defendant to the plaintiff, thus bringing antidiscrimination jurisprudence more into conformity with the rest of the judicial system.

However, the battle against quotas was not over. These decisions immediately came under sustained attack from "civil rights" groups, powerful voices within Congress, and legal scholars.[47] Senators Edward Kennedy and Howard Metzenbaum, longtime supporters of set-asides, wrote a "Civil Rights Act of 1990" with the explicit intention of overturning these and several other such decisions and reinstating the guilty-until-proved-innocent standard set by *Griggs*. The "Civil Rights Act of 1990" was vetoed by George Bush on the grounds that it would create hiring and promotion quotas. Congress failed to override his veto by the slimmest of margins—one vote. A "1991 Civil Rights Act" rose phoenixlike from the ashes of the 1990 version. Bush, under attack for his negative record on "civil rights," signed this one.

Meanwhile, the impact of decisions such as *Croson* and *Wards Cove* has been greatly exaggerated. As our survey of the construction industry makes clear, "quotathink" has come to permeate contracting and hiring practices in both public and private sectors and is too deeply entrenched to be dislodged by anything less than a revolution in our thinking. The issue of whether the 1991 Civil Rights Act "will create quotas" is therefore moot.

Consider the strange case of *Equal Employment Opportunity Commission v. The Daniel Lamp Co.,* featured on a segment of the CBS television news program *60 Minutes*.[48] Daniel Lamp is a small company located in a poor, mostly Hispanic area in southeastern Chicago. It manufactures lamps from used parts and then sells them to furniture stores around the city. Owner Mike Welbel is a self-made entrepreneur, a one-time traveling salesman who had borrowed $3,000 on a Chevy station wagon and started his own business nine years earlier. Welbel is white; his workforce, which varies in size from under twelve to over thirty employees, has always been nearly all Hispanic and black. This did not prevent the Equal Employment Opportunity Commission (EEOC) from accusing him of racial discrimination and filing suit based on an allegation made by a black woman who applied for a job with the company in early 1989 and was not hired. As Welbel tells it, one day EEOC representatives showed up at his office and demanded to see his employment records. He cooperated fully, believing he had nothing to hide. The EEOC then demanded that Welbel pay not only $340.01 to the woman who was not hired, but also $123,991 to six other blacks who allegedly applied for jobs at Daniel Lamp during 1988 and 1989 but weren't hired. In addition, Welbel was ordered to buy newspaper advertisements at the cost of around $10,000 of his own money to locate these individuals!

Welbel's description of his initial reaction as told to Morley Safer of *60 Minutes* is worth repeating:

> I froze. I froze in my chair. I— I— I was— I was— I— I got— I started feeling my chest bouncing around. I don't— I don't think it was a heart attack, but I'll tell you something. It was the next thing to it. I just was frozen with shock.[49]

The following exchange between Safer and Jim Lafferty, director of legislative affairs at the EEOC, occurred during the program:

> SAFER (interviewing): . . . quite apart from records, doesn't your nose tell you that this really isn't much of a case and that Mike Welbel is probably not a racist? He's a little guy trying to . . . make a living . . .

> LAFFERTY: Well, unfortunately, we have to rely on, not only the statistics, but on the word of Lucille Johnson and seven other people who've come forward since then telling us that they had also experienced discrimination during that period at Daniel Lamp.

SAFER (voiceover): What helped to make Lafferty's case against Mike Welbel was the EEOC's computer. It told the agency that, based on 363 companies employing 100 or more people and located within a three-mile radius of Daniel Lamp, Daniel Lamp should employ at any given moment exactly 8.45 blacks, which to Mike Welbel sounded like a quota. And the law says the EEOC can't set quotas.

LAFFERTY: We really haven't said that. What we've said is, "These are what the companies around you are doing. You've discriminated against this—"

SAFER: Stop being a federal bureaucrat for a minute and tell me what you're really telling him. What are you really telling him?

LAFFERTY: Don't discriminate. Obey the law.

SAFER: But if he has three black employees and doesn't hire a fourth for whatever reason and that fourth accused him of discrimination, do you prosecute?

LAFFERTY: Yes, we do. It's not that there's a magic number. Please believe me. We don't set magical numbers for people like Mr. Welbel to meet.

SAFER (voiceover): That's what Mr. Lafferty says, but, in a sense, it did set numbers by telling Mike that, based on other larger companies' personnel, Daniel Lamp should employ 8.45 blacks.

WELBEL: Any way you slice the pie, it's a quota system.

SAFER: But if they say, "Look, Mike, you've got to have eight blacks working for you," could you live with that?

WELBEL: Could I live with it? Yes. Is it more difficult than hiring by qualification? Yes. What the government is asking me to do is hire by color. They're saying, "Look, this black individual may not be as qualified, but that's who we want to see in your workplace." What they've become is— They do the hiring and I run the place under their direction. I no longer decide who's good and who's bad.[50]

Daniel Lamp eventually reached a settlement with the EEOC.[51] This was fortunate, for had the lawsuit gone to court and Welbel lost, he would have been out of business and his minority employees would have been out on the street—put there by the very organization that purports to represent their interests. The details of the settlement have been kept secret but, needless to say, Welbel now employs a numerically correct number of blacks at Daniel Lamp.

The struggle to eliminate racial quotas from our legal system has so far failed. Defenders of the 1990 and 1991 Civil Rights Bills continue to maintain that this legislation does not create quotas and that complaints about quotas are inherently racist. The exact opposite is the case. Race and gender quotas have existed in American society ever since the Nixon administration. They have devastated the lives and careers of countless people with limited legal resources to fight back.

It is also increasingly clear that quota legislation is not the boon to women and minorities that its advocates maintain. The problems created by past discrimination against women and minorities do not seem to lend themselves to solution by top-down legislation. The assumption that they can be so addressed has brought enormous harm to numerous small businesses, many of which have employed minorities in large numbers.

How could our society commit such a series of colossal blunders? I believe those who drafted Section 105(f) of the STAA were unable to distinguish the concept *minority* from that of *disadvantaged*. This left no room for the distinction between members of minorities who were relatively well off and owned firms and (the probably larger number of) minority individuals who worked for nonminority-owned firms. Firms were designated either as DBE or non-DBE depending on the race and gender characteristics of their *ownership*, not their *workforce*. The set-aside steamroller has probably flattened the livelihoods of as many women and minority members as white men.

TWO

The Numbers Game in Higher Education

Storm over Campus: the "New Racism" and the Official Response

During the 1980s and 1990s, racial hostilities have invaded college and university campuses—including some of the nation's most prestigious institutions. Hundreds of reports of racial incidents have surfaced over the past several years. Consider the following:

- One day in 1988, University of Michigan undergraduate Michael Wilson arrived early for a French class and saw a poster on the blackboard that read: "Support the K.K.K. college fund. A mind is a terrible thing to waste: especially on a nigger." A month or so later, a satirical poem written in phony black English and entitled "If Duh Dean Don't 'Pologize" was circulated to university officials and the affirmative action office. In April 1989, anonymous fliers appeared all over campus, including the office door of the Department of Afro-American Studies, announcing "White Pride Week."

- At Yale University in 1988, an unidentified person or persons painted a swastika on the door of the school's African-American student center next to the words *"white power."*

- At the University of Wisconsin's main campus in Madison, the Zeta Beta Tau fraternity held a mock slave auction in which pledges painted their faces black and wore wigs in imitation of black hairstyles.

- At Northern Illinois University, white students driving by in a pickup truck yelled racial slurs at blacks attending a Jesse Jackson speech. Later, fliers reading "Niggers Get Out" and "Get Your Black Asses Back to Africa" were found on campus buses.

- At Purdue University, what would have been a cross burning in front of the Black Cultural Center was interrupted by campus police who chased perpetrators into the woods.[1]

- In April 1989 at prestigious Smith College, four black women received anonymous notes containing racial epithets. Ensuing events, including rallies, led to shouting matches between black and white students and retaliatory antiwhite letters.[2]

- At a prominent Midwestern university in 1989, a speaker reading from Dr. Martin Luther King, Jr.'s speeches paused as eight white students got up and walked out to the sound of muffled snickers and other signs of approval from white students in the lecture hall.[3]

- In November 1989 at MacMurray College in Jacksonville, Illinois, forty anonymous letters containing racial slurs were sent to black students and a black staff member, prompting a protest by around 400 students.[4]

- Two fraternities at the University of Texas in Austin were temporarily suspended in April 1990 as a result of two incidents. The first occurred when Delta Tau Delta fraternity members painted a car with racial slogans and destroyed it with a sledgehammer. The second involved Phi Gamma Delta fraternity members handing out T-shirts with racial caricatures.[5]

- At Wesleyan University in 1990, someone spray-painted racial slurs on the walls of a black cultural center. This occurred just days after two firebombings at other campus buildings that rumor had attributed to black students.[6]

- Sabrina Collins, a freshman at Emory University in Atlanta, contended that she had been repeatedly victimized by racial slurs and returned to her dormitory room one day in early March of 1990 to find it vandalized, with racial epithets scrawled all over it. Though she went to the hospital for emotional trauma, there is some nonconclusive evidence that the incident was staged.[7]

- At Brown University a white student, Douglas Hann, was expelled for yelling antiblack, antisemitic, and antihomosexual remarks while drunk.[8]

- At George Mason University in 1991, members of the Sigma Chi fraternity staged a fundraising event in the student union building in which a student appeared in blackface, arousing the wrath of black students. According to the university's assistant vice president for student services, the organization would have to go through "formal training on cultural diversity issues."[9]

- A similar incident occurred at the University of Alabama during a sorority event in 1991 when sorority women attended a Kappa Delta "Who Rides the Bus" party in blackface and dressed as poor, pregnant black mothers. Black students were joined by faculty members as they marched in protest.[10]

- In March of 1992 at Bloomsburg University of Pennsylvania, over 2,000 people attended prayer services and a candlelight vigil following a cross burning in front of the administration building.[11]

- In April of 1992 at Olivet College in Olivet, Michigan, the majority of black students left campus following a brawl in a residence hall involving seventy black and white students following weeks of racial tension.[12] The incident prompted the resignation of the college's president, Donald A. Morris, who had served the campus for fifteen years.[13]

- In May of 1992, police used tear gas to break up a fight between black and white students at Ohio State University during an annual spring festival that according to Martin Jischke, Iowa State's president, would probably be discontinued.[14]

- White student unions sprang up on several campuses, including Temple University, the University of Florida, and the University of Minnesota, during the late 1980s. Such organizations have elicited intense hostility from faculty, administrators, and other student groups.[15] On occasion, fist fights have broken out between members of opposing student groups.[16] Mark Wright, the founder of the Florida group, complained of a campus double standard in racial matters. As he put it, "when whites decide to stand up for issues that are important to them, they are labeled racists. When blacks do so, they are labeled civil rights activists."[17]

Minority students and supporters have grown increasingly militant in response to perceived slights and offenses. At Vassar College, students protested an alleged remark by Senator Patrick Moynihan that a black Jamaican woman "should pack her bags and go back where she came from" if she didn't like the United States. A Moynihan aide denied his making the remark; nonetheless, militant students demanded his ouster from his position as Vassar's Eleanor Roosevelt Chair, a visiting lectureship.[18]

An anthropology class at Berkeley was disrupted by a student group calling itself Direct Action Against Racism, claiming that the professor had promoted racist views in a Berkeley alumni magazine.[19] At Auburn University, the Kappa Alpha fraternity's annual Old South parade, a seventy-year-old tradition, came under fire from black students who decried it as racist and insensitive to those whose ancestors had been slaves during the Confederacy.[20]

Protests and marches are often used to force administrations to make stronger commitments to diversity. Following the racial incident at Wesleyan, eleven students went on a hunger strike to force the administration toward that end.[21] A sit-in by students demanding more women and minorities on the faculty occurred at Berkeley in 1990, leading to the arrest of fifty-six people.[22] A Harvard Law School commencement was disrupted by graduates demanding that the school hire more women and minorities, and calling for the resignation of Law School Dean Robert C. Clark.[23]

In one extreme case, Chino Wilson, a sports writer for the Penn State campus paper *The Daily Collegian*, wrote a column proclaiming that "white people are devils" and advising blacks to arm themselves. He also repeated Louis Farrakhan's contention that AIDS is a "diabolical plot to exterminate black people."[24]

Militant feminist students occasionally go to similar extremes, as when University of Colorado graduate student Kristen Asmus offered her solution to the problem of sexual harassment: "Women will start fighting back. Women will begin to react with as much violence as men have mustered against them. Women will begin to stop talking about castration, and make it a reality. Women will begin to abandon their life-giving, caring inner nature and start carrying guns. Women will begin to kill men if they have to."[25]

Racial incidents continue to erupt on campus and often do reveal a double standard in how administrators deal with white and black students. Two widely publicized incidents occurred at the University of Pennsylvania in 1993. In one, student Eden Jacobowitz was accused of shouting racial slurs at five black women who had been partying under his dormitory window. He had used the phrase "water buffalo," the closest English translation of a Hebrew word meaning any thoughtless, inconsiderate person, and which scholars both black and white confirmed had no racial connotation whatsoever.

In the second case, a group of black students seized and destroyed all the copies they could find of an issue of the undergraduate newspaper *The Daily Pennsylvanian*, which contained a column by firebreathing conservative columnist Gregory Pavlik denouncing preferential policies, the Martin Luther King holiday, and black student organizations. Virtually nothing was done to the black students despite the fact that their actions obviously abrogated freedom of speech and of the press. Jacobowitz, on the other hand, found himself in serious trouble and facing a possible expulsion, had the charges not eventually been dropped in the face of adverse publicity. Penn's then president, Sheldon Hackney, had recently been nominated by President Clinton to head the National Endowment for the Humanities.[26]

These and many similar incidents have erupted alongside extensive efforts to recruit more women and minorities to campuses as well as similar efforts to promote cultural diversity through curricular reforms, adjustments of admissions standards, and similar measures.[27] According to the Baltimore-based National Institute Against Prejudice and Violence, over 300 campuses have experienced racial incidents since around 1986.[28] The number has continued to grow, with fresh cases reported almost weekly.[29]

All have been considered compelling evidence of widespread "campus racism," the generic term for a variety of activities ranging from ethnic slurs and other forms of hate speech to acts of vandalism and occasionally violence directed primarily (but not exclusively) at black individuals, black student unions and cultural centers, departments of black or African-American studies, and affirmative action offices. Such actions seem calculated to offend, to be insensitive. But what is behind them?

Have we seen the emergence of a new and particularly virulent form of racism? Or just the frustrated response of some white students to what they instinctively perceive as injustice? Is such frustration justified, or is it purely racist? The issue has now been discussed and debated in articles, editorials, and studies too numerous to cite individually. However, it is clear that what might be called the Official Response to campus racial tension has emerged. The Official Response is manifest in administrative decisions and in student complaints that there are too few minority faculty and that the curriculum is too white, too male, and too European. This response explains campus racism as follows: What we have here is an outgrowth of Reagan-era conservative politics, which created a cultural ambience hostile to minorities. Racial disturbances indicate a residuum of racism that the civil rights movement failed to eradicate. Such disturbances prove that the educational system has failed in its mission of inculcating the wrongness of racial stereotyping in a generation too young to remember the civil rights struggles of the 1950s and 1960s.

Today blacks, Hispanics, and women are making more gains in the workplace than ever before; the diversity of faces on our campuses is increasing by leaps and bounds. The new racism is surfacing in reaction to this. It is a product of white males who feel threatened by the erosion of their status as the dominant group.

The Official Response is implemented in several ways. One is the strengthening of policies aimed at recruiting more black and Hispanic students, which in practice has usually entailed

preferential treatment. Another is the mounting of equivalent efforts to recruit and hire more faculty from groups designated as disadvantaged. Still another is renewed emphasis on educating for correct attitudes on racial and ethnic questions.

When anonymous racist fliers appeared on the campus of the University of Wisconsin during 1987 and 1988, then chancellor Donna Shalala announced a plan to double the number of minority freshmen, hire seventy new minority faculty members, require mandatory cultural orientation for all incoming students, and revise the curriculum to include materials by black and Hispanic authors.[30]

A recent article describes the emergence of racial tension as "a problem in moral education, not merely a problem in public relations or policy" and argues for "respectful engagement . . . [We] must use our skills as educators to devise sound programs that give students enduring reasons for respecting one another's racial backgrounds and identities," drawing "all our students into such programs and not just those who are spontaneously so inclined." Despite the author's denial, on second glance it is clear that his "respectful engagement" is a form of reeducation to inculcate the view that affirmative action and similar policies are not *really* strategies for favoring members of certain groups at the expense of others. This is his solution to the problem of racial tension on campus.[31]

Is the Official Response adequate? This question in turn raises subquestions: Is it true that the Reagan era inaugurated a cultural climate hostile to minorities? Can one assume that purely moral arguments for affirmative action overrule its effects on white males and that offering still more preferential protections to minority students will defuse hostility? Do the presumed social benefits of preferential recruitment and hiring of university faculty, including quotas such as Dr. Shalala's, outweigh the social costs? Have programs of moral education, curricular reforms, efforts at sensitivity training, and educating for diversity actually improved the campus racial climate, or have they made matters worse by fostering heightened racial consciousness, militancy, and censorship? Until we are willing to confront these questions, the racial climate both on campuses and in the country generally can be expected to deteriorate.

The answers may not please campus moralists. Let us consider first the question of whether it is reasonable to blame Reagan administration policies for growing tensions between groups. It is true that the Reagan administration was staffed with people who favored a rejection of preferential policies and a return to color-blind and genderblind ones. At the same time, our look at the construction industry should make us skeptical of the view that Reagan or his appointees really rolled back preferential treatment. Ronald Reagan *signed* the Surface Transportation Assistance Act of 1982, which *increased* the effects of preferential policies on an entire industry.

At least one pathbreaking study of civil rights under the Reagan administration, that of Robert Detlefsen, refutes the claim that the Reagan era turned back the clock on affirmative action.[32] His research found that opposition to preferential policies during the 1980s encountered a bureaucratic stone wall; the policies themselves grew ever stronger. The only threat to them came during 1989 with Supreme Court decisions such as *Croson*. We have seen how long these decisions were able to withstand the assault of the advocates of preferential policies. Reflexively blaming the Reagan era for racial tensions is increasingly unconvincing.

What is really bothering white students? Consider the generic comment reported by Joseph Berger to the *New York Times*: "My old man is paying through the nose to send me to school, while [minorities] get Pell grants and talent search grants."[33] This reflects an accurate perception that there exist countless efforts on behalf of blacks in higher education that are unavailable to whites. Such efforts range from awards for which only blacks are eligible to minority-only scholarships. Most have the backing of national task forces and federal, state, and local governments and are defended by prominent state politicians.[34]

For example, at Pennsylvania State University there are $580 "black achievement awards" for black students who maintain a *C or C+ average*. If the average goes up, so does the award—to $1,160![35] At the University of Texas at Austin, President William H. Cunningham travels around the state recruiting Hispanics and blacks and once offered a prospective black student a $20,000 scholarship *on the spot*.[36]

At Harvard, blacks and other minorities can receive almost unlimited financial support regardless of need. As Abigail Thernstrom noted drily, "Bill Cosby's children would be eligible for full support."[37] It is hardly surprising that such practices arouse resentment. In public institutions, many white students' parents are doubly subsidizing these programs first through taxation and then through the tuition they pay for their own children. But the most serious objections to these programs derive from their adverse impact on the supposed beneficiaries—minority students. For, *by themselves, these programs do not qualify anyone to do college work.* For a variety of reasons, at present the majority of black teenagers are unprepared to do college-level work.[38] Thus the major effect of special programs aimed at blacks has been the institution of either *racenorming* or else an across-the-board lowering of standards. So far, racenorming appears to be more prevalent.[39] Racenorming is the practice of relativizing admissions standards to group identity, so that members of groups compete against one another but not against members of other groups. As a result, *no* admissions standards are universally applied to *all* races and groups. Thus has the illusion of minority advancement been created on many campuses.

Powerful forces protect such practices from exposure to the public. When Georgetown University third-year law student Timothy Maguire published an article exposing such practices in the *Georgetown Law Weekly*, he received an official reprimand from the university. Some black students demanded his expulsion, but the administration did not go that far.[40] Statistics on the lower grades and test scores of minority students also found their way into print at Touro College, a private liberal arts school in New York City.[41] These incidents are telling us something—that preferential policies are a primary cause of the racial troubles haunting American college and university campuses.

After researching preferential policies in several countries, Thomas Sowell observes that whenever and wherever such policies are instituted, they incur the resentment of the nonpreferred—a resentment that builds until violence erupts between preferred and nonpreferred groups. This has occurred in many countries between different nonwhite groups, not just in the United States between white and other groups.[42] In other words, some white students in this country are reacting in basically the same way human beings everywhere react to similar situations.

At least one psychological study supports the existence of a direct connection between perceptions of reverse discrimination and aggressive behavior.[43] Thus racial incidents will probably continue to accumulate as long as preferential programs remain the dominant policy. They may represent a kind of guerrilla warfare against racial preferences. It is unfortunate that the main targets of this guerrilla warfare are minority students, most of whom did nothing to build this kind of system.

Affirmative Action and "Moral Education" Arguments

Some respond that the reaction to preferential policies on college and university campuses nevertheless reflects a moral vacuum. The present generation of students had not even been born when this country's civil rights breakthroughs occurred. Hence they are not sensitive to the fact that while important victories were won at that time, the war against racism in American society is far from over. This brings us back to moral education arguments. Are preferential policies justified on moral grounds, grounds of justice? This question has perplexed philosophers and policy analysts and has provoked an enormous literature across disciplines from philosophy to the social sciences to law.

Two major arguments have emerged to justify affirmative action on moral grounds. *Backward-looking* arguments observe that African Americans began their existence in this country as slaves, despite our nation's dedication to the principle that "all men are created equal." Even after slavery ended, discriminatory laws systematically kept black Americans on the bottom rungs of society. Women, too, were once prevented from voting and were treated as property. Justice demands that reparation be made to these groups for decades of discrimination, and since these can only be made to women and blacks attempting to obtain education or employment today, preferential policies are justified to balance the books.

Forward-looking arguments approach the situation from the point of view of the society we hope to build, one from which all traces of discrimination have been eradicated. Affirmative action is justified to the extent it can contribute to the building of the kind of society that would now exist had there been no discrimination against women and minorities.[44] Affirmative action sees to it that members of formerly excluded and marginalized groups gain and retain access to centers of power, particularly in government and the educational system. Since white men presently dominate these centers of power and have subtle methods of retaining that dominance, preferential policies are required.

There are also several subsidiary forward-looking arguments. The *role model argument* holds that if black undergraduates can see black adults in positions of authority and influence, they will come to believe that success is possible for them, and such confidence breeds success. Thus preferential policies are justified because they supply minority communities with role models for minority youth to emulate.

The *argument from cultural bias* maintains that many of the standardized tests of individual achievement used as entrance requirements to better colleges and universities were devised by white men and reflect only their values and standards. This argument joins multiculturalism in reducing "objective standards" to a device for perpetuating white male hegemony. A college or university curriculum aiming to correct for this bias should incorporate, and even favor, previously neglected perspectives, which are assumed to correlate with ethnic categories. Since such perspectives are best presented by members of the oppressed groups, affirmative action for women and minority faculty as a means of improving the curriculum follows, as do preferential admissions of minority students, perhaps according to standards tailored to their special needs.[45]

A final forward-looking rationale for affirmative action and kindred policies may be termed the *argument from changing demographics*. This argument observes that, on the basis of demographic data, we can state that the number of women, blacks, Hispanics, and other nonwhite groups in the American population is steadily increasing. As we approach the turn of the century, their numbers can be expected to increase until white men are no longer a numerical majority.

Thus, more and more members of groups other than white men will be entering the workforce. However, white men continue to hold key positions of power and influence in all major institutions, public and private; hence the need for affirmative action to break their stranglehold on power. Preferential policies reflect the changing needs of a society in demographic transition, one whose corresponding transition in the ethnic composition of its power centers would not otherwise keep pace.

Do these arguments bear close examination? The examination of the construction industry in Chapter 1 should suggest something seriously wrong with the backward-looking arguments. Unfortunately, those who were most seriously wronged through the institution of slavery have been dead for over a hundred years, as have those who perpetuated the wrongs. The white men whose careers have been sacrificed to the social agenda of increased parity have not perpetrated any wrongs against black people, nor have they benefited demonstrably from wrongs committed in the past. And those who reap the greatest benefits have usually been least harmed by discriminatory practices. As a tool of social justice, affirmative action is a blunt instrument at best.

Backward-looking rationales for affirmative action focus on *groups* and regard them as organic, homogeneous units, so that one entire group (white men) can be held responsible for wrongs committed by some of its members in the past against members of another group (blacks). Somehow the very loosely defined descendants of the sinning group must make reparations to the very loosely defined descendants of the sinned-against group.

This argument commits two hasty generalizations, an informal fallacy in reasoning. In the first, it argues that because *some* whites are morally culpable for having enslaved or discriminated against blacks, *all* whites are morally culpable and should be expected to pay. In the second, it states that because *some* blacks were oppressed and deserved reparations, *any* black person can be justifiably offered reparations now. Thus an inherited, collective guilt is inculcated in white students as part of the moral education, along with an inherited sense of victimization and consequent group entitlement to reparations in black students.

The forward-looking rationales also defy logic. They overlook a basic fact: *No one can possibly know how our society would look had there been no discrimination.* Affirmative action is based on the assumption that discrimination is the only reason for differences between groups, but no evidence has been produced in support of this assumption. In fact, Thomas Sowell has noted evidence to the contrary in many parts of the world. Different ethnic groups have different cultural histories not reducible to differences in political power.

They have, for instance, over long periods of time, responded to different physical environments. Such different histories often predispose different groups to tend to excel in different occupations. Thus there is an odd incompatibility between multiculturalists' celebration of diversity and the belief—often fervently held by the same people—that a just society would produce no statistical differences between groups. This is likely to be true only to the extent that the groups are no longer groups in the sense of having different cultures.

The *role model argument* raises (or should raise) the question of whether a person who is known to have obtained his or her position due to a government program can possibly be as good a role model as someone who obtained the position on merit without such assistance. Optimistic role model assumptions are also called into question by two facts. First, several generations of black public school students have now had many black teachers and administrators, yet academic performance indicators remain low and dropout rates remain high. Second, Asian and Asian American students have excelled in public schools with virtually no role models at all.

The *argument from cultural bias* is contradicted by the well-documented fact that these students tend to score higher on standardized tests than whites, despite having originated from a cultural milieu more different from that of American whites than is the case with American blacks. The majority of blacks entering American colleges and universities were born here and grew up speaking English. Many Asians, on the other hand, arrived unable to speak English and possessing nothing but the clothes on their backs. Today their children are earning Ph.D.s in physics and computer engineering. The claim that objective standards for success are instruments of white male hegemony simply does not hold up.

The *argument from changing demographics* fails to confront the reality that government programs that put members of nonwhite groups in positions of influence *cannot legislate qualifications for these positions into existence by fiat.* Attempts to do so will only result in a group of people who, though in influential positions, are unable to do the work required. This may be why more black students are attending college than ever before, yet their attrition rate remains high.

For moral arguments that command the equivalent of involuntary sacrifice, leaving a trail of shattered careers and dreams in their wake, the social payoff had better be exceptionally good. Thus far, it is not. We have found little increase in either overall social well-being or minority well-being to offset the harm done to innocent third parties, such as younger white men who had no hand in earlier practices of discrimination. Moreover, many innocent third parties are neither white nor male.

The Other Invisible Victims: Asian Americans

By the middle of the 1980s, evidence had surfaced that affirmative action policies in admissions to elite universities were working to the disadvantage of Asian-American applicants. (The term *Asian American* here refers to people of Japanese, Korean, Taiwanese, Chinese, Vietnamese, Cambodian, Thai, or Filipino descent, many of them immigrants or children of immigrants who have adopted this country as their new homeland.) The phenomenon has been especially noteworthy on such campuses as Berkeley, Harvard, Stanford, Princeton, Yale, and UCLA. We will focus on Berkeley.

Long a center of social experimentation and radical-left political agitation, Berkeley is the kind of place where one would expect to find a deeply entrenched commitment to strong affirmative action. Indeed, this is what we do find. The controversy over the effects of strong affirmative action on Asian Americans was ignited by the discovery that Asian Americans with virtually straight-A secondary school grade averages and high test scores were being refused admission to Berkeley in favor of blacks and Hispanics of far more modest accomplishments.[46]

While the number of Asian-American applicants for admission to Berkeley increased dramatically from 1978 to 1983, there was no corresponding increase in their actual enrollment. In fact, their enrollment declined despite their being among the most highly competitive and qualified of all applicants by any reasonable standards. Their test scores, on average, were higher than those of whites.[47] This fueled the suspicion that affirmative action at Berkeley had led to a de facto ceiling on Asian-American admissions, in effect discriminating against them, and on alarming grounds: They were *achieving too much*. John H. Bunzel and Jeffrey K. D. Au wrote:

> . . . a much higher proportion of Asian Americans than Caucasians is actually eligible for college admission. In 1983 . . . 26 percent of California's Asian American high school graduates were academically qualified for freshman admission to the University of California, compared to only 15.5 percent of their Caucasian counterparts. Not only do Asian Americans have a high level of performance in terms of

national standardized test scores and high school grade point averages, but the proportion that takes the Scholastic Aptitude Test (SAT) is much higher than that of Caucasians.[48]

In late 1984, Professor L. Ling-Chi Wang of Berkeley led a task force to investigate the fact that the number of newly enrolled Asian students dropped 21 percent during the academic year 1983–84. His group, the Asian American Task Force on University Admissions, spent six months studying the problem and concluded that "deliberate policy changes" on the part of university officials had led to a reduction in the number of Asian Americans admitted to Berkeley.[49] These findings pointed straight to university affirmative action policies. Two unannounced policy changes that adversely affected Asian Americans (particularly new immigrants) were: requirement of a 400 minimum score in that portion of the SAT that measures one's mastery of English; and the automatic redirection of Asian Americans eligible for the University of California system's Educational Opportunity Program to other, less prestigious campuses around the state.

The task force verified that the admission rate of Asian-American applicants did not correspond to the increase in the applicant pool and concluded that the two-tiered admissions system introduced in the fall of 1985 discriminated against Asian-American students, particularly recent immigrants. (The first tier consisted of students admitted under the most stringent academic criteria; the second consisted of athletes and members of designated affirmative action groups, primarily blacks and Hispanics, who did not have to meet such criteria.)

Asian Americans found themselves treated no differently from white males for affirmative action purposes. Though a numerical minority, Asians and Asian Americans were not an *official* minority. So they were excluded from affirmative action benefits. The task force observed that Berkeley had "violated the public trust" by keeping the policy changes secret and by not including Asian Americans in discussions of decisions affecting them.[50]

The response to these charges is worth more than a passing glance. Berkeley Chancellor Ira Michael Heyman justified the university's admissions policies as follows: "Berkeley must provide effective leadership in an increasingly multiethnic society. . . . We must prepare a diverse student body to govern a state which will increasingly demand a diverse group of leaders."[51] We have encountered the term *diversity* (or *cultural diversity*) several times now. By the late 1980s it had become one of the three official code words for affirmative action, the other two being *inclusiveness* and *multiculturalism*. Giving priority to diversity meant that the quest for statistical equality, not individual qualifications, had become primary in determining who would be admitted to Berkeley.[52]

Heyman accepts the equation of lack of proportional representation with covert discrimination and sees himself led to take, in his own words, "a little social engineering to reach deeply felt needs."[53] His *social engineering* led to the most aggressive affirmative action program anywhere, with the result that a student body approximately 90 percent white in the late 1960s became one where whites were a minority group themselves.[54]

This was achieved through racenorming under which whites and Asians existed at one level and had to meet one set of admissions standards, while blacks and Hispanics subsisted at another and were held to lower standards. The former groups were labeled "overrepresented," that is, tending to be well prepared for college work in large numbers, while blacks and Hispanics were labeled "underrepresented," that is, tending to be underprepared in large numbers. Asians tended on the average to be more prepared than whites. One administrator remarked, "If we keep getting extremely well-prepared Asians . . . we may get to the point where whites are an affirmative action group."[55]

That anyone set out to discriminate against Asian Americans is doubtful. It just happened that the value placed on hard work and academic achievement within Asian and Asian-American families has placed them and anyone else with such values at a disadvantage. This is likely to occur in any climate in which political considerations are awarded priority over substantive ones.

Regardless of whether we call it affirmative action, inclusion, diversity, multiculturalism, or racenorming, this procedure will result in quota ceilings for some groups and open-door admissions for others. In effect, affirmative action at Berkeley penalized highly prepared Asian Americans for coming from groups whose inculcated values place stress on individual initiative and achievement, while rewarding less prepared blacks and Hispanics for coming from groups whose most visible leaders actually discourage individual initiative and achievement.

Sadly, such a program inevitably casts doubt on blacks and Hispanics who would have gained access to Berkeley without a preferential program. It undermines their claim to genuine merit. It will also cause great harm, perhaps even psychological devastation, to underprepared members of these groups who find themselves in college but unable to do college work.

It is almost as if the real target of affirmative action were not white men, but *achievers*. Affirmative action penalizes achievers for being achievers and rewards nonachievers for being non-achievers—without regard to race, ethnicity, gender, religion, or creed.

Hiring Faculty by the Numbers

Preferential admissions for student members of "underrepresented groups" are paralleled by relentless policies of preferential hiring of college faculty. This began when the U.S. Department of Health, Education and Welfare (now the Department of Health and Human Services) issued Revised Order No. 4, requiring colleges and universities to embark on aggressive programs to recruit and hire women and members of minority groups. The directive required faculty search committees "to reject male (white) and non-minority applicants who might have better credentials than female and minority applicants so long as the latter have qualifications *better than the least qualified member presently employed by a department*."[56]

What are the results? In the words of philosopher Nicholas Capaldi, we are now seeing "the slow strangulation of the modern American university."[57] For decades, educators and politicians have lamented the decline of public education in the United States. Perhaps this decline is not unrelated to the emphasis on parity that began over twenty years ago. Since one cannot legislate qualifications for university faculty positions into existence any more than one can legislate the ability of students to do college work or the skills to engage in a demanding occupation, the endless quest for correct statistical outcomes has brought dual standards at the level of faculty hiring, as well as student admissions, and—as night follows day—attacks on the idea of standards.

Such attacks predate the publicity surrounding them in the

wake of the political correctness controversy. Consider the following extract from a letter an HEW official sent to the president of the University of Arizona, dated March 31, 1971:

> Department Heads should be advised that, in addition to the active recruitment of females, affirmative action requires that Government contractors consider other factors than mere technical qualifications.[58]

A similar policy was put into effect at Cornell University, as reported in a letter to the *New York Times:*

> . . . that policy, as described in a letter from the president of the university to the deans and department chairmen, is "the hiring of additional minority persons and females" even if "*in many instances, it may be necessary to hire unqualified or marginally qualified persons.*"[59]

Entire subject matters, skills, and areas of expertise are expendable:

> At one Ivy League university, representatives at the Regional HEW demanded an explanation of why there were no women or minority students in the Graduate Department of Religious Studies. They were told that a reading knowledge of Hebrew and Greek was presupposed. Whereupon the representatives of HEW advised orally: "Then end those old-fashioned programs that require irrelevant languages. And start up programs on relevant things which minority group students can study without learning languages."[60]

Clearly, critics of affirmative action have not simply made up the charge that these measures result in lowered standards. Rather, calls for lowered standards seem to have originated with those charged with enforcing compliance to "hard" affirmative action.

The drive to increase the representation of women and minorities on college and university faculties has become an end justifying any means. It is written into laws that would never have stood up to legal challenge a few short years ago: A state law in California requires that at least 30 percent of all new employees, faculty, and staff of the state community college system be ethnic minorities.[61] To aid the search, the California Community Colleges system created a *Faculty and Staff Diversity Registry*.[62]

In 1988, the University of Wisconsin under the leadership of Donna Shalala publicized its Madison Plan aimed at increasing the number of minority faculty and staff by 75 percent in five years, with the specific goal of hiring seventy minority faculty. The plan stated the school's intent to replace retirements and resigning faculty with minorities whenever possible; to add twenty-five total faculty by fall 1991, including fifteen new tenure-track junior faculty; to hire or promote 125 minority members to staff positions; to institute an Ethnic Studies requirement for students.[63] (It is significant that in the first year of this plan the university hired eighteen minority faculty, but lost seven to retirements and other job offers.[64] By the following year, the net gain was twenty.)[65]

Duke University promised to have one minority faculty member in place in every department by 1993. (Duke did not attain its goal.)[66] Wellesley college administrators are considering a stipulation that every department hire a minority group member along with its next appointment.[67] In desperate efforts to fill quotas, California colleges hold affirmative action job fairs; colleges and universities all over the country place their names on minority vita banks. An affirmative action register is circulated nationwide to three and a half million people. These are routinely advertised in publications such as *The Chronicle of Higher Education*.[68]

At Harvard Law School, Professor Derrick A. Bell announced in 1990 that he would take an extended leave without pay until the school appointed a "woman of color."[69] (Apparently any "woman of color" would do.) Bell actually relinquished his tenure at Harvard in defense of this cause, moving to New York University.[70]

Unfortunately, the people sought by these methods simply don't exist in the numbers sought. Purveyors of the doctrine of covert discrimination would have us believe that there is a pool of highly qualified and available blacks who cannot find teaching positions at major universities because of discrimination. Statistics show this to be untrue. In 1988, approximately 16,000 doctorates were awarded to American citizens by American universities. Only 357 of these went to blacks.[71] The majority were in the social sciences. Many fields ranging from hard sciences such as astronomy to the humanities (for example, comparative literature) awarded no Ph.D.s to blacks at all. In 1986, no Ph.D.s were awarded to blacks in mathematics, astronomy, theoretical chemistry, aerospace engineering, or computer engineering. Of more than 8,000 awarded in engineering and the physical sciences, only fourteen went to blacks. Between 1978 and 1988, the number of blacks receiving Ph.D.s actually declined by 23 percent.[72]

What makes these statistics demand a better explanation than discrimination is that today there are countless efforts on behalf of blacks in postgraduate education. In Pennsylvania, black students are promised full-tuition scholarships to study for advanced degrees anywhere in the state.[73] The California State University system offers minority and female student loans of up to $30,000 to study for doctorates at other schools and waives repayment if they return to the system to teach.[74] Advertisements for fellowships and scholarships aimed exclusively at qualifying ethnic minorities for faculty positions and scholarly careers are routinely published and circulated to millions of readers.[75] Still, colleges and universities are unable to recruit enough black faculty to satisfy the activists.

These mad scrambles have led to serious suggestions that the Ph.D. requirement be waived for prospective black faculty and an explicit double standard instituted.[76] This would bring racenorming to faculty hiring, perhaps as a logical final step from its start in student admissions, where it is now routine.

Secrecy now permeates many academic searches. One recent article, published pseudonymously, recounts a search in which the search committee members were indirectly told that they had to hire a black (preferably a black woman) or funding for the position would be withdrawn.[77] It is unknown how common such "nonsearches" really are, but that they exist can no longer be doubted. White men applying for such reserved positions in good faith seldom learn that they had no chance of being considered. Such searches rarely increase the overall number of blacks in academe—they usually end up raiding other departments.

The minority individuals lured to such positions are sometimes paid much higher salaries than white men can obtain. A plan to lure women and minorities with higher salaries was adopted in 1991 by the University of Texas at San Antonio.[78] Not surprisingly, some minority scholars have become nomads moving at will in search of ever more lucrative pastures. Henry Louis Gates, Jr., offers probably the best-known case study of such an individual. In a few short years Gates went from Yale to Cornell to Duke to Harvard, where he now heads the African-American studies program.[79]

Critics of Affirmative Action and the Ad Hominem Argument

With affirmative action in higher education producing these kinds of results, the eruption of protest is not surprising. Resistance takes various forms from ugly incidents to reasoned critiques. Dissident students like Timothy Maguire have been joined by established scholars with impeccable credentials. Detailed criticism of preferential policies from scholars both black (Thomas Sowell) and white (Nathan Glazer) began to appear after the strong interpretation of affirmative action became dominant. As for the general public, it has been overwhelmingly sympathetic to the idea of compensatory measures for *proven* acts of discrimination from which individual blacks and women had personally suffered . . . but resistant to quotas, set-asides, and any other policy that favors some at the expense of others without regard to individual responsibility.

The official response can be summed up in one word—stonewalling. In a thorough study,[80] sociologist Frederick R. Lynch has documented how affirmative action programs have been protected throughout federal and state governments, in the universities, and in the media by an informal but rigidly enforced system of taboos he calls the New McCarthyism, surrounded by a "spiral of silence." The term New McCarthyism suggests parallels between the actions of today's defenders of affirmative action and those of the late Senator Joseph McCarthy, whose anticommunist witch hunts in the 1950s ruined the careers of innocent people.[81] The "spiral of silence" refers to the secrecy in which the details of affirmative action initiatives are enshrouded; as Lynch puts it, "Word comes down but does not go out."[82]

The New McCarthyism, like the old, has bred intense pressure to conform to the prevailing orthodoxy. This orthodoxy holds that American institutions are not merely guilty of racist and sexist *acts* but are inherently racist and sexist, and affirmative action is therefore needed to counterbalance both. This article of faith is an integral component of political correctness and has insinuated itself into contemporary scholarship in the humanities and the social sciences, where it has become what we may call the New Establishment. The selection process for top university posts operates in such a way as to weed out anyone who is not committed to achieving "cultural diversity" on campus, that is, committed to "strong" affirmative action.[83]

Those who submit the orthodoxy to critical analysis lay themselves open to serious repercussions and reprisals, no matter how reasonable their arguments or evidence. Some backers of affirmative action and other race-conscious policies propagate the view that *anyone critical of these policies is, at heart, a racist*. The charge of racism was thrown at Maguire for exposing the racenorming at Georgetown. The same charge was hurled at the Penn student newspaper that published a column critical of affirmative action. *Racist* has become one of the most damaging epithets that can be hurled at someone defending an unpopular point of view, as was the epithet *communist* in the 1950s.

When Norman Podhoretz raised objections to quotas at a Harvard colloquium in the early years of the post-*Griggs* era, he reported that the questions he received "were so charged with hatred that I found myself wondering if a public reading of *Mein Kampf* could have elicited greater outrage. Almost everyone who took the antiquota position in those days had similar tales to tell."[84] Similarly, when sociologist Lee Nesbit published some objections to affirmative action in *The Humanist*, the response in the magazine's letters column was denunciatory.[85] Duke University's President Keith Brodie was denounced as a racist when he expressed initial hesitation about the value of setting minority hiring quotas that no one believed could be met. He pointed out that departments would find themselves hiring faculty who were not qualified and who

> may not be motivated to carry out the research activity that would be required for a tenured appointment. . . . At the end of the day, we would have benefitted from their presence and then run into the awkward situation of not granting them tenure. . . . We do no one any favors by lowering our standards.

"That's just insulting," Melvin Peters of the University's Committee on Black Faculty retorted. "It's visceral and unwitting racism."[86] Brodie caved in and recanted.

Dissenting minority individuals come under especially fierce attack. Thomas Sowell has long been a pariah to the "civil rights" establishment. Other dissident black scholars such as Anne Wortham, William B. Allen, Walter Williams, Kenny J. Williams, Shelby Steele, and Stephen J. Carter have all come under fire for displaying "false consciousness" by questioning the continued necessity of affirmative action, or for other offenses such as insisting on strict writing standards for undergraduates. One need only recall the furor that erupted in December 1990 when Michael L. Williams of the EEOC suggested that most government-funded minority or "race-exclusive" scholarships were illegal. Williams's "mistake" was to read the Civil Rights Act of 1964 literally.

These maneuvers are textbook examples of the logical fallacy known as the *argumentum ad hominem*. An argument ad hominem attacks the arguer personally instead of addressing whatever substantive issues the arguer has attempted to raise. Dismissive claims that students are in need of moral education if they object to preferential policies, or that white scholars are covert racists if they question affirmative action, or that blacks with similar doubts suffer from false consciousness are all ad hominem.

Perhaps the longest single example of this approach was written by Harvard Law School's Randall Kennedy (it runs to more than eight pages).[87] His conclusion is that while proponents of affirmative action "know that not all of their opponents are racists; they know that many of them are. . . ."[88] Can one imagine an approach more poisonous to the "reasoned discourse" Kennedy says he wants? Given the evidence amassed for the existence of quotas and preferences and about their far-reaching effects, the charge that only an irresponsible racist would draw attention to these realities can no longer be accepted.

Affirmative Action and Accreditation

In 1989 Bernard M. Baruch College, the largest college of the City University of New York, was notified that it was remiss in its duty to improve the diversity of its faculty.[89] The source of this mandate was the Middle States Association of Colleges and Secondary Schools, the largest and most powerful of the country's six accrediting agencies. It is responsible for the accreditation of 600 colleges and universities, 1,800 secondary schools, and 900 elementary schools throughout Delaware, Maryland, New Jersey, New York, Pennsylvania, the District of Columbia, Panama, Puerto Rico, and the Virgin Islands as well as American-style schools and colleges in Europe, Africa, and the Middle East.[90]

Until 1988, accrediting agencies approached universities with questions such as: How many Ph.D.s are on the faculty? How many are publishing articles in the leading journals of their fields? How many courses are they teaching, and what kinds of courses are they? How many volumes are in the library? Does the institution have the financial resources necessary to support the kinds of academic programs it offers?

In 1988, however, Middle States adopted a new set of standards aimed at promoting diversity among faculty, students, and trustees. The new policy mandated that

> to be eligible for accreditation, an institution must . . . have a governing board which includes a diverse membership broadly representative of the public interest and reflecting the student constituency. [Members] should represent different points of view, interests, and experiences as well as diversity in age, race, ethnicity, and gender.[91]

Until Baruch's accreditation was held up for three months during 1990, this new mandate received little attention. But since a college or university must be accredited by an agency recognized by the Department of Education to be eligible for federal money and its students eligible for financial aid, the incorporation of diversity mandates into the accreditation process gave these mandates and their executors immense power. To have its accreditation renewed, Baruch had to submit a plan to hire more minority faculty members and retain more minority students. The plan included recruiting minorities to fill administrative positions and allowing minority lecturers extra time to pursue their doctorates.[92]

Baruch's student body at the time was 36 percent white, 26 percent black, 20 percent Asian, and 18 percent Hispanic. The college had 18 percent black faculty, higher than that of more prominent colleges and universities in the New York City area or the state generally. While Middle States claimed there were no minorities in tenure-track positions at Baruch, Professor James Guyot who teaches political science and public administration there pointed out that 37 percent of recent tenure-track hires had been Asians. "In other words," concludes one recent observer drily, "[Middle States]'s diversity standard was not used to foster a multicultural environment: Such an environment already existed."[93]

An ad hoc committee on Middle States was formed at Baruch and brought complaints to Secretary of Education Lamar Alexander about the accrediting organization's misuse of its power to further political goals rather than educational ones. Alexander responded by delaying renewal of the accrediting bureau's own federal recognition until its diversity mandates had been reviewed. The subsequent review concluded that Baruch had excellent academic standards and that the only reason for the delay of its reaccreditation was its "failure to hire an adequate proportion of minority faculty and administrators."[94] Like Daniel Lamp, Baruch had not filled its quota.

When the school filled two vacancies in the administration with members of minorities, Middle States relented. This kind of interference by accrediting bureaus leads logically to the adoption of quotas, not merely for faculty hiring and student admissions, but for the *graduation* of minority students as well.[95] When two minority candidates were hired in a situation that altogether excluded white males from consideration, Guyot observed that "such race-based discrimination in hiring by a public university is quite likely unconstitutional."[96]

Joel Segall, who had been president of Baruch until April, suggested that Baruch had been made a test case. Baruch's rate of recruiting and retaining minorities on its faculty and its student body was statistically comparable to that of similar institutions. There could be no reason to think other institutions would fare better. "Part of the reason," he said, "is I don't know how many minority faculty members are enough. I don't know what retention rates are acceptable."[97]

Spokespersons for Middle States deny that they are attempting to impose quotas. "Poppycock" was the word used by Peter J. Liacouras of Temple University. "Agencies . . . may not tell you that you have to have a faculty that is 10 percent black or 47 percent women. But they can tell you you must achieve fairness and cultural pluralism. . . ."[98] Liacouras did not go on to enlighten us as to what nonnumerical criteria might establish the presence or absence of *fairness* and *pluralism.*

Howard L. Simmons, executive director of the Commission on

Higher Education at Middle States, similarly defended the mandates. The new standards, he said, made clear "that there had to be language that was much more specific dealing with the issue of equity and nondiscrimination for all students, with particular emphasis on underrepresented minorities and women. . . . The bottom line is that we want to promote the creation of an affirmative learning environment for students in every way."[99]

At least two dozen other colleges and universities have had their accreditation threatened by Middle States' interjection of political goals into the accreditation process. Another notorious instance was Westminster Seminary, a private Presbyterian school located in New Wilmington, Pennsylvania. Middle States threatened to withdraw Westminster's accreditation because there were no women on its board of ordained trustees.

Westminster was founded in 1929 for the purpose of training Presbyterian ministers. The Confession of Faith and Catechisms of the Presbyterian Church of America forbids the ordination of women. While not all Presbyterian denominations honor this commitment, some do, and Westminster sees itself as serving that constituency. In an interview, the school's president, Samuel T. Logan, outlined what would happen if Westminster lost its accreditation.

First, students would lose their Stafford Loans, by which the federal government guarantees repayment of privately obtained student loans. Second, since it is "unlikely that the Immigration Service would approve a visa to study at an unaccredited school," foreign students would risk having their visas revoked, actually damaging the *genuine* diversity and multiculturalism at Westminster. Third, students studying for the military chaplaincy could lose their eligibility to serve as chaplains when they graduate.[100] Consequently, the diversity requirements Middle States was trying to impose on Westminster forced the school to choose between the free practice of its religious tradition and the good of its students. (Many other church-affiliated schools have found themselves in the same predicament.) Westminster obtained legal counsel. Finally, with its own approval as an accrediting agency undergoing scrutiny from new Secretary of Education Lamar Alexander, Middle States backed down by passing a resolution that "diversity standards will not be 'mandatory conditions' or the sole basis for adverse actions." Rather, it would enforce diversity standards "consistent with institutional mission and sponsorship."[101] On June 19, 1990, the accrediting agency withdrew its demand that women be placed on Westminster's board of trustees, while Westminster approved a plan that would allow women to serve on some board committees.[102]

However, this battle is far from over. A second accrediting bureau, the Western Association of Schools and Colleges, adopted standards similar to those of Middle States. Stephen S. Weiner, president of the Western Association, defended the move. His argument was the familiar demographic one:

> American colleges and universities are undergoing massive changes in the racial and ethnic composition of their student bodies. . . . Our commission recognizes that today's college students will come to maturity as parents, workers, voters, and professionals in a world that has no majority.[103]

He therefore endorses the addition of "appreciation of cultural diversity" to competence in written and oral communication, quantitative skills, and so forth, as educational goals. There is the usual disclaimer regarding quotas:

> [W]e ask both institutions and our teams not to define the challenge of diversity—or its attainment—solely in terms of numbers of minority-group students or faculty, staff, or governing-board members. Contrary to the fears expressed by some, we are not pressing for the adoption of quotas.[104]

Yet from this point, Weiner's article descends into the usual vagueness about what he *is* advocating. He tells us that "Having members of minority groups in each constituency of an institution, especially in leadership positions, is essential and a prerequisite for a meaningful dialogue about diversity." Plans to achieve greater diversity must "have been subjected to broad and searching discussion" on curricula, recruiting, retention strategies, student-life programs, and academic support. . . . [The plans] must have goals and some way of assessing whether the goals are being achieved."

Weiner assures us that "diversity does not mean a narrow effort to benefit only members of minority groups, but a commitment of talent and resources to widen everyone's intellectual grasp and personal understanding." Diversity shouldn't be taken as "a code word for granting preferences to one group over another," but rather setting the stage for "campus cultures where individuals and groups are deeply committed to teaching one another and learning from one another."

Whatever he means, Weiner further assures us that "diversity and educational quality are intertwined, and therefore, both are the proper concern of the regional accrediting commission." Consequently:

> Presidents and faculty leaders *need to attend to the requisites of affirmative action in employment and admissions policies*, support candid assessment of the existing campus climate concerning diversity, and take the lead in articulating a vision of how a diverse and educationally challenging campus community can develop."[105]

One is unsure how to evaluate policy recommendations this vague. Regarding the policy at Middle States, sociologist William R. Beer observes that their result in practice will surely

> increase the arbitrary power of the accreditors. The use of an unstated but *de facto* racial graduation quota puts university administrators in a vulnerable position, since there is no way to tell whether Middle States will charge them with not having satisfied the goal of graduating sufficient numbers of designated minority groups. The lack of precision allows Middle States to deny that they are seeking any exact outcome, thereby avoiding legal action. At the same time, when it suits them they can use the "outcomes-based approach" as a potential threat to colleges seeking accreditation. Knowing that they will be held to an inexact but real racial graduation quota, residents and deans will be inclined to design programs to increase graduation prospects for protected groups.[106]

Weiner's article is clear only in that the Western Association is following in the Middle States Association's footsteps.

Finally, Weiner informs us that his organization "has under-taken new efforts to recruit, select, and train team members" and that by 1989 "more than 20 percent . . . were people of color, and more than 30 percent were women. *Almost 50 percent . . . were new to the accreditation process. . . .* "[107] Thus immense power has been placed in the hands of mostly untested recruits who are largely free in practice to interpret the standards as they see fit.

Accrediting agencies, in their role as a conduit through which money flows from government to educational institutions, are ex-tremely powerful. Their subversion by advocates of preferential treatment for government-designated minorities is dismaying. But the ramifications of affirmative action go far beyond the imposition of quotas. For, as has become increasingly evident with the publica-tion of books such as Roger Kimball's *Tenured Radicals* and Di-nesh D'Souza's *Illiberal Education*, many of the individuals now being hired for permanent faculty and administrative positions under diversity mandates of one sort or another are using their positions to advance ideological agendas unrelievedly hostile to the roles of scholarship and teaching as traditionally conceived, that is, the search for universal truths about the world and the human condition, and the transmission of the accumulated knowledge and wisdom of the past two millennia to the next generation.

Instead, students are being "educated" to demonize Western civilization and institutions while romanticizing nonwestern cul-tures; to see American history exclusively as the history of race, gender, and class oppression; and to censor those who question these dogmas. The result is a narrowing, rather than a broadening, of the educational project. This new narrowness is the subject of our next chapter.

THREE

Multiculturalism and the Rise of Antischolarship

Antischolarship

Affirmative action's impact on higher education is not limited to hiring and admissions. Its influence has reverberated through scholarship and teaching and brought about either a revolution of major proportions or a steep decline in standards for politically protected groups working on politically protected topics—depending on your point of view. The areas of teaching and scholarship most affected have been those charged with transmitting our historical, philosophical, legal, and cultural heritage to the next generation. It is thus reasonable to submit the revolution's assumptions and methods to scrutiny.

In 1990, articles and exposés on what became known as *political correctness* began to appear.[1] Originally a Leninist expression of disdain for those who followed the party line too closely, it is now widely used to refer to those accused of politicizing scholarship and polarizing campuses. A number of academic whistleblowers argued that by the late 1980s college and university administrations, curricula, academic departments, and disciplines—particularly in the humanities, the social sciences, and law—had fallen under the sway of a coterie of hard-left intellectual activists, a "rainbow coalition"

(Henry Louis Gates, Jr.'s term[2]) of deconstructionists, radical feminists, multiculturalists, Afrocentrists, and a few leftover Marxists and neo-Marxists.[3]

The members of this coterie came of age during the student uprisings of the late 1960s, stayed on campus as graduate students, and became full-time faculty members who eventually won tenure and set about changing the curriculum to incorporate their political agendas.

These changes include sweeping curricular reforms including required ethnic studies courses and sensitivity training. The changes have been protected by an arsenal of speech codes, intimidation, and censorship—the same "spiral of silence" that once protected affirmative action alone. The roots of this movement extend in one direction to classical Marxism (suitably modified to include race and gender as well as class oppression); in another, to recent French philosophy (including Jacques Derrida, Paul De Man, Michel Foucault, Louis Althusser, Jacques Lacan, and Jean-Francois Lyotard); and in still another, to a number of writers from groups designated as "disenfranchised" (Malcolm X, Alice Walker, Toni Morrison, and Franz Fanon are favorites).

Defenders of the new scholarship admit that there is more focus than ever before in the humanities and social sciences on issues of race, ethnicity, gender, class, and sexual orientation. They contend, however, that talk of political correctness embodies nothing more than the right-wing paranoia of white men who are losing their dominant status in a multicultural America whose scholarship is only gradually and haltingly coming to reflect cultural change.

Who are these new scholars? Prominent voices include deconstructionist Stanley Fish, who heads Duke University's English department and also holds a chair in Duke's School of Law; his colleague and wife Jane Tompkins, architect of the "new historicism"; other colleagues Barbara Herrnstein Smith, a former president of the powerful Modern Language Association and author of a book called *Contingencies of Value*;[4] Frank Lentricchia (whom the *Village Voice* once proclaimed the "Dirty Harry of literary criticism"); and Eve Sedgwick, purveyor of "homosexual studies" (she recently published a book entitled *Between Men*).[5]

African-American "superstars" include Harvard's Henry Louis Gates, Jr.; Houston Baker of the University of Pennsylvania English department; Leonard Jeffries of the Afro-American Studies department at City College, CUNY; Martin Bernal of the Department of Government at Cornell University; and Molefi Kete Asante of Temple University.

Other prominent voices are archfeminist legal theorist Catharine A. MacKinnon of the University of Michigan Law School; her sometime collaborator Andrea Dworkin; radical feminist philosophers Alison Jaggar of the University of Colorado at Boulder and Sandra Harding of the University of Delaware; Paula Rothenberg of Women's Studies at William Paterson College and editor of the controversial text *Racism and Sexism: An Integrated Study*;[6] and Catharine Stimpson of English and Women's Studies at Rutgers University. This is far from a comprehensive list. There are many, many more.

Critics of the movements led by such individuals contend that although these movements claim the mantle of disenfranchisement and marginalization, they actually wield more clout in the humanities, social sciences, and legal studies than any other group. Their supporters and followers at less prestigious institutions are innumerable, and their agendas now have representatives in nearly every major department of English, comparative literature, social sciences, and philosophy, and every major law school in the country.

Jay Parini, a poet and novelist residing at Middlebury College, has stated:

> After the Vietnam War, a lot of us didn't just crawl back into our library cubicles; we stepped into academic positions. With the war over, our visibility was lost and it seemed for a while— to the unobservant—that we had disappeared. Now we have tenure, and the job of reshaping the universities has begun in earnest.[7]

Other new scholars are equally up-front about their intentions. Elizabeth Ellsworth of the University of Wisconsin has spoken of the need "to appropriate public resources (classrooms, school supplies, teacher/professor salaries, academic requirements, and degrees) to further various 'progressive' political agendas." One of her courses, innocently entitled Curriculum and Instruction 607, was actually a course in political demonstrations. Students could earn three credits putting their skills to use by "interrupting business-as-usual (that is, social relations of racism, sexism, classism, Eurocentrism as usual) in the public spaces of the library, mall, and administrative offices."[8]

Donald Lazere, professor of English at California Polytechnic Institute at San Luis Obispo, described his pedagogical technique for inculcating in students the view that the United States is a society of class divisions:

> Under the rhetorical topic of learning to examine issues from viewpoints differing from their own ethnocentric one, they can be exposed to sources delineating the gross inequities between the upper class and themselves; the odds against their attaining room at the top; the way their education . . . has channeled them toward a mid-level professional and social slot and conditioned them into authoritarian conformity. . . .[9]

Andrew Ross of Princeton has stated, "I teach in the Ivy League in order to have direct access to the minds of the children of the ruling classes."[10] Significantly, Charles Paine of Duke University rejects critical thinking on the grounds that it will not bring students around to "radical visions of the world." Instilling such visions requires the professor to "recognize that he or she must influence (perhaps manipulate is the more accurate word) students' values through charisma or power."[11]

What are these "radical visions"? What do these new scholars believe? Their beliefs are not identical. Some, such as Henry Louis Gates, Jr., are fairly moderate. Others can reasonably be situated out on the lunatic fringe (Catharine MacKinnon, Andrea Dworkin, and Leonard Jeffries). Yet there are common themes that run through their published statements.

These include the following:

1. American institutions, from universities to those of government and business, have not merely engaged in racist and sexist acts that can be corrected by liberal reforms but are inherently racist, sexist, classist, and homophobic. Founding documents such as the Constitution, for example, were

written to protect the class interests of white, wealthy, land-owning men.

2. The basic unit in society is not the individual but the group; thus race, gender, ethnicity, class, and sometimes sexual preference are the defining features of human cognition and experience and the primary determinants of one's personal identity.

3. Universal truth, objectivity, and neutrality (sometimes even reality) are myths designed to disguise the longstanding Eurocentric bias of scholarship and education in Western universities. All reading, writing, cognition, and inquiry express no more than the historical particularity and group-identity of the reader, writer, or inquirer, and thus are wholly political.

4. All groups are in some sense moral equals and have contributed equally to human progress. All are therefore entitled to a representation in the college and university curriculum equal to their percentage of the population. The apparent superiority of western European civilization can be explained entirely as the result of centuries of exploitation of other cultures by white men, who are therefore not to be honored as history's builders, shapers, and achievers, but rather denounced as its worst villains.

5. American institutions, especially educational ones, must be radically restructured along multicultural lines in order to give voice to those previously marginalized—women and minorities.

This dogma has created an Orwellian academic universe where "valuing diversity" really means uniform support for the "politics of difference" and all its assumptions; where intolerance toward the slightest deviation from this norm passes for *tolerance* and *sensitivity*; where academics aspire to be superstars who can stay on the "cutting edge," that is, offer slightly more extreme pronouncements this week than last week, instead of attempting to produce works that will stand the test of time; and where in the name of tolerance, an ever-increasing militancy among protected groups is actively encouraged.

During this period we have seen potentially worse violations of academic freedom than those that took place during the McCarthy era—worse because McCarthy never had the support of the dominant intellectual culture in this country. Stephan Thernstrom, for example, stopped teaching a once-popular course in American ethnicity after accusations of racial insensitivity followed his class reading from white plantation owners' diaries, which allegedly painted slavery in a benevolent light. Reynolds Farley, a University of Michigan sociologist and authority on racial demographics, was confronted with similar charges for having remarked that Malcolm X spent some time as a pimp.

Ian MacNeil, while visiting at Harvard Law School, was confronted by radical feminists angered over alleged "sexist language" in a textbook he had written. Murray Dolfman of the University of Pennsylvania found his class occupied by militant black students and was forced to undergo "racial sensitivity training" following a jocular reference to "ex-slaves" who should know where the term *servitude* could be found in the Constitution. Alan Gribben—once a student radical himself—encountered such a climate of hostility at the University of Texas in Austin's English department, after opposing efforts to politicize the teaching of composition there that he abandoned a tenured position at a major research university for a small commuter campus (Auburn University at Montgomery).[12]

Many students have similar stories to tell. We have encountered Timothy Maguire's experience at Georgetown Law School when he exposed the racenorming there. Dinesh D'Souza has collected numerous and sometimes poignant accounts of students who have inadvertently run afoul of the new speech and behavior codes. Nina Wu, for example, was expelled from her dormitory at the University of Connecticut after putting a poster on her door using the word "homos"—which the university contended violated its policy against "slurs or epithets based on race, sex, ethnic origin, religion or sexual orientation." She had to sue to return to campus.[13]

Pete Schaub, a business major at the University of Washington at Seattle, found himself physically barred from attending a women's studies class after he challenged the instructors, radical feminists Donna Langston and Dana-Michele Brown, to produce evidence for a claim they had made in class that lesbians raise children better than married couples.[14]

Jerome Pinn of the University of Michigan checked into his dormitory room and found that his roommate, a militant homosexual, had plastered its walls with pictures of nude men. He complained to housing authorities and found himself threatened with discrimination charges:

> [Housing officials] asked what was wrong with *me*—what *my* problem was. I said that I had a religious and moral objection to homosexual conduct. . . . Finally they agreed to assign me to another room, but they warned me that if I told anyone of the reason, I would face university charges of discrimination on the basis of sexual orientation.[15]

Sometimes the reprisals for expressing politically unacceptable points of view are borderline sadistic. A student at Mount Holyoke College was subjected to such an attack after writing an article for the campus newspaper objecting to the politicizing of a philosophy class she was enrolled in:

> Her professor's response was, without any advance warning to the student, to leave class early one day so that the student's classmates could let her know what they thought of her ideas. The newspaper for which the student had written described what ensued as "a verbal lynching":
>
> With the absence of a moderator, and in the midst of so many angry student activists . . . the "discussion" quickly degenerated into an *ad hominem* denunciation of a single student. As [the student] put it, "They were no longer attacking my political beliefs; they were attacking my character."[16]

Marc Shachtman of Oberlin College described the similar experience of a classmate:

> In a course I took last year, a maverick student said he agreed with a Supreme Court justice's view that a particular affirmative action program would unconstitutionally discriminate on the basis of race. During the next few minutes, a couple of students vehemently objected. One raised her voice significantly, the other began to yell at him. In the following fifteen minutes, the professor did not speak; instead, he took other volunteers. Almost all of these students jumped on the bandwagon, berating the one maverick student. The professor gave

him one more chance to speak. By this time the student was quite flustered and incoherent.[17]

The publicizing of these and many similar confrontations with purveyors of the new orthodoxy prompted Benno Schmidt, then president of Yale University, to remark in 1991 that

> The most serious problems of freedom of expression in our society today exist on our campuses. . . . The [new] assumption seems to be that the purpose of education is to induce correct opinion rather than to search for wisdom and liberate the mind.[18]

Retiring President Derek Bok of Harvard warned of the need to "resist . . . deliberate, overt attempts to impose orthodoxy and suppress dissent. . . . In recent years, the threat of orthodoxy has come primarily from within rather than outside the university."[19]

In short, during the past decade we have seen the rise of *antischolarship* in academic research, teaching, and activism. Antischolarship, as the term suggests, is resolutely hostile to every method and value that previously facilitated open, reasoned discourse in a climate of academic freedom. Antischolarship has gone beyond advocacy of race and gender preferences to waging what Peter Shaw has described as a "war against the intellect."[20]

Why has this happened? It has happened because in the choice between merit-based criteria—whether for hiring, subcontracting, admitting to college, or for any other purpose—and the demand for proportional representation of groups as an end in itself, something must give. It is simply not possible to focus on both at once. This fundamental dilemma has given rise to the antischolar. Antischolars aim to obliterate, as much as possible, all intellectual grounds for upholding impartial criteria. In its more extreme forms, antischolarship attempts to do away with such concepts as intellectual truth and literary or artistic merit altogether.

The results go beyond rationalizations for preferential treatment for women and minorities. We have actually seen the emergence of a new entitlement—to cultural achievement. In antischolarship's wake, we have seen new "disciplines" created and existing ones altered almost beyond recognition. Whole curricula have been bent to fit the political agendas of pressure groups.[21] One must guard one's speech very carefully to avoid offending the sensitivities of any politically protected group. Such protections are no longer limited to those who can plausibly claim historical victimization, and a pseudolanguage of euphemisms has issued from the culture of hypersensitivity. Some of the terms (for example, "differently abled" for *handicapped*, "follicularly challenged" for *bald*) are so absurd as to positively invite satire.[22]

One core belief seems, more than any other, to animate antischolarship. It concerns the human cognitive condition, our ability to assimilate and transmit genuine knowledge about reality. This view holds that group characteristics (race, gender, class, and sometimes sexual orientation) are the primary "ways of being in the world" and hence the primary determinants of consciousness, experience, and thought—thus also of our language, writings, inquiries, and social institutions. As Diane Ravitch recently explained, multiculturalism

is unabashedly filiopietistic and deterministic. It teaches children that their identity is determined by their "cultural genes." That something in their blood or their race memory or their cultural DNA defines who they are and what they may achieve.[23]

Barbara Herrnstein Smith informed Dinesh D'Souza that

Minorities and women perceive and experience the world differently. These perspectives now collide with those of white males. My teaching emphasizes the new perspectives, which are a necessary solution to our invisible procedures of discrimination.[24]

This position, which I call *Strong RGC-Relativity* (RGC for race, gender, and class),[25] holds that one can no more transcend one's race, gender, cultural context, or economic class than step outside one's skin. Every person is locked inside a cognitive prison created by group identity. There are no knowable, universal truths or values that transcend these contingencies. Such universals could only be attained by beings who were raceless, genderless, classless, and ahistorical—that is, by beings who were not human. Antischolars have borrowed Harvard philosopher Hilary Putnam's adage that there is no God's Eye point of view.[26]

Three varieties of antischolarship are worth a closer look in light of their considerable influence on contemporary thought. They are *deconstructionism, radical feminism*, and *Afrocentrism*. Each has close links with affirmative action in higher education.

Varieties of Antischolarship I: Deconstructionism

Deconstructionism is not easy to characterize, partly because of the paradoxical nature of its doctrines, partly because of the impenetrable writing style of its gurus, and partly because of their sometimes belligerent insistence that any attempt to describe deconstructionism clearly is by nature a misrepresentation. Nevertheless, let us try![27]

Deconstructionism asserts a thesis about language: Language can never get outside itself to represent or make contact with an extralinguistic reality. Thus deconstructionism takes a militantly skeptical view of our cognitive capabilities and recommends that the search for truth be given up. Jacques Derrida claims, "[Reading] . . . cannot legitimately transgress the text toward something other than it, toward a referent (a reality that is metaphysical, historical, psychobiological, etc.) or toward a signified outside the text whose content could take place, could have taken place outside of language."[28]

Derrida stands Aristotle on his head by denying both self-identity and the law of contradiction. Contradiction (or *differance*), for Derrida, is built into everything, because a statement or concept can only take on a semblance of identity and determinateness by excluding other things. (For example, the concept "man" derives its identity and determinateness only by excluding "woman." Yet this exclusion reveals that the concept "woman" was inside that of "man" all along, contradicting and subverting it.)

Thus any concept or statement is "contaminated" by what it excludes; the excluded concept "decenters" it, denies its integrity, wholeness, or self-identity. No "center" can hold: The center created by "logocentrism" and "Eurocentrism" is decentered by those forms of writing that it has marginalized and excluded.

Thus certain aspects of deconstructionism lend themselves to support of affirmative action, the multiculturalist revolution, and the politicizing of inquiry. As Derrida has remarked, "Deconstruction . . . is not a discursive or theoretical affair, but a practico-political one."[29]

The human social world is made up of texts (il n'y a rien hors du texte, says Derrida: "Nothing exists but the text."). A text has no determinate meaning or intrinsic merit. Both are always derived from the judgment of some group. Since one group (white men) has exercised domination over all other groups, the assigning of any merit to texts written by white men merely rationalizes this domination.

Deconstructionist Stanley Fish contends that "history is the crucible in which standards emerge and become sociologically and politically established."[30] There is in Fish's view no such thing as objective knowledge or standards. Belief in either is a product of historical and sociological conditioning, so that "the best we can hope to do is convert someone from their [*sic*] set of beliefs to ours. This is persuasion. It has nothing to do with truth or knowledge. It is an art, as the old rhetoricians knew."[31] With no neutrality, there can be only interpretation from within a cultural (racial, sexual, or economic) perspective. When asked, then, "Does might make right?" Fish responds:

> In a sense, the answer I must give is yes, since in the absence
> of a perspective independent of interpretation, some interpre-
> tive perspective will always rule by virtue of having won out
> over its competitors.[32]

Dinesh D'Souza has commented that "In other words, Fish seemed to recognize, relativism paves the way for a toppling of the old rules, and the establishment of new ones based on political strength."[33]

Fish is one of the most influential figures on the contemporary literary scene and is much in demand on the lecture circuit. His views wield considerable clout within his discipline. Fred Siegel recently reported one of Fish's performances, which was dedicated to demonstrating the deconstructionist view that language never represents reality:

Asked during the question period if the First Amendment isn't something more than an expression of power, Fish rasps, "Free speech? Yeah, tell me another one." A graduate student, puzzled by the way Fish has folded the world into the alphabet, asks the professor where his kind of "academic leftism" is going. "I want them," responds Fish, referring to students and faculty, "to do what I tell them to." Later, he explains to a small group: "I want to be able to walk into any first-rate faculty anywhere and dominate it, shape it to my will. I'm fascinated by my own will."[34]

I want to be able to walk into any first-rate faculty anywhere and dominate it, shape it to my will. I'm fascinated by my own will.

This is where deconstructionism has taken us. The response that Adolf Hitler would have approved is difficult to resist. Deconstructionist Denis Donoghue has admitted that "nothing in deconstruction provides an ethical criticism of Nazism."[35] For ultimately it is not merely legal concepts such as free speech that are "decentered" by their opposites: The deconstructionist wrecking ball can be wielded against any ethical notion whatsoever.

Derrida cites German philosopher Friedrich Nietzsche as a precursor. This is understandable: Nietzsche sometimes made statements like "It is perhaps dawning on five or six minds that physics, too, is only an interpretation and exegesis of the world (to suit us, if I may say so!) and *not* a world-explanation. . . ."[36] But Nietzsche regarded the consequences of this awareness as extremely serious and viewed what he took to be their inevitability with trepidation. For when truth was abandoned, we would have to create our own "truths," moral and otherwise. This was *not* something to play games with: It placed enormous responsibility on humanity, for nihilism threatened to render human lives trivial and meaningless. Civilization could reap a joyous rebirth or ultimate annihilation, and the heavy burden of choice was on us as *persons*.

In contrast, Derrida and Fish regard the consequences of their views as not only untroubling but unquestionably liberating: We will be free of "logocentric repression." Theirs is perhaps the first joyful nihilism, a nihilism with a tone and jargon especially suited to contemporary academic gamesmanship, which aims not at enduring intellectual accomplishments but rather tenure and promotions, grants and accolades.

In other words, recent years have seen the appearance of a major movement within the humanities whose militantly relativistic and nihilistic world view not only denies our ability to even partially control and transcend the contingencies of our own language, but also celebrates the void . . . and its inevitable filling with the worship of power. This perspective is being widely disseminated to college students today in English and comparative literature classes and has become enormously influential even among people who have never so much as heard the word *deconstruction*.

Varieties of Antischolarship II: Radical Feminism

The brand of *feminism* produced by antischolars differs from its predecessor in being *radical*. Feminism of the 1960s—liberal or equity feminism—emphasized similarities between men and women, similarities that implied that in many workplaces a woman can do what a man can do. Feminists relied on such similarities and came up with very reasonable arguments against discrimination.

By contrast, in keeping with the adoption of "strong" affirmative action and the need to justify preferences, the new breed of feminist uses a deconstruction-like approach to focus not on similarities between the sexes, but on differences. It hints that the "different voice" of women is morally superior to that of men.[37] Earlier feminists claimed that some of our social and cultural practices have been unfair to women. Radical feminists claim that our institutions are inherently unjust to women and must be totally restructured or abolished to eliminate "patriarchy."

Radical feminists contend that women's experience of the world is categorically different from men's. One such feminist writes,

Research on gender suggests . . . that men and women in contemporary Western societies are differently constituted as human subjects; that they inhabit, experience, and construct

the sociopolitical world in different, and often incommensurable ways. . . . that what has passed as a gender-neutral vocabu-
lary of reason, morality, cognitive development, autonomy,
justice, history, theory, progress, and enlightenment is imbued
with masculine meaning.[38]

Claims for the "gendering" of thought and experience are sweeping. Feminist "philosopher of science" Sandra Harding asserts:

Feminism proposes that there are no contemporary humans
who escape gendering. . . . Feminism also asserts that gender
is a fundamental category within which meaning and value are
assigned to everything in the world, a way of organizing
human social relations.[39]

This approach opened the door for radical feminism to conduct
incursions into one academic discipline after another. One of the
unique features of radical feminism is its attack on science. As
"feminist standpoint theorist" Mary E. Hawkesworth puts it:

[Knowledge] is always mediated by a host of factors related to
an individual's particular position in a determinate sociopolitical formation at a specific point in history. *Class, race, and
gender necessarily structure the individual's understanding of
reality and hence inform all knowledge claims.*[40]

Thus radical feminism does not stop with the claim that women
are underrepresented in science (the "woman question in science,"
Harding calls it); it contends that *science itself* is inherently alien to
feminine consciousness (the "science question in feminism"). "Science as usual," as Harding calls it, must therefore be criticized and
repudiated, and the way paved for its replacement by a "feminist
science."

Science, she tells us, has from the start been the tool of white
male oppressors: "classist, racist, and sexist social relations are as
central to the organization of science as they are to the organization
of social life more generally"; there is a "symbiotic relationship
between racism, classism, and science."[41] Her conclusion wonders

if "there is anything morally and *politically* redeeming in the scientific world view, its underlying epistemology, and the practices these legitimate."[42]

This conclusion is based on bizarre analyses such as the following, of the scientific revolution:

> [When] Copernican theory replaced the earth-centered universe with a sun-centered universe, it also replaced a woman-centered universe with a man-centered one. . . . In the new Copernican theory, the womanly earth, which had been God's special creation for man's nurturance, became just one tiny, externally moved planet circling in an insignificant orbit around the masculine sun.[43]

Or consider:

> Traditional historians and philosophers have said that [rape metaphors] are irrelevant to the *real* meanings and references of scientific concepts. . . . But when it comes to regarding nature as a machine, they have quite a different analysis: Here, we are told, the metaphor provides the interpretations of Newton's mathematical laws: It directs inquirers to fruitful ways to apply his theory. . . . But if . . . mechanistic metaphors were a fundamental component of the explanations the new science provided, why should we believe that the gender metaphors were not? A consistent analysis would lead to the conclusion that understanding nature as a woman indifferent to or even welcoming rape was equally fundamental. . . . Presumably these metaphors, too, had fruitful . . . consequences for science. In that case, why is it not as illuminating and honest to refer to Newton's laws as "Newton's rape manual" as it is to call them "Newton's mechanics"?[44]

Harding's interpretation of the Copernican revolution suggests that the Copernican theory of the solar system owed its rise not to the slow breakdown of the old Ptolemaic model along with a gradual accumulation of new evidence, as traditional historians of science have thought, but to the triumph of masculinity (as if there were no powerful men before). Her interpretation of Newton concludes that

"Newton's mechanics" and "Newton's rape manual" are equally valid interpretations of Newton's laws!

Harding is not an isolated case. Feminist "philosopher" Alison Jaggar tells us how to get past those troublesome differences between the sexes:

> Just as sexual segregation in nonprocreative work must be eliminated, so men must participate fully in childrearing and, so far as possible, in childbearing. . . . the ultimate transformation of human nature at which socialist feminists aim goes beyond the liberal conception of psychological androgyny to a possible transformation of "physical" human capacities. . . . This transformation might even include the capacities for insemination, for lactation, and for gestation, so that, for instance one woman could inseminate another, so that men and nonparturitive women could lactate and so that fertilized ova could get transplanted into women's or even into men's bodies.[45]

If we turn to how radical feminists handle issues of concern to most women (for example, rape or sexual harassment), we find equally strange statements. Liberal feminism wanted equal and fair treatment for women in the workplace. Nearly all reasonable people were sympathetic to its goals. Liberal feminism did not touch basic institutions such as dating, courtship, marriage, motherhood, and family life, which form the warp and woof of the lives of most women, and in which most place a great deal of value. Not so with radical feminists. When they turn their attention to these institutions, radical feminists find them to be bastions of male domination. Women who accept them are dismissed with a degree of contempt that is absolutely stunning.

Again radical feminists take their cue from deconstructionists: Nothing is what it seems. "Average" (that is, nonfeminist) women are hopelessly immersed in "false consciousness" and so don't realize that dating and courtship are akin to prostitution, and that marriage, childrearing, and family life are inherently oppressive and should be forcibly abolished.[46] As Alison Jaggar puts it, "women [are] deluded, tricked, or bewildered by the patriarchal culture, patriarchal science, and even the language of patriarchy."[47] Thus

they do not realize that "prostitution is the archetypical relationship of women to men," or that "the ideology of romantic love has
now become so pervasive that most women in contemporary society probably believe they marry for love rather than for economic
support."[48]

The more extreme radical feminists are preoccupied with
power, domination, and degradation of women to a degree that
suggests psychological pathology. Catharine MacKinnon has attempted to blur the distinction between consensual sexual intercourse and rape by blurring the difference between sex and violence
and combining this with the thesis of "gender inequality"—the
contention that in sexual situations a woman's role is invariably an
exploited one. In her book *Feminism Unmodified* she wrote that
"the mainspring of sexual inequality is misogyny and the mainspring of misogyny is sexual sadism. . . . This, at least, is my
understanding of the popular denial that sexual violation is a sexual
practice."[49] And:

> . . . men who are in prison for rape think it's the dumbest thing
> that ever happened. . . . It isn't just a miscarriage of justice;
> they were put in jail for something very little different from
> what most men do most of the time and call it sex. . . . It seems
> to me we have here a convergence between the rapist's view of
> what he has done and the victim's perspective on what was
> done to her. That is, for both, their ordinary experiences of
> heterosexual intercourse and the act of rape have something in
> common.[50]

And, more recently:

> Feminists have reconceived rape as central to women's condi-
> tion in two ways. Some see rape as an act of violence, not
> sexuality, the threat of which intimidates all women. Others
> see rape, including its violence, as an expression of male sexu-
> ality, the social imperatives of which define all women. . . .
>
> The problem remains what it has always been: telling the
> difference. The convergence of sexuality with violence, long
> used at law to deny the reality of women's violation, is recog-
> nized by rape survivors, with a difference: Where the legal

system has seen the intercourse in rape, victims see the rape in intercourse. *The uncoerced context for sexual expression becomes as elusive as the physical acts come to feel indistinguishable. Instead of asking, what is the violation of rape, what if we ask, what is the nonviolation of intercourse? To tell what is wrong with rape, explain what is right about sex. . . . Perhaps the wrong of rape has proven so difficult to articulate because the unquestionable starting point has been that rape is definable as distinct from intercourse, when for women it is difficult to distinguish them under conditions of male domination.*[51]

If these remarks strike you as products of the extreme fringe of the extreme fringe, you're wrong. MacKinnon was quickly outflanked on the left by her colleague Andrea Dworkin. Dworkin's writings describe human relationships in the most nauseating manner possible (her book *Intercourse* is filled with casual obscenities that would make a sailor blush). Consider:

Dirty words stay dirty because they express a hate for women as inferiors . . . a hate for women's genitals, a hate for women's bodies, a hate for the insides of women touched in fucking. . . . The next question—a real one and a fascinating one—then is: With women not dirty, with sex not dirty, could men fuck? To what extent does intercourse depend on the inferiority of women?[52]

A few more paragraphs, and Dworkin is contending that sexual intercourse is more degrading to women than Hitler's treatment was to the Jews. "No one," she was recently quoted as saying elsewhere, "not even Goebbels, said that the Jews liked it."[53]

This is where radical feminism has brought us, led by antischolars like Harding, Jaggar, MacKinnon, and Dworkin. There seems little reason to believe that they could resist the temptation to exercise totalitarian control not only over men but also over *women*, or that they could resist the temptation to implement their matron saint Simone de Beauvoir's dictum: "No woman should be authorized to stay at home and raise her children . . . *one should not have the choice precisely because if there is such a choice, too many women will make that one.*"[54]

Radical feminists have grown influential in the academy to the point where administrators and other faculty virtually live in fear of crossing them. Horror stories abound of unsuspecting administrators, faculty, and students trespassing against the new orthodoxy and suffering consequences ranging from ostracism (in the case of faculty) to threat of expulsion (in the case of students).[55]

Varieties of Antischolarship III: Afrocentrism

A third type of antischolarship goes by the name *Afrocentrism*. According to Molefi Kete Asante, one of its major voices in the academy, Afrocentrism means "placing African ideals at the center of any analysis that involves African culture and behavior."[56] It rejects all attempts to reach common ground with European cultures, let alone universality or objectivity:

> Without severe criticism, the preponderant Eurocentric myths of universalism, objectivity, and classical traditions retain a provincial European cast. Scholarship rooted in such a tradition obviously lacks either historical or conceptual authenticity. The aggressive seizure of intellectual space, like the seizure of land, amounts to the aggressor occupying someone else's territory while claiming it as his own.[57]

And finally: "The protectors of the basest Eurocentric theory, with its racist focus, describe their ethos as the universal ethos, encompassing the only correct view."[58]

Afrocentrists insist that Westerners have achieved nothing on their own. Rather, they stole central components of their heritage from other cultures, especially those of Africa. The ancient Egyptians were really black! Afrocentrist historian Asa Hilliard of Georgia State University has stated, "Very few doctors . . . are aware that when they take their medical oath, the hypocratic [*sic*] oath, they actually swear to Imhotep, the African God of Medicine. He contends that there has been a massive conspiracy by Western whites to suppress African contributions to Western civilization: "African history has been lost, stolen, destroyed, and suppressed." The Greeks stole African philosophy and science from the Egyptians, and when the library at Alexandria was burned by Christians this hid their theft. . . . Napoleon's soldiers then destroyed the nose and lips of the Sphinx to obliterate its Negroid features. . . . Both Beethoven and Robert Browning were blacks whose real ethnicity has been suppressed."[59]

Martin Bernal, son of the late Marxist intellectual J. D. Bernal, is writing a work entitled *Black Athena: The Afroasiatic Roots of Classical Civilization*, projected to run to three volumes when complete. The first volume, entitled *The Fabrication of Ancient Greece 1785–1985*, claims that classical Greek culture is derived primarily from earlier Egyptian and Phoenician cultures.[60] As his title suggests, however, Bernal's topic is not so much the classical Greeks as modern and contemporary scholarship about them. Bernal distinguishes between the Ancient and Aryan models of classical Greek scholarship and castigates nearly all classical Greek scholars of the past two centuries for the racism and anti-Semitism that he maintains has blinded them to the truth of the Ancient model. He tells us up front that his primary aim is not intellectual but political: "The political purpose of *Black Athena* is . . . to lessen European cultural arrogance."[61]

George Ghevarughese Joseph goes further. According to him, Eurocentrism amounts to an "intellectual racism" that forms the basis of an "imperialist/racist ideology of domination" tainting every academic discipline. Mathematics, Joseph argues, was invented in Egypt, Babylon, and India long before the Greeks were supposed to have developed it. Furthermore, the discoveries credited to Harvey, Newton, and Darwin should actually be attributed to Arab scientists.[62] Afrocentrism recommends that black Americans reject European-derived thought and cultural practices altogether in favor of distinctively African-derived ones, including adopted African names and modes of dress. (But one can't resist wondering: If European culture is really derived from Africa, can it be all bad?)

Other Afrocentrists carry anti-Western ideology to even greater extremes: Leonard Jeffries caused a stir in the late 1980s with his distinction between "ice people" and "sun people" as ancestors of modern ethnic groups. The two ancestral groups, according to Jeffries, had vastly different perceptions of the world and hence diametrically opposed philosophies of life.[63] The groups descended from ice people are materialistic, egoistic, imperialistic, and violent. Those descended from sun people are spiritualistic, communitarian, cooperative, and nonviolent. Jeffries contends that blacks, Asians, and the indigenous peoples of Latin America and the Caribbean are the direct descendants of sun people, Europeans of ice people.

Sun people are superior because they have more melanin, which regulates intellect and health. White scientists do not carry out research on melanin, Jeffries contends, because the results would confirm the superiority of blacks to whites. The current preeminence of descendants of ice people, says Jeffries, threatens the world with nuclear annihilation. Jeffries has been quoted as having applauded the explosion of the *Challenger* space shuttle on the grounds that it would deter whites from "spreading their filth throughout the universe."[64]

This is where Afrocentrism has led us. That university intellectuals would be capable of this sort of malice would have stunned Dr. Martin Luther King, Jr., and other early civil rights leaders. One has to ask: *how do people like MacKinnon and Jeffries obtain tenured academic positions in the first place?* Certainly not on merit! This brings us to the antischolarship–affirmative action connection.

The Antischolarship–Affirmative Action Connection

At least one antischolar, Sandra Harding, is explicit about the link between her views and affirmative action, telling her readers that "affirmative action is a scientific and epistemological issue as well as a moral and political one." She adds that "the social group that gets the chance to define the important problematics, concepts, assumptions, and hypotheses in a field will end up leaving its social fingerprints on the picture of the world that emerges from the results of that field's research processes."[65] She rejects the view that knowledge is knowledge, whether you are white or black, male or female, heterosexual, or homosexual, saying that this has "antidemocratic consequences":

If all knowers are interchangeable [i.e., knowledge is the same for everybody regardless of race, ethnicity, gender, sexual orientation], then affirmative action in the sciences can be "only" a moral and political agenda. It can have no possible consequences for the content or logic of the natural sciences; the scientific work of men and women, blacks and whites, Nazis and

Ku Klux Klanners will be equally supervised and disciplined by scientific method. If all knowers are in principle interchangeable, then white, Western, economically privileged, heterosexual men can produce knowledge at least as good as anyone else can.... Thus affirmative action, and the civil rights and women's movements appear to have no relevance to the picture of the world produced by the sciences....

Even worse, from the conventional perspective it can appear more likely that affirmative action policies will endanger the sciences. . . .[66]

Harding is simply being true to the logic of her position. Concepts such as objective truth, reason, logic, and even justice are only "white male heterosexual social constructs" when viewed through the lens of antischolarship. Let us be clear about what the antischolar means by racism, sexism, and homophobia: The antischolar does not mean mere hatred or contempt for another person because of that person's race or gender or sexual orientation. For the antischolar, the critical variable is institutional power. White heterosexual men have institutional power; blacks, other ethnic minorities, women, and homosexuals do not. Hence only white heterosexual men can be racists, sexists, and homophobes. Even the most extreme remarks of a Chino Wilson or a Leonard Jeffries cannot be condemned as racist, or those of a Catharine MacKinnon or Andrea Dworkin as sexist. According to antischolars, American society has always been built on power and relations of domination, with white men the dominators and other groups the dominated. White men appeal to universal principles and impartial criteria to mask their bid to stay in power. In this case, concludes the antischolar, scholarship and teaching should do whatever needs to be done to expose the existing power structure, as a prelude to dismantling it. Hence the deconstruction of what white men of European descent have said about universal principles and impartial criteria.

By offering an intellectual justification for denying the validity of impartial criteria, deconstruction supplies a useful intellectual link between antischolarship and affirmative action. Stanley Fish seems to agree, saying "Our *modus operandi* is not independent of the minority, affirmative action consciousness," followed by the typically obscure comment that the Duke hiring plan helps realize "our historicist, postmodernist, poststructuralist moment."[67] He dismisses those who would speak of hiring by merit or qualification:

They want a definition of quality that excludes considerations of race, sex, and so on. . . . But once you have subtracted from the accidents of class, race, gender, and political circumstance, what is it that you have left? [Merit is] a political viewpoint claiming for itself the mantle of objectivity. . . . All educational decisions are political by their very nature.[68]

The concepts of individual rights, individual achievement, and individual responsibility are conspicuous by their absence from the world according to antischolars. Consider the politically correct response to a student at the University of Pennsylvania who, in support of holding "racism seminars" there, wrote a memo expressing her "deep regard for the individual and . . . desire to protect the freedoms of *all* members of society." An administrator returned her note, circled the passage, underlined the word *individual* and stated that

This is a RED FLAG phrase today, which is considered by many to be RACIST. Arguments that champion the individual over the group ultimately privileges [*sic*] the "individuals" belonging to the largest or dominant group.[69]

Thus the educational system can only "celebrate our diversity" by treating all races, ethnic groups, and cultures as inherently equal. The fact that the traditional literary and philosophical canon is composed substantially of works by white men only confirms that white men have oppressed, stolen from, and exploited the rest of the world.

Thus we arrive at the following goals for the multiculturalist agenda:

- Locate previously unknown literary works or other alleged achievements by members of disenfranchised groups including women, blacks, Hispanics, native Americans, "third world" writers, gays and lesbians, and so on. These will be used to "reload" the canon—to the extent that we want a "canon" at all; antischolars disagree among themselves on this point. The reloaded canon would give proportional representation to both sexes and to all racial, ethnic, and cultural groups and would become the basis for a redesigned core curriculum throughout the school system. Multiculturalism thus in effect extends affirmative action retrospectively to the literary, cultural, historical, and even scientific arenas.

- Analyses of the traditional canon should consist of efforts to mine it for evidence of the ethnic, gender, and class biases of its white male authors. We do not simply forget about Aristotle, Shakespeare, Locke, Joyce, Conrad, Madison, Twain, and their ilk; we deconstruct their writings by isolating and exposing expressions of their biases.

- The ultimate goal of education is political activity that targets these biases in "bourgeois" society at large, as a prelude to instituting a new order.

This approach is now the mainstream in the humanities. Barbara Herrnstein Smith says of herself and her colleagues at Duke: "We are the mainstream—what we are doing here is what most of the best colleges do, or aspire to do." Her use of the term "best" here may be puzzling, as it actually implies a standard. "Best," though, may just mean "popular" or "exciting," for as Frank Lentricchia adds, "We are hot and everyone knows that." Administrators, too, are in a tizzy: Malcolm Gillis, vice provost for academic affairs at Duke, was quoted as saying, "Look, what we wanted was academic excitement, and these fellows sure knew how to generate that. They're cutting edge. Whatever they're doing, they get attention. That's our objective."[70]

What are some of the consequences of the preference for excitement over substance? The transformation of disciplines such as legal studies and English, along with the smorgasbord of new ones such as African-American studies, women's studies, Hispanic studies, and gay or lesbian studies, has created the possibility of a new discipline for every group that can claim to be marginalized. From the perspective of advancing affirmative action politics in the academy, this accomplishes four things:

1. It creates new faculty positions and even entire departments for which only members of politically designated disenfranchised groups are qualified.

2. The new disciplines then serve as forums for eliciting or inculcating resentment against white heterosexual men.

3. Their practitioners can inculcate guilt in white men—students, faculty members, and administrators—as descendants of history's villains and oppressors, thus ensuring their sometimes reluctant but nonetheless adequate support for the politicizing of education.

4. Newly tenured chairs in these disciplines, which are often joint appointments with more traditional disciplines, can serve as impregnable home bases from which to extend the influence of the radical-left agenda throughout the university community, and ultimately into American "bourgeois" society at large. For example, MacKinnon and Dworkin were commissioned by the city of Minneapolis to craft a pornography code. The result, which openly advocated censorship, was struck down by the courts as unconstitutional on First Amendment grounds.[71]

We are seeing nothing less than the restructuring of the academy by a resolutely anti-intellectual clique that holds in contempt the very standards of scholarly discourse its members have been entrusted to uphold. While portraying themselves as Western society's victims, members of this clique wield enormous power. They have tenured chairs at some of the most prestigious universities in the country. Their writings are published by leading university presses (Harvard University Press has handled Catharine MacKinnon's two most important books, *Feminism Unmodified* and *Toward a Feminist Theory of the State*) and win prestigious awards (Sandra Harding's *The Science Question in Feminism* won the American Sociological Association's Jessie Bernard Award for 1987). As a result, academic disciplines from comparative literature to law are being transformed from fields of inquiry and instruction into launching pads for political activism and indoctrination.

The Incoherence of Antischolarship

One of the primary objections to affirmative action has been that it lowers the standards of every institution it touches, and our findings more than confirm this. We have seen not just the lowering of standards in scholarship, but a systematic effort to abolish them altogether. Antischolars forestall criticisms of their theories and methods by claiming that any invocation of standards is inherently racist, sexist, homophobic, or simply an effort to conceal one's own agenda. This has the effect of foreclosing further discussion—who, after all, wants to be publicly denounced as a racist? There are good reasons for antischolars to try to prevent discussion, for if their theories and methods are discussed on intellectual terms, they prove to be riddled with logical inconsistencies and factual inaccuracies. No wonder they reject the ideas of logic, objectivity, and reality!

Recall that Derrida described deconstruction as "not a discursive or theoretical affair but a practico-political one." Surely such an exclusionary, categorical definition—which claims that deconstruction is *this* and definitely not *that*—is vulnerable to its own method: it itself cries out to be decentered and deconstructed.

The claim that "there is no such thing as universal intellectual truth" is meaningless unless the claim itself is the one example of a universal intellectual truth. To deny the possibility of truth is self-contradictory: Why should we believe this denial, unless it is true? But if it is true, its truth disproves its denial of the possibility of truth. . . . Claims that "objectivity and impartiality are impossible" similarly imply their own objectivity and impartiality—to the extent that they can purport to have serious meaning at all—and so are similarly self-refuting.

Likewise, the claim that we can never rise above the contingencies of race, ethnicity, gender, and class (or, in antischolar jargon, that we can never "decontextualize" the historically particular) looks suspiciously like a decontextualized universal claim intended to hold true independently of the race, ethnicity, gender, and class of the speaker. Otherwise, why should we take it more seriously than any opposing view?

Finally, if the whole meaning of a text is in my reading and not in the author's intention in writing—then if I decide that the texts produced by Jacques Derrida, Paul de Man, Stanley Fish, and other deconstructionists are so much waste paper, on what grounds can they object? For if all texts are of equal value, there is no reason to prefer their texts over any others—indeed, over *Mein Kampf* or even racist restroom-wall graffiti.

Antischolars evade these fundamental objections or answer them in impoverished ways. They trivialize the probable consequences of widespread internalization of their nihilism. For example, Fish said of those whom he dismisses as "objectivists":

They worry that there will be young people walking around acting in a random, nihilistic way, or perpetually perplexed by life. But that doesn't follow from my position at all. I'm just saying that our standards are acquired through socialization. My critics assume a world in which persons are not socialized. Actually, it is impossible to live without standards. The only question is, where do the standards come from, how are they realized, whose standards prevail?[72]

In reality, anyone who has spent time observing today's college students and other young people—who has frequented their bars, listened to their music, or studied the various youth subcultures—realizes there are indeed plenty of "young people walking around acting in random, nihilistic ways."[73]

Fish says, "The only question is, where do the standards come from, how are they realized, whose standards prevail?" But this is not the only question or even the most important question regarding standards. The most important question is: What standards have the best historical and contemporary track records of sustaining prosperous, free, and secure societies? The question "*What* standards *should* prevail?" cannot be collapsed into "*Whose* standards *do* prevail?"

Fish and other antischolars are not "just saying that our standards are acquired through socialization." They are saying—and they say it in a hundred ways—that since standards are acquired through socialization, any set of standards is nothing but a bid for power by a specific group. But—to use Fish's words—"that doesn't follow." Many people who are well aware that all standards are acquired through socialization nonetheless have concluded that some standards can be reasonably demonstrated to be preferable to others, not just for a narrow group but for a whole society.

Fish is unable to provide valid reasons why we should prefer his standards—whatever they are—to those of an objectivist. Fish can only respond that advocates of one set of standards will always have more power and influence than advocates of another. In other words, for Fish, power is the ultimate standard. Power does not have to submit itself to any ethical standard. There are no superior standards by which to judge the different means of achieving or holding power, or the uses to which it is put. Does this view really represent social progress?

Among other things, the deconstructionist denial of objective truth or widely applicable values is in conflict with affirmative action's implicit premise of the value of intergroup equality of condition. After all, that form of equality is just one of many social values. Why should our polity give it precedence over other values such as equality before the law, individual rights, or economic productivity? To say that we should do so implies a claim that equality (and of a specific kind at that) is a superior (why? more nearly universal?) value—and that such a value hierarchy (one that places intergroup equality of condition at the top) is more socially constructive (by objective criteria?) than others.

The prevailing approach to multiculturalism implies that there is a fundamental rift between the experiences of any two groups and that nothing—educational or otherwise—can overcome it. This is the view I call *Strong RGC-Relativity:* Group identity being the core determinant of all experiences, different racial and ethnic groups (as well as men and women) are epistemically alienated from one another. Nothing, including education, can overcome these fundamental rifts at the very root of our being. The experiences of blacks and whites become globally incommensurable: They have no logical or experiential points of contact.[74]

In that case, what is to be done? Affirmative action and the celebration of diversity in such contexts as literature are surely naive in this event. For there seems little point in having white students read works by black authors—or, for that matter, in having black students read white authors—if their cultures and experiences are radically incommensurable. What is read will surely seem nothing more than words on paper that cannot even in principle be understood and assimilated.

It is hardly surprising that multiculturalism and affirmative action have led not to genuine tolerance of, or willingness to learn from, differences—but instead to our present situation of mutual distrust and sometimes open conflict. In the final analysis, if there are no truths or values members of different ethnic groups (or different sexes) can all appeal to, the only way of resolving disputes is force. This is as ironic as it is frightening, given that doing away with repression and putting an end to hatred and ethnoviolence were all original goals of multiculturalism.

The various forms of antischolarship exhibit other serious problems in logical consistency. Milton, Shakespeare, Locke, Adam Smith, Conrad, and others are treated as fair game for deconstruction (that is, debunking), while Marx, Engels, Foucault, Althusser, Derrida, and De Man remain largely exempt from such treatment. Antischolars further exempt their own writings from deconstructive analysis and react with belligerence to anyone they claim has misrepresented their ideas![75] Radical feminists occasionally tinker with Marx's and Engel's writings to incorporate race and gender into their collection of oppressed groups,[76] but the premises of Marxism are not touched.

What protects Marx, Engels, and certain others is their ideological correctness. But if experience and thought are relative to race, gender, and class, Marx and Engels—European white males, after all—ought to harbor all the biases the breed has always displayed. The same would be true of Foucault, De Man, Derrida, and Fish. Given the cognitive determinism at the heart of multiculturalism, the political correctness of these white men is a mystery.

Any such view that relativizes consciousness and cognition to race, ethnicity, gender, and class, *and offers no specific means of liberating oneself from the resulting cognitive prison*, leads one to believe that voices of liberation among white, European males ought not to exist at all. And the voices of antischolars who are not white males should seem to have emerged out of nowhere, without Western antecedents . . . but this is hardly the case.

Equally unfortunate for the multiculturalist equation of cultural perspective with race, gender, and class is the existence of women and members of minority groups who reject the ideas we have been examining. They distrust affirmative action; reject the contention that American institutions are so permeated with racism and sexism that a black woman cannot prosper by her own merits (Oprah Winfrey was recently reported to be America's richest entertainer—obviously the legions of American racists and sexists have been asleep on the job); and would join William Bennett, Allan Bloom, and other dissident intellectuals in condemning the decline of intellectual standards and of general literacy during recent years.

To explain this, antischolars invoke the Marxist notion of "false consciousness" (false by objective criteria?) and contend that such individuals are engaged in denial. This response is grotesquely ad hoc, not to mention ad hominem. It would have to apply to some of the most prominent and best-trained black and female intellectuals in the country. It would have to apply to economists Thomas

Sowell and Walter Williams, both of whom have written many books on the economics and politics of race; to political scientists Glenn Loury and William B. Allen (Allen is a Straussian, the school of thought that also produced Allan Bloom); to Shelby Steele, English professor and author of *The Content of Our Character,* and legal scholar Stephen J. Carter; to sociologist Anne Wortham and to Kenny Williams, a black woman in Duke's English department who has aroused the ire of her colleagues by dissenting from the party line and insisting on good writing standards. It would have to include philosophers Lisa Newton, Christina Sommers, Marguerita Levin, and Ellen Klein; political scientist Linda Chavez; educator and former National Endowment for the Humanities chair Lynne Cheney; diplomat Jeane Kirkpatrick; libertarian feminist Joan Kennedy Taylor; educator and author Camille Paglia, and many more.

According to the multiculturalist depiction of human cognition as race- and gender-specific, such people ought not exist. There should be *no* black or women intellectuals who are distrustful or ambivalent about affirmative action or who question the prevalent voices bemoaning institutional racism and sexism, oppression and domination.

Within the various oppressed groups are many who can claim membership in not one but two such groups (blacks and women, for example, or Hispanics and women). Which category of oppression is the determinant of their consciousness? Race or gender? Both together, perhaps generating yet another specific form of cognition? Some radical feminists have taken these questions seriously. Harding, for example, has asked:

Can there be a feminist standpoint if women's (or feminists') social experience is divided by class, race, and culture? Must there be Black and white, working-class and professional-class, American and Nigerian feminist standpoints?[77]

And Mary E. Hawkesworth observed that

Objections raised by Third World women and women of color to the political priorities of white, Western feminists generate profound skepticism about the ability of any particular group of women to "know" what is in the interest of all women.[78]

These are reasonable questions and have generated what could be described as the "postmodern" fragmentation of discourse, which Harding attempts to resolve by intoning that "feminist claims are more plausible and less distorting only insofar as they are grounded in a solidarity between these modern fractured identities and between the politics they create."[79] That such a solidarity can be achieved is clear—the existence of the antischolar "rainbow coalition" is proof. However, this solidarity is surely achieved at the expense of logical consistency. The view that one's chromosomes and racial genes constitute global determinants on cognition seems more plausibly to entail the degeneration of discourse into a Babel of incommensurable voices with nothing in common except the claim to victimhood.

There are now probably well over a million offspring of interracial marriages in the United States alone. Is one set of cultural genes dominant? Or do individuals of mixed parentage have a different mode of cognition altogether? To my knowledge only one writer has tried to face the mixed-race problem, or attempted to show how such individuals fit into their view of social/cognitive reality (apart from facile claims that "society" informs individuals whether they are "black" or "white").[80]

Radical feminism and multiculturalism cannot explain how members of different races and sexes seem able to communicate across ethnic and gender barriers, especially when their interaction is voluntary and when they have common, agreed-upon goals or a common subject matter. Black undergraduates, for example, have routinely enrolled in my logic courses and many have no more difficulty understanding "Eurocentric" Aristotelian logic than do white students—though both suffer from underpreparedness because of the deterioration of secondary education.

Finally, there is a deeper self-contradiction at which all these arguments hint. When a radical feminist claims that women have been subjugated by men, when a black backer of affirmative action makes the same claim on behalf of blacks, and when Martin Bernal claims that conventional Eurocentric historians have ancient history all wrong, all are appealing to *facts of the matter* of the very sort that cannot exist (or, at least, cannot be perceived by humans) if there are no race-neutral or gender-neutral truths. If there are no such facts of the matter that hold for all groups concerned, on what grounds can feminists or blacks appeal to *evidence* or *data* to argue their cases? These facts or events must occur in a world common to all groups. If regarded as nothing more than social constructions, they need convince no one. Courts in particular, where white men remain superior in both power and numbers, could never have been persuaded to adopt the various planks of the civil rights agenda without appeals to both a common American cultural heritage that values equality and to factual evidence of deleterious effects of discrimination.

The various forms of antischolarship, whether of the deconstructionist or the radical feminist or the multiculturalist brand, are logically incoherent. It remains to be seen how long they will be able to hide this fundamental incoherence behind "everything-is-political" cliches. That they have been able to do it as long as they have is a sorry commentary on the present state of the American academy. Only someone locked into an ideology with all four claws can overlook so many embarrassingly obvious problems. The systematic refusal to address, or even formulate in a serious way, fundamental objections to prevailing views suggests that at the heart of antischolarship is something more than the desire to rationalize race and sex quotas.

Harding's attack on the "interchangeability of knowers" hints strongly at it. I suggest that embedded in multiculturalist ideology is a deep and abiding hostility to rational thought and its achievements. For rational thought recognizes immediately the difference between *states of affairs* and *language about* states of affairs: Rational thought will find unintelligible the claim that we are locked into cognitive prisons created by ethnicity or gender or even language. It does not shy away from uncomfortable questions such as whether racism really is the primary cause of economic differences between blacks and whites, or sexism the reason why there are more housewives than female scientists and engineers.

Rational thought seeks to approach impartiality as nearly as possible, in establishing criteria for distinguishing first- from second-rateness, excellence from mediocrity, genuine contributions to thought from intellectual fads. It seeks to distinguish better from worse in any discipline or human endeavor and hence follows Aristotle in "treating equals equally and unequals unequally."

To attain the sort of equality sought by the dominant voices in the humanities and social sciences today, one has to insist that anyone claiming superiority for some standards over others is biased (while evading the question of why anyone ought to accept the superiority of *this* idea). To make the charge of universal bias stick, one must undermine the concept of impartial criteria. To do that, one ultimately must negate cognitive abilities, that is, one must attack human reason itself—and by institutionalizing this attack, take it to a level that no previous philosopher has approached, not even Nietzsche.

In other words, we see here—for the first time in our nation's history—open war being declared on the intellect by precisely those whom our educational institutions have placed in charge of safeguarding and transmitting its products to the next generation. Those who have tried to inform the public that a suffocating blanket of political correctness has descended upon the academy are right on the mark. The barbarians really are inside the gates. Whether exciting or not, their products ought to receive short shrift by rational minds. One can only hope that the aforesaid rational minds constitute a silent majority only temporarily intimidated by the decibel level of antischolars.

Why "Multiculturalism" Is Not Multicultural

There are two further observations to be made on multiculturalism. First, a genuine multiculturalism would recognize that peoples are different in some but not all respects and can learn from each other. It would recognize that a pluralistic, multiethnic culture cannot prosper without mutual tolerance and willingness to work together to identify and solve mutual problems.[81] Therefore a genuine multiculturalism, unlike the prevailing approach, would accept the realist or "objectivist" view that different peoples nevertheless have common truths and values that arise from our inhabiting a common world.

A genuine education for diversity, multiethnicity, and tolerance will work toward identifying those very things that multiculturalism rejects: truths, concepts, experiences, and principles that are widely shared because they speak to the human condition. It will, in short, endorse what I call *Weak RGC-Relativity*: Race, gender, and class have the *potential* to influence cognition and thereby bias perception, but these factors can be transcended by becoming conscious of tendencies toward unwarranted assumptions (for example, racial stereotypes) and taking actions to correct them.[82]

Multiculturalists deride this approach to multiculturalism as ceding too much to the "enemy." They point out that a multicultural curriculum of this kind will still be dominated numerically by authors who are white men of European descent. This is true. White men of European descent built Western civilization by developing the moral and practical concepts prerequisite to Western political, legal, scientific, and technological achievements.[83] It is nonsense to read into this historical fact a threat to exclude authors or other achievers of genuine merit solely because of different skin pigmentation or different sex.

Genuinely multicultural inquiry committed to the search for points of commonality is entirely consistent with the affirmation of value in black writers such as Richard Wright and Ralph Ellison, or in understanding the contrasting philosophies of Booker T. Washington and Frederic Douglass (it adds that one need not be black to appreciate this value and these philosophies). Humiliation by those in power is, after all, endemic to the human condition; no race or sex has a monopoly on it.

I recall reading Wright's *Black Boy* and Ellison's *Invisible Man* in grade school English classes long before multiculturalism was heard of and before Black History Month became an annual February institution. I recall my surprise at the lack of antipathy toward his former masters in Washington's *Up from Slavery*. These and other works sensitized many of us to the plight of blacks during the eras of slavery and segregation.

Such works were not suppressed or excluded from study by a repressive Eurocentric literary establishment. By the same light, no one repressed Madame Curie's scientific discoveries. Multiculturalists cannot claim credit for the respect accorded these contributions to knowledge nor make sense of their warm reception, because these realities do not fit into their racial-genetic determinism.

Few would deny the importance of the study of alternative cultural, philosophical, and religious traditions, especially since improved technology and telecommunications (thanks to Western science) in an increasingly global economy (thanks to capitalism) are bringing different traditions into contact with one another to a degree seldom before seen. But the kind of study that would emerge from a genuine multiculturalism is not what antischolars have in mind. Their assumptions of race-gender-class determinism and the moral equality of cultures are Western through and through and are among the logically weakest and morally most pernicious concepts that Western thought has yet produced.

This brings us to a second set of observations. The objectives of feminists who are serious about justice for women inevitably clash with the objectives of multiculturalists who insist on the moral equivalence of all cultural traditions. A recent lecture by writer and columnist Cathy Young highlights this quandary by exposing the way girls and women are often treated in non-Western cultures. Referring to a *New York Times* review of anthropologist Kenneth Good's memoir of life with a Venezuelan tribe, the Yanomamo, Young observes:

> It is a tribe that treats women in an incredibly brutal way. If a female past puberty is not attached to a male, if she is unmarried or even widowed, or if she has the audacity to run away from her husband, she is considered fair game for anyone. She will be routinely gang-raped and sometimes mutilated. The critic summarized all this and then went on to quote, approvingly, Good's assertion that "violence [was] not a central theme of Yanomamo life."[84]

Young goes on to note that in traditional African cultures women are usually relegated to a status lower than that of men. Polygyny, child marriage, wife beating, and genital mutilation of girls (for example, clitoridectomy, that then causes bleeding during intercourse) are common practices. Young cites another *New York Times* story about women and AIDS in Africa that included an account of how "a woman who refuses to have sex with her AIDS-infected husband—who, by the way, has three other wives—is seen as rejecting her proper wifely role."[85]

A *60 Minutes* segment (first aired January 31, 1993) documented the systematic brutalizing and mistreatment of women in India. Infanticide of female babies has become so common there, because of the low regard in which girls are held, that the female population has actually begun to decline! Similar situations abound throughout Eastern cultures. Such harsh realities reveal multiculturalists to be either surprisingly ignorant about non-Western cultures, or surprisingly dishonest.

That at least some multiculturalists practice out-and-out lying is suggested by a *Washington Times* report of a program to train federal employees in "sensitivity to cultural diversity." Young reported that this program included seminars by a retired industrial psychologist, Edwin J. Nichols, who fed the audience the standard Afrocentrist line:

> White males are the bane of civilization, whites are cold and acquisitive and logical—apparently being logical is a bad thing—whereas for Africans, African-Americans, Hispanics, and Arabs, the highest value lies in interpersonal relationships and being intuitively attuned to the rhythms of the universe. . . . Mr. Nichols . . . tells people in his seminars that women in African societies have a higher status than in European societies and are more equal to men. He explains that white women became submissive to men because in the cold climates of Europe, they had to depend on men for survival. On the other hand, "African women see themselves as equal to men" because food in Africa was readily available to them on trees whenever they wanted it.[86]

This would be news to the women of Uganda and other parts of Africa where women are not permitted to speak or show their faces unveiled in public.

Cultural defense arguments sometimes use the undeniably low status of women in many non-Western cultures to reduce homicide charges:

> In 1987, a Chinese immigrant named Dong Lu Chen killed his wife, Jian Wan, smashing her head with a claw hammer after she confessed to an affair. At the 1989 trial, which included the testimony of an anthropologist, the defense argued that Chen's cultural background—"the special high place the family holds in the Chinese community" and "the shame and humiliation" of a wife's infidelity—made him lose control. Mostly on the strength of this "cultural defense," a Brooklyn judge sentenced Chen to five years probation on a reduced manslaughter charge. (I might add that the "cultural defense" has since cropped up in several spousal homicide and rape

cases involving immigrants from Laos, Ethiopia, and other Third World countries.)[87]

In the face of these accounts, the shrill outcry from radical feminists about the oppression of women in American society is as hollow as claims of the moral equivalence of Western and non-Western cultures are dishonest.

What drives multiculturalism is the desire for power, not justice. Advocates of this ideology seek to impose it on top of the various relations different groups and individuals might otherwise develop spontaneously in accordance with what they rationally perceive to be in their best interests.

We have seen how questionable it is that radical feminists really have the interests of ordinary women in mind. Their views, like those of Afrocentrists and deconstructionists, appear to be born almost entirely of resentment toward WASP-male Eurocentric culture and the intellectual discipline by which its achievements were brought about. The supposedly monolithic character of WASP-male Eurocentric culture is a mythical creation of antischolarship. Western European civilization, which includes dozens of indigenous peoples, has produced dozens if not hundreds of independent movements in philosophy, literature, art, music, and culture. Anglo-Saxon culture constitutes only a small range of these, and even it is not monolithic, but integrates diverse sources. Multiculturalists insinuate that the achievements of Anglo-Saxons and others of European descent are either beyond the reach of nonwhite people or are inherently hostile to their interests. This reductionism once again points up the essentially racist assumptions underlying multiculturalism.

Affirmative action has been a major factor in the decline of serious scholarship over the past twenty-five years and the concomitant rise of politically motivated forms of irrationalism. Since coercive government programs never gave anyone a single intellectual skill or new idea, affirmative action in practice has lowered standards throughout higher education. In an effort to obfuscate this reality and intimidate potential critics, multiculturalism in its currently irrational form developed. Its claim to fame has been its aggressive effort to discredit the very idea of objective standards for scholarship, hiring, or admissions.

FOUR

The World according to Affirmative Action

It Didn't Start with Affirmative Action

By now, many readers probably are wondering: *How on earth did our country get into this mess?!* We can now examine this question in some detail. There is good reason to conclude that affirmative action is just the latest battle in a centuries-long conflict between two visions of human social reality and human possibilities.

Affirmative action is a product of what Thomas Sowell calls an *unconstrained vision* of human moral and social possibilities, a vision "in which man was capable of directly feeling other people's needs as more important than his own, and therefore of consistently acting impartially, even when his own interests or those of his family were involved."[1] According to this vision, the egocentric predicament has resulted from particular social and economic arrangements and thus is not an essential or permanent feature of the human condition. A society can transcend the egocentric predicament by changing its social and political institutions.

In contrast, the *constrained vision* of human possibilities accepts the existence of a self-interested human nature and takes the egocentric predicament as a given. It recommends policies and procedures that innovate within broad parameters and, in so doing, attempt to maximize social benefits, but that recognize that efforts to "change human nature" are futile and create more problems than they solve.

Preferential policies derive from an unconstrained vision. Their dismal failure provides indirect but compelling support for a contrasting constrained vision, whose outlines we will explore later.

Most discussions of affirmative action don't raise such issues. Its proponents assume that its justification or critique can be accomplished without examining deeper assumptions about human nature and the world we inhabit. Most contemporary scholarship is done within a framework of separate, largely autonomous fields of inquiry. This approach, sometimes called *specialism*,[2] is widely endorsed in the academy. Leading moral philosopher John Rawls has explicitly defended it.[3]

Despite lip service paid to multidisciplinary studies, academic intellectuals are discouraged from attempting to develop integrated, comprehensive views of the world and our place in it. Philosophers who have tried to do so have either been ignored or dismissed out of hand by the "mainstream."[4] Today, with the emergence of applied, "practical philosophy," as philosopher and intellectual historian Stephen Toulmin calls it,[5] the situation has improved a little. But the structure of academic inquiry still makes little room for those with comprehensive visions.

Thus questionable philosophical assumptions have come to be embedded in legislation and in public policy proposals. To the extent these assumptions are noticed at all, they are treated as self-evident truths. This suggests the need for a more penetrating and integrated philosophical approach to policy problems. Such an approach will enable us to discern how affirmative action has become entrenched in our society, despite producing far more negative than positive results. We will learn that some of the ideological assumptions underlying affirmative action are almost as old as Western civilization; others, though not so old as that, nevertheless extend back to well before the twentieth century.

Behind affirmative action lies a worldview exemplifying a particular unconstrained vision I call the *Philosophy of Social Engineering*. According to this philosophy, human social reality can be comprehended by these theses:

1. a *collectivist* view of human society that subordinates individuals to groups both morally and metaphysically, and hence also as a matter of policy

2. a *sociocultural determinism* that denies individual free agency and thereby shifts responsibility for the identity, behavior, cognition, and actions of individuals to their social and economic environment

3. a *psychology of victimization* that equates inequality with oppression and posits that Western cultures achieved their success only through the oppression of other cultures

4. an *egalitarianism* about social relations and outcomes that forms the supreme moral regulative ideal against which actual states of affairs are to be evaluated

5. an *elitism* that implicitly claims that there is a privileged group or vanguard of human beings that has grasped the human situation as defined in (1) through (4) and that has both the moral superiority and the complete knowledge that will enable it to liberate victims of oppression

One may note in passing that *every one* of these ideas is Western through and through—one need not go outside the history of Western philosophy to identify their main antecedents. I do not maintain that the Philosophy of Social Engineering constitutes a unified movement or one that explains all of history. Major philosophers and social theorists have constructed its various components, but the components have been brought together not by an integrative logic but by the emotional needs they fulfill. On the stage of history, the Philosophy of Social Engineering has been a blind, blundering force, its foot soldiers driven by the resentments directed against the achievers of any culture by its nonachievers.[6]

Collectivism

Collectivism is one of the oldest Western moral and political philosophies. Its roots go back at least as far as the ancient Greek philosopher Plato's vision of a perfectly just society in his famous dialogue *The Republic*, one of the most influential works in the Western world. Plato began with the reasonable suppositions that human beings are social creatures and that within civil society there is specialization and division of labor. One of the central thrusts of the relevant portions of Plato's dialogue is that we can draw an analogy between the individual and society as a whole: "The state is the individual writ large." (Plato assumed the identity of state and society, an identity that history has emphatically disproven.)

An individual is composed of different elements that must work in harmony if each is to advance and not hinder the whole person's best interests. Those characteristics that make a state harmonious, balanced, just, and wise are essentially the same as those that make an individual harmonious, balanced, just, and wise.

In other words, society is not merely a collection of individuals who are pooling their resources in a division of labor, but rather an organism of which the individuals are components like the organs in one's body, and thus ultimately inseparable from the whole. Within this whole, they are naturally suited to perform different tasks just as the organs in one's body are suited to different functions. Some are fit to rule, for example; others more suited to be artisans; still others, to be soldiers or "guardians." Society can succeed only if individuals perform the tasks for which they are suited by innate abilities. In other words, the ideal state has a place for everyone and everyone in his place, and these places can be known. At the helm of Plato's perfect society is the Philosopher King, a person ideally suited to rule, educated specifically for the task of becoming sovereign, and kept isolated from distracting influences during his education.

Plato's overall aim in *The Republic* was to articulate and defend a conception of justice that he believed to be the same in the state as in individuals, and in so doing answer the skeptical Thrasymachus, whose position was that justice is merely "the will of the stronger," that is, the will of those who have the might to impose their views on society and *call* them justice. The end result, however, is that in Plato's society individuals and their interests are entirely subordinate to the interests of society as a whole, under the assumption that there is no fundamental conflict.

"In any case," Socrates tells one of his interlocutors at one point, "in establishing our city, we are not aiming to make any one group outstandingly happy, but to make the whole city so, as far as possible. We thought that in such a city we would most easily find justice. . . ."[7] The focus of this vision of justice, then, is no more on its individual components than our vision of *health* is on the health of individual cells or organs as opposed to the health of the whole human body. A collectivist subordinates the needs and interests of individuals to those of the whole in the belief that the real needs and interests of individuals are best satisfied when we try to satisfy the needs and interests of the whole—just as an organism's overall health engenders the health of its component parts.

Plato's vision has more than a hint of otherworldliness about it, and he had no illusions about its possibility in this world. Nevertheless, the vision of perfect justice attainable through a kind of social blueprint thought out in all its details by intellectuals has continued to exert enormous direct and indirect influence through the ages— even among multiculturalists who believe themselves to have overcome the influence of Western ideas on their thought.

The first influential *modern* collectivist vision was Romanticist philosopher Jean-Jacques Rousseau's *Le contrat sociel* (*The Social Contract*). Rousseau had earlier distinguished himself by having won a prize for an essay entitled *Discours sur les sciences et les arts* contending that the revival of the arts and the sciences had corrupted rather than enhanced morals. This essay put forth the idea that what appeared to be progress was sometimes actually regression, and man had been happier and more virtuous in the "state of nature." Of the ancient Greek polities, Rousseau most admired Sparta, as the most austere and frugal. Significantly, he shared this admiration with Plato.

In his next major essay, the *Discours sur l'origine de l'inegalite parmi les hommes* (*Discourse on the Origin of Inequality between Men*), Rousseau further developed his theme that the state of nature is one of innocence while civil society is fundamentally corrupting, for with civil society comes the institution of property: "The first man who, after fencing off a piece of land, took it upon himself to say, 'This belongs to me,' and found people simple-minded enough to believe him, was the true founder of civil society."[8] He equated civil society with the institution of property rights and titles of nobility, which created massive inequality and gave it the force of law.

In the time period between the writing of *Discours sur l'inegalite* and the writing of *The Social Contract*, Rousseau studied the writings of Thomas Hobbes and modified his views on the state of nature. Following Hobbes, he concluded that the freedom available in the state of nature is vastly inferior to that available in civil society, for in the state of nature one is only free, but in civil society one can be both free and virtuous. For Rousseau, virtue presupposes action taken within civil society; virtue makes no sense apart from civil society. Furthermore, virtue requires action taken not just within any civil society—for Rousseau remained convinced that the European society he saw around him was deeply corrupted rather than virtuous. So, like Plato, he set out to theorize about the lines along which an ideally virtuous community would be organized.

Rousseau took Hobbes to task for holding that our only choice was between a freedom that led back to the anarchic state of nature on the one hand, and submission to the absolute rule of a sovereign on the other. He believed that one could be both free—not ruled by a sovereign in Hobbes's sense—and a member of a civil society. His way around the Hobbesian dilemma sounds almost commonplace in our modern democratic era: People rule themselves rather than submit to being ruled by a sovereign. But things are not so simple as this. For what does it mean to assert that the people rule themselves?

The most important contribution Rousseau made to the development of modern collectivism was his doctrine of a citizenry's general will as something standing over and above the private wills of individuals—a will that is given force by representatives of the state and that ultimately constitutes Rousseau's "sovereign" and the source of freedom as he understands it. To be free in civil society amounts to one's willingness to subjugate one's private will to this general will and the laws it prescribes for itself. Consequently, we need not choose between the barbarous freedom of the Hobbesian state of nature and the rule of a sovereign.

One cannot avoid sensing that Rousseau's conception of *freedom* is quite different from our familiar one, especially in this crucial passage:

> Now as the sovereign is formed entirely of the individuals who compose it, it has not, nor could it have, an interest contrary to theirs; and so the sovereign has no need to give guarantees to its subjects, because it is impossible for a body to wish to hurt all of its members, and, as we shall see, it cannot hurt any particular member. . . .
>
> But this is not true of the relationship of subject to sovereign. Despite their common interest, subjects will not be bound by their commitment unless means are found to guarantee their fidelity.
>
> For every individual as a man may have a private will contrary to, or different from, the general will that he has as a citizen. His private interest may speak with a very different voice from that of the public interest; his absolute and

naturally independent existence may make him regard what he owes to the common cause as a gratuitous contribution, the loss of which would be less painful for others than the payment is onerous from him; and fancying that the artificial person which constitutes the state is a mere rational entity (since it is not a man), he might seek to enjoy the rights of a citizen without doing the duties of a subject. The growth of this kind of injustice would bring about the ruin of the body politic.

Hence, in order that the social pact shall not be an empty formula, it is tacitly implied in that commitment—which alone can give force to all others—that *whoever refuses to obey the general will shall be constrained to do so by the whole body, which means nothing other than that he shall be forced to be free. . . .*[9]

Scholars of Rousseau have offered various interpretations of this passage. But it is clear that Rousseau has developed a conception of *freedom* fundamentally different from that of Hobbes and other British theorists. Rousseau's version of freedom became the cornerstone of what has been called the Continental (as opposed to the English) theory of freedom.[10] According to the English tradition, freedom is a possessed by individuals and means freedom from external coercion. But in the Continental tradition, freedom is achieved through laws that a collective agency uses to bind individuals to the collective will, freeing them from the vagaries of their private wills. Only with such a conception of freedom does it become logically possible for an individual to be forced to be free.

Like Plato, Rousseau saw no ultimate conflict between the needs and interests of society as a whole and the needs and interests of the individuals that make it up. Like Plato, he held that if the philosopher attended to the Big Picture, the needs of individuals would almost automatically be met. A recalcitrant individual becomes comparable to a cancerous cell or defective organ. This "organic conception of society" entered German philosophy by way of Immanuel Kant who, a generation later, would formulate the Categorical Imperative: One should always act as if legislating for oneself as both sovereign and subject, in a "kingdom of ends" (Kant's term for a society whose members consistently obey the moral law out of respect for the law as relevant to all actions). The organic vision appeared again in Hegel's *Philosophy of Right,* which contains alarming passages such as the following:

> A single person, I need hardly say, is something subordinate, and as such he must dedicate himself to the ethical whole. Hence if the state claims life, the individual must surrender it.[11]

It seems unavoidable that this is the sentiment toward which the collectivist vision tends: Individuals are expendable. Virtually all of modern collectivism has manifested this sentiment in varying degrees—whether in the extreme Hitlerian, Stalinist, or Maoist forms, which regarded millions of individual lives as routinely expendable, or in the comparatively moderate forms that have emerged thus far in America. There is a parallel between collectivist ideology and affirmative action: The careers of individual white men are expendable in service to the greater good of a society built around the ideal of statistically verifiable intergroup equality of condition.

Sociocultural Determinism

Determinism is another critically essential component of the Philosophy of Social Engineering. *Universal determinism* is the thesis that all of reality is contained in the physical world as a closed system of mechanical causes and effects. The universe is seen as more like a machine than anything else in its basic operation. (This view need not assert that the universe *is* a kind of machine; it need only introduce the machine as a kind of universal root-metaphor in Stephen Pepper's sense.[12])

Suppose the universe is in some initial state S at time t. In the determinist view, given the laws of physics and chemistry and nothing more, one can calculate any other state of the universe S' at any other moment in time t'. In other words, it is possible in principle to supply sufficient as well as necessary antecedent conditions for every event that has ever taken place or will ever take place. In the physical sciences, this idea became the most successful in history.

Gradually, especially with Julien Offray de la Mettrie's tract *L'Homme Machine* (*Man, the Machine*), it dawned on philosophers that what was successful at explaining and predicting physical phenomena might also work in the human world. Thus was born the doctrine Friedrich A. Hayek would come to call *scientism*, the thesis that concepts and methods of the physical sciences can be imported directly into the human sciences. This thesis came to animate the social theories of Henri de Saint-Simon and Auguste Comte, in whose hands it became integral to the social engineer's view that social problems are basically technical problems to be solved by manipulation of antecedent conditions.[13] Scientism clearly follows from universal determinism, for if determinism is true universally and not just for restricted domains such as Newtonian macrophysics, it is true for human beings. It means that sufficient as well as necessary antecedent conditions can be given for every human *action* (the preferred term is usually *behavior*).

There are several forms of determinism with regard to human beings, and not all suit the social engineer's purposes. For example, *sociobiological determinism* regards the determinants on human behaviors as ultimately genetic (not so much race-specific as species-specific). Since this implies a stable human nature, it suggests a variety of constrained vision: Certain social arrangements and practices are rooted in human biology, making the optimistic visions of most revolutionaries unrealizable. Thus, sociobiological determinism is anathema to the intellectual movements we have been considering. Edward O. Wilson, the world's leading advocate of sociobiological determinism, has endured nearly as much invective as have critics of affirmative action and once had a pail of water upended over his head by radicals.

Sociocultural determinism locates the determinants on human behavior not in genetics or biology but in the social environment, including the sociological and economic circumstances in which a person was raised, the kind of upbringing he had, the kind of schools she went to, the kind of occupation he or she engages in, and so on. These conditions are enormously complex, and no one claims to have given a complete account of them. But according to the sociocultural determinist, such an account is possible in principle. In this scheme of things, human nature has no stable core but is instead entirely a product of social influences. The thoughts, desires, motives, and behaviors of individuals are inevitable outcomes of specific socioeconomic conditions.

The factors that shape individuals are thus beyond their control. But these conditions are not unknowable and not beyond the control of *other* individuals. Suppose these factors can be brought under the control of those who can claim knowledge of the determinants on human life and thus of the universal social conditions for human happiness. Perhaps they can manufacture a new kind of human being with a new form of consciousness by subtly instituting a new set of controls. This is what follows from the idea that human nature is unstable: Change the social environment, and you change human nature.

This form of determinism, however it has been cashed out on different occasions,[14] is the unofficial metaphysics of twentieth-century social science and of much modern "scientific" philosophy. Its hegemony has made it difficult for social scientists and philosophers to discuss such matters as free choice and moral responsibility apart from reference to cultural conditioning.

Philosophers have given us an enormous literature on the problem of free will and determinism and the relationship between this problem and moral responsibility. Some of this literature is of the highest quality, technically speaking.[15] The dominant position which has emerged, though, is *compatibilism*, the thesis that universal determinism as defined above (or in some equivalent way) is logically compatible with human free agency in some sense and hence with moral accountability. There are different forms of compatibilism, but our concern here is with their similarities.

The most influential forms of compatibilism refuse to identify an *explanation* of behavior with a *compulsion* to behave in some way. That is, they maintain that identifying the conditions that prompted—and thus in a sense caused—a given behavior does not mean that these conditions *forced* the behavior. This, compatibilists maintain, is a misuse of the word *forced*. The person was not forced to do something if he was free from coercion by someone else, even though his inclination to do it can be given necessary and sufficient antecedents. This leads directly to the idea that if a group of individuals can rearrange the social determinants operating within society on a large enough scale, they can change people's inclinations, and so produce desirable forms of behavior without being said to *compel* them.

Karl Marx combined collectivism with his brand of *economic* sociocultural determinism, which claimed the sociocultural determinants to be mainly economic. The result was dialectical materialism, essentially an attempt at a deterministic theory of history. In his scheme, the fundamental units for social analysis are *classes*, defined by the distinction between those who own the means of production in a society and those who have only their labor to sell. Marxism soon became the most important vehicle for advancing collectivist ideas within a framework that aimed at overturning of capitalism while maintaining an appearance of scientific, intellectual respectability. Marx explained the history of his own century as the history of the growing exploitation of the proletariat by the bourgeoisie, a process that would inevitably bring violent revolution (though late in life Marx modified this position and stated that socialism could be brought about in incremental stages).

Beginning with Lenin and continuing with Stalin, Mao, Castro, Pol Pot, and others, this view proceeded to enslave every society in which its advocates were able to seize power. It had enslaved roughly a third of the world before it unraveled. Finally it ran its course, and the Soviet Union went out of business in 1991. Today the Marxist ideology that powered the Soviets for seventy years is being repudiated all over the world, even by peoples raised with no tradition of freedom.

It would be simplistic to call our affirmative actioneers closet Marxists. But, at the most fundamental level, their premises—that individuals are metaphysically as well as morally subordinate to groups, and ultimately they do not control their own thoughts and actions—are the same. Deterministic doctrines are very influential in today's academic world. According to classical Marxism, all individual thought, consciousness, and motivation can be explained in terms of class interest. In short, cognition can be assigned necessary and sufficient social conditions just as can overt behavior. When *race* and *gender* are added to *class* in the equation, we arrive at Strong RGC-Relativity.

Toward Social Engineering: the Psychology of Victimization, the Egalitarian Imperative, and the New Philosopher Kings

We can now formulate the third thesis at the heart of defenses of affirmative action, the thesis that ties determinism and collectivism to doctrinaire liberalism. We may call it the *psychology of victimization*. Capaldi has stated, "The heart of doctrinaire liberalism is the belief that man is the victim of circumstances greater than himself—social, political, and psychological. The masses cannot comprehend these great impersonal forces that guide their destiny."[16] These "great impersonal forces" are the forces that lead some groups to seek and maintain power over others.

The subordinated groups are *historically* (that is, *collectively*) victimized, as opposed to being victimized by specific acts taken against them by individuals. The social situations of oppressed groups are what they are through no actions of their own, and they cannot transcend their circumstances without outside help . . . without being liberated . . . without the addition of new, liberating variables to their environment.

Popular works such as William Ryan's *Blaming the Victim*[17] helped articulate the psychology of victimization as part of the official ideology of the Democratic party, and the psychology of victimization was incorporated into the civil rights movement as it evolved through the 1970s and 1980s. One consequence was the rapid entrenchment of the view that we do not merely live in a society in which racist acts have been committed, but rather in one that is racist through and through—racism being built into the superstructure of American capitalism itself because the capitalists are white and have a white man's consciousness. This in turn supports the view that discrimination can be covert as well as overt— built, for example, into the very standards for employment and into the idea of "merit."

Covert discrimination thus will never be remedied from within, because in the absence of an outside point of view—from a victim's consciousness—it will simply not be noticed. Hence it can be remedied only from outside the affected institutions, by political and legal power that is more formidable than that of the institutions and that operates from within the oppressed perspective. In the absence of blacks from the centers of power, covert discrimination will ensure that even good faith efforts to end discrimination will fail. Hence nondiscrimination is simply not enough.

Government properly informed by the perspectives of groups that were once discriminated against must take "affirmative action" to help those unable to help themselves by forcing employers to hire members of such groups according to specific goals and timetables, to place them on university faculties, to admit them into student bodies, and so on. It must ensure that their perspectives receive attention—for in so doing, we further expose the discriminatory cultural biases that have warped and distorted every endeavor and every field of inquiry. By exposing them, we may place ourselves in a position to get rid of them.

Two more ingredients complete the philosophical justification for preferential policies. One is an ethic of *egalitarianism*, as a regulative ideal by which existing societies and economic systems are to be judged. The final ingredient is the view expressed by Capaldi that "Understanding is necessarily limited to a vanguard of enlightened men and women who can free mankind by obtaining control of the state machinery and using their new-found power for the purpose of breaking the chains that have always fettered mankind."[18] In other words, the twentieth-century incarnations of Plato's Philosopher King.

The ethic of egalitarianism is intended to answer the question: Why should anyone care that different groups are unequally represented in the centers of power and influence in American society? Egalitarianism mandates not merely as much equality of *opportunity* as is possible, but as much equality of *condition* as is possible. The redistribution of job opportunities and income then becomes necessary for justice. We encounter in new forms the Rousseauian assumptions that equality is a morally superior condition to inequality and that it would exist in an ideal setting in which there had never been oppression of one race, class, or sex by another.

This justifies measuring equality of opportunity by equality of results and the success of an affirmative action program by the attainment of proportional representation. The egalitarian ethic concludes that when proportional representation is lacking, equal opportunity must be lacking as well. Proportional representation becomes the only acceptable state of affairs, whether in the schools, in the workplace, or the literary canon.

When egalitarianism and determinism are married, the immediate consequence is statism, the doctrine that the state is the only institution capable of rectifying undesirable social conditions. Inequality exists because the current social determinants have led to the oppression of blacks by whites, the exploitation of women by men, and so on—and *the oppressing group can do nothing on its own* to solve the problem. The oppressing factors can be eliminated only by using the state to realign the determinants on various social groups. If the right combination of determinants can be found and instituted, inequality will vanish.

Who is qualified to serve as the agent of the state? Who is most likely to succeed at creating equality of condition? This question is answered by *elitism*, the thesis (whether defended openly or implicit in policy) that there exists a special class or privileged elite of individuals who are educated in the proper way and who have the knowledge, the wisdom, the vision, and the virtue to use the state to rectify injustice.

Political programs that offer preferential treatment to the previously powerless must be designed and managed by those enlightened cultural leaders and social activists who alone have the knowledge and insight to carry them forward to social justice (conceived as equality of condition).

Thus do we arrive at a complete justification for social engineering, with the role of Philosopher Kings being played by an alliance of left-leaning intellectuals, college administrators, politicians, lobbyists, judges, and bureaucrats, comprising what Capaldi calls the "academic-bureaucratic complex." Their methods—the politicization of scholarship, the stigmatizing of dissent, the calls for censorship—are justified by their superior level of knowledge and moral insight, which others do not have.

The Errors of Collectivism

It should be increasingly clear that the intellectual roots of affirmative action lie within a body of ideas fundamentally alien to those values and principles on which the United States was founded, and which shaped its development until the early part of this century. Those whose philosophies composed the foundation of American liberty—John Locke, Adam Smith, Thomas Paine, and Charles Montesquieu—all saw the individual as being a free agent with a capacity for autonomous rationality, as being the most fundamental unit in society, and as inhabiting a universe where morality amounted to more than social conditioning. They saw freedom as freedom to act according to one's own desires, as choices controlled by one's sense of responsibility. Freedom was not absolute but limited by the laws of nature (including human nature) and the provision that one not act so as to infringe on the freedom of others.

The Anglo-Saxon philosophers did not accept the Rousseauian concept of freedom as conformity to legislation by some collective agency. They saw the primary function of state power as the protection of individual liberties, not as the manifestation of a collective will with an agenda of its own.

Of course, no one openly defends anything exactly like the Philosophy of Social Engineering as described above. But what defenders of affirmative action *do* believe, and the arguments they offer, logically commit them to something very close to that position. In any thorough discussion of affirmative action, we find ourselves encountering components of the Philosophy of Social Engineering again and again.

Take collectivism: In contemporary forms, collectivism entails the reification of groups as agencies deemed capable of suffering from oppression and therefore of being owed reparation. But can groups be moral agents? Before we can answer this question, we must ask in turn what it means to be a moral agent. What kinds of properties and capacities must something have to be deemed worthy of respect on moral grounds?

Philosopher George Sher (who incidentally supports affirmative action on other grounds) has argued that collective entities such as races and sexes "simply do not *have* needs or merits of the appropriate sorts" to be considered legitimate moral agents as such.[19] To say that some entity needs some good, he tells us, is to say that this good is necessary for its well-being; this means that only entities that can enjoy well-being can have needs.

What does it take for an entity to enjoy well-being? At the very least, such entities must be able to experience the world around them, with the resulting range of sensations ranging from happiness and pleasure to discomfort or pain. This means the entity must have a certain internal organization or configuration, including a nervous system capable of processing information from the outside and reordering it in appropriate ways. Racial and sexual groups have no such organization.

Such groups, unlike their members, do not satisfy the preconditions for attaining any of the states of well-being with which we are familiar. They do not have single organized bodies, and so can neither sustain good bodily health nor suffer illness. They do not have nervous systems, and so cannot experience the various states of comfort and discomfort which these systems make possible. They do not have consciousness, and so cannot experience either amusement, happiness, interest, or self-esteem, or the less pleasant states which stand opposed to these.[20]

In other words, groups are not conscious and so cannot feel plea-sure or pain; consequently, they cannot be harmed by other groups at least not in any ordinary usage of the term. Because these in-gredients are missing, there is a serious problem with claiming that racial and ethnic groups, or the two genders have the moral proper-ties their individual members have.

Another problem emerges when we focus on the role of action in moral agency, and in whatever moral properties we attribute to such phenomena as skills and abilities. "Skills and abilities," adds Sher, "are exercised only through actions. Hence it would be sense-less to speak of either the abilities or the skills of a non-agent. For similar reasons, non-agents can neither exert effort nor produce goods."[21] There are, of course, certain animal species, especially social insects, that have evolved the equivalent of a kind of collec-tive consciousness and could perhaps be said to act as a collective agent. But humans are not social insects.

There do exist collective agencies, such as corporations and other organizations, that for some legal purposes are treated as if they were acting agents. That common moral properties apply to such agencies has occasionally been argued with some plausibility.[22] But these organizations have clearcut structures, and we can iden-tify senses in which they can be well-off or harmed. Even here, we are really talking about the individuals of which they are composed; an organization as such is not conscious, has no feelings, and cannot act autonomously apart from its members.

Racial or ethnic groups and the two genders are far less orga-nized and far more diffuse. Hence, in their cases there is even less sense to be made of the claim that they can have moral properties, that is, be held accountable for moral wrongdoing or be considered deserving of moral reparations. Only individuals are conscious and have capacities of reason and action. Only individuals can even understand moral concepts; only individuals can initiate action, and hence possibly harm others. And what harm they do cannot be taken against groups as a whole (unless the individual is a Hitler or a Stalin or a Mao), but only against individual members of groups.[23]

And yet, a defender of collectivism might ask: What reasons do we have for taking the view that individuals are the most basic units of society? For no one denies that most human groupings consist of individuals with many traits in common besides the obvious physical ones. People become members of communities by being born into similar surroundings, growing up in similar environments, speaking the same language or dialect, employing the same concepts to order experience, and developing similar outlooks. Furthermore, individuals may derive great benefit from cooperating for various purposes, dividing their labors, and working to achieve common goals.

It is doubtful that civil society would be possible were not this much true. But we must not place more weight on these observations than they can carry. From none of them does it follow that an involuntary collective takes on an autonomous existence in any morally interesting sense. As Tibor Machan recently put it:

> . . . we are . . . essentially individual human beings. We are significantly different from other human beings, from all human beings. That is indeed part of our nature, to be different from others, to create in ourselves a unique being, a self-made entity that is both in harmony with others but is also significantly independent of them.[24]

The first target of the individualist, then, is the Platonist doctrine that "society is the individual writ large" and that individuals are merely components of a larger organism. For there simply is no such supervening organic entity, such as Rousseau's general will, that can act on the individual in any real sense. Actions taken in the name of the common good are in fact taken by the state, that is, by individuals who hold the reins of power. This is the case even in Rousseau's republic.

Moreover, actions taken by individuals on behest of the state in an effort to smother others' individuality, in order to pave the way for a new type of human being, seem doomed to failure. Philosopher Mary Midgley argues:

> Individuality cannot be trained out of us like a bad habit. Either it persists as the mainspring of our energies or, if it is crushed, its collapse destroys the rest of our capacities. Human

beings, in fact, are not blank paper at birth and cannot be conditioned to be social insects. The selfless communal consciousness which perhaps pervades a beehive is simply not an option for us.[25]

And yet a dogged defender of affirmative action might wonder if he really needs to posit a collective agency. Perhaps all he need do is defend the "shackled runner" argument, which holds that a greater number of blacks are in bad shape economically than whites, and for different reasons: Whites, no matter how badly off, never suffered from systematic discrimination. Because of the discrimination against their ancestors, the majority of blacks are economically well behind the majority of whites even if legal barriers are down. In this case, affirmative action may be needed as a condition of equal opportunity. Even Thomas Sowell observed that

Even the most ardent believer in individual merit must recognize that where you happen to have been born, how you were raised, or where you happen to have been located when opportunity or disaster came along, can make all the difference in the world.[26]

This argument can be strengthened. Consider the following hypothetical situation: A black woman from an impoverished background with a broken family, poor nutrition, and poor schools, and a white man from a middle-class background may have roughly equal innate abilities and make roughly equal efforts to exercise them, but because the black woman's starting point is so far behind, the white man will come out ahead. Indeed, the black woman may actually have *more* innate ability than the white man and work harder, yet arrive at the same place economically that he has reached with less ability and effort.

And this doesn't even take into account the possibility of overt discrimination against the black woman. Consequently, so the argument goes, demonstrated merit or credentials cannot be decisive in determining who should get a position or contract and cannot be directly connected to either effort or innate ability. If we rely on the latter, then the position or contract should go to the black woman:

Having worked harder to reach the same point, she shows more promise of future success. Furthermore, such a person could serve as a role model demonstrating that blacks who exercise their abilities can succeed, when given the opportunity that an affirmative action program can provide.

This defense of affirmative action is probably the strongest available. Not only does it recognize the role of action and effort in human life, but it recognizes what is undoubtedly true: Many blacks, starting further back on the economic and educational scale than most whites, must make greater efforts to succeed. The argument acknowledges that some are successful with these efforts and recommends that we attempt to single out such individuals and reward them accordingly. No doubt there are affirmative action programs that have helped at least some women, blacks, and other minorities in this way. I would be prepared to accept this argument if it stood up to full scrutiny . . . but it does not.

This argument does not take into account the fact that many whites also come from impoverished backgrounds and also receive little encouragement to develop and apply whatever innate talents they have. They too must rely on inner resources. A poor white man might also have to exercise greater effort to reach the same place, educationally and economically, as his middle-class counterpart; nevertheless, poor white men are ineligible for programs aimed exclusively at women and minorities. Likewise, there are black individuals who do not come from deprived backgrounds but who will be eligible for such programs.

The "middle-class white man" and the "poor black female" are in fact statistical abstractions, not flesh-and-blood human beings. While we may cite social tendencies based on statistics, these tell us little about any particular individual. Policies that are based on such abstractions ignore the efforts of many real individuals while undeservedly overcompensating others.

Another problem is the impossibility of measuring how much innate talent a given individual began with, and therefore how much personal effort has gone into her achievements. An employer assessing job applications can see only the concrete achievements— and those often imperfectly (because of such contingencies as the fact that some people are better at preparing resumes than others). It will clearly be unreasonable to require that a hiring decision be based on effort alone. What must count is concrete, demonstrable results, regardless of the subjective effort made by the individual to achieve them.

So while it is reasonable to hope that one's efforts will meet with substantial rewards and to work to see to it that personal effort is rewarded to the greatest extent possible, it is also reasonable to realize that it is part of the "natural order" that some have to work harder than others to achieve the same results.

No affirmative action program can take such contingencies of individual circumstance into account. Since there will be no way to determine whether a given black woman who has been hired for a reserved position actually worked harder than the white man who was not eligible for it, under affirmative action the hiring will be based exclusively on a presumed group situation, whether or not it applies in this case. Once again, intentionally or not, affirmative action will have assumed that historical harm has been done to entire groups; thus lapsing back into collectivism, sociocultural determinism, and the psychology of victimization. In short, the central error of affirmative action is that it faces a knowledge problem. Its makeshift solution is collectivism. However, societies and racial or ethnic groups are not homogeneous, organism-like units. They are composed of real, live, inescapably *individual* flesh-and-blood human beings, all slightly different from one another despite social planners' classifications. These differences add up. They make it impossible to predict what a given individual is going to need, want, or do. The result is that social plans, even sophisticated ones such as that found in Plato's *Republic*, can never be more than academic games. Collectivism remains a utopian fantasy—which is why Plato never pretended that the society constructed in the pages of the *Republic* could actually exist.

Social Engineering: an Incoherent Agenda

Let's look at another component of the Philosophy of Social Engineering: sociocultural determinism. The sociocultural determinist view is that individuals are entirely products of their economic and social environments and therefore entirely malleable in that if it is possible to redesign the environment, it is possible to produce a new kind of human being.

Sociocultural determinism contains a kernel of truth. People who have very limited exposure to circumstances outside, for instance, a ghetto—with shaky or nonexistent family structures, poor schools, and crime-ridden neighborhoods—will tend not to know what their options are, not be motivated to find out, and model their lives on the people they see around them and leave matters at that. To an extent, they are products of their environment.

Nonetheless, many individuals of all races and both sexes have transcended such disadvantages and climbed the social ladder. A black middle class, for instance, has been growing steadily for several decades. Accounts of black success stories fill the pages of magazines such as *Black Enterprise* and *Ebony* (which are written, edited, and published by blacks for blacks). This is not new; in fields such as education there have been successful blacks in the United States since the time of the Civil War, as Thomas Sowell has documented.[27]

To account for such things, determinists invoke "hidden variables" of one sort or another—for example, a few words spoken at the right time by a respected uncle or other mentor when the person was a teenager. The difficulty is that such posited variables are entirely ad hoc and untestable. No one has ever been able to point to specific environmental determinants that in some sense "cause" a person to want to escape poverty, or "cause" another person, well-off to begin with, to begin sliding down the economic ladder as soon as his parents cut him loose.

Sociocultural determinism cannot offer us more than a promissory note. It does not provide a convincing explanation of those individuals who escape from their immediate circumstances or refuse to play the role of victim. So why is sociocultural determinism so influential? The reason, I think, is the widely held assumption that some form of determinism offers the only genuinely scientific account of human behavior in society. But we do not actually have to choose between the epistemic authority of science and that of the individual rights–based tradition on which our society was founded. For sociocultural determinism is not synonymous with science; it is a *philosophy* of science and way of applying it in our culture, rooted more in a priori assumptions rather than actual scientific findings. This is why I refer to determinism as a metaphysic and the unofficial ideology of modern social science. From it follows scientism, the doctrine that concepts and methods applicable in the physical sciences can easily be transferred to the human sciences.

Our real choice is thus not between *science* and free agency but between *scientism* and free agency. We are being asked to choose between a set of principles that became the cornerstones of our national heritage and a philosophy that considers every problem an empirical one solvable by methods that proved successful in the physical sciences. This philosophy, in its strongest form, holds that every meaningful statement is capable of being confirmed or disconfirmed by scientific means alone.

Yet if we examine this statement itself, we sense that something is amiss: Can *it* be confirmed or disconfirmed by scientific means? It would seem not. The statement fails its own test of meaningfulness. (That is, it is meaningless by its own standard of meaningfulness.) In that case, since presumably we all understand it, the source of its meaning is not found in a capacity for scientific testability. (In addition, the problem of the epistemic authority of science is not itself a scientific or technical problem.) So there are some intellectual problems that scientific method by itself cannot solve.

The modernist view of science is seamlessly empiricist: It holds that whatever knowledge we have comes to us through our five senses. We have no other sources of knowledge. Thus we cannot arrive at any general truths about the nature of the universe simply by thinking about it. But if this argument is sound, radical empiricism is in error at a crucial junction—*its* truth cannot be discovered or verified through our five senses. Like determinism, empiricism is a philosophical thesis, lent partial support by the obvious fact that much knowledge *does* come to us through our five senses.

Furthermore, science neither does nor can judge potential contributions solely on the basis of empirical findings. This has been clear to philosophers of science for some time now.[28] Determinism itself is an example of a global hypothesis acting as a guiding nonempirical assumption.

We have seen the self-refuting character of "All meaningful statements are confirmable or disconfirmable by scientific means." Many such statements are self-refuting because they are self-referential: They are about all statements and hence include themselves in their scope of reference. If what they say about themselves is not true (or cannot be true if the statement is to be credible), we may reject them as self-refuting.[29] Statements made by human beings about human beings have such properties. For example, there could be no possibility of rationally justifying the claim "No statement ever made by a human being is rationally justifiable." A logical dilemma arises for such statements and for the philosophical stances and social theories from which they logically derive.

Let us apply these observations to determinism. To the extent that determinism is assumed to be universally true for human beings, it applies to its own defenders: determinists. But this yields the result that all *their* actions, physical and cognitive, are caused by factors for which antecedent necessary and sufficient conditions can be identified, at least in principle, including their formulation and defense of determinism.

For purposes of evaluating an idea, we distinguish between the causes of our beliefs (social, psychological, and so on) and the reasons we can give for thinking them true or probable. This distinction was long enshrined in the view that in considering a scientific or other kind of theory, we must distinguish between the "context of discovery," wherein is to be found the causal antecedents of our beliefs, and the "context of justification," in which is offered the reasons for thinking them true. An account of this distinction can be found in any good philosophy of science text.

Applying it to determinism, we begin with the realization that causal processes do not establish truth. If we add the assumption that determinism is true and apply determinism to itself (more exactly, to determinists and their formulations and defenses of determinism), we arrive at the result that we can never escape the context of discovery. We can never transcend the descriptive realm of identifying casual antecedents to reach the evaluative one of showing that there are reasons for thinking determinism true. We have arrived at the result that if determinism is true, then there can be no rational justification for believing it true. The determinist can claim to have "reasons" resulting from his own deliberations, but this claim cannot be conclusive. Determinism—sociocultural or otherwise—means that in the last analysis, individuals have no control over their cognitive processes and hence over the content and evaluation of their own beliefs.

The determinist's only recourse is to grant this much and go on to add that he was influenced to accept determinism as true by his scientific training, which exposed him to the kinds of factors that indeed show the universe to be built up as the determinist describes it. But to accept this is to accept the view that cognition works automatically and that if the conditions are right, error is impossible. This amounts to the claim that under the appropriate conditions the determinist is infallible—but no sane determinist claims infallibility or completeness for his knowledge. Errors in perception and judgment are always possible.

Rational deliberation on and acceptance of a thesis both seem by their very nature to require that determinism be false. The formulation, articulation, defense, and acceptance of a thesis are all *actions* of a sort and hence volitional. The concept of a *rational defense* or *rational acceptance* of determinism is thus self-contradictory. Determinism as a theory of the universe and everything in it—including human beings and their cognitive processes—conflicts with something that must be true about human beings before *any* theories can be considered true or justified.

Does this constitute an absolute refutation of determinism? Not quite. For it was not the thesis of determinism itself that was self-contradictory, but the thesis of determinism in conjunction with the claim that it has been rationally defended and justified. Thus the thesis could be true, and it would follow that the very idea that we are agents with rational capacities is a grand illusion. Yet given the advances of science, engineering, and civilization generally over the past two thousand years, the claim that we are entirely driven by impulses beyond our control seems unlikely to be true; such a claim would make our increased mastery of the physical environment more or less a complete mystery. So while we may not have produced an absolute refutation of determinism, we have cast serious doubt on it. At the very least, its defense seems pointless.[30]

The logical obstacles to sociocultural determinism mount in the realm of social policy. If sociocultural determinism is true, then we can give the actions of social engineers antecedent necessary and sufficient conditions just as we can anyone else's actions. This precludes their gaining the kind of control over the social environment they need to realign determinants on all the groups that compose civil society. For doing so would require them to perform the deterministically impossible feat of "bootstrapping": picking themselves up by their own bootstraps, as it were, and gaining control over the causes of their own behavior. Social engineers must thus exempt themselves from determinism and from their own societal blueprints. This option, pressed a bit further, takes on overtones of the technocratic totalitarianism found in such works as Aldous Huxley's *Brave New World*. For the falsity of universal determinism does not mean that large numbers of people cannot be controlled by other people. But what (or who) controls the controllers? If they are truly free to bring about social change—to make society different from what it would have been without their special insights and efforts—in so doing they disprove determinism.

Absolute determinism is thus incompatible with elitism. Elitism assumes that a certain group of individuals—"progressive social reformers," "technologists of behavior," "liberal Democrats," or whatever label is chosen—has the know-how to redesign society and is not controlled by the determinants that rule ordinary mortals. Members of such an elite might maintain (as did behaviorist B. F. Skinner) that they are nevertheless controlled by determinants—different ones. But this means there will always be at least one set of sociocultural elements beyond their control, which vitiates the possibility of *universal* social planning. Social planning based on sociocultural determinism is inherently self-contradictory. Remember, sociocultural determinism was the main premise for the psychology of victimization. If sociocultural determinism falls, the psychology of victimization falls with it. It will then make perfect sense to say that a black crack dealer, rather than being a victim of a racist society, is instead a criminal and an insult to his law-abiding black neighbors.

The social engineer is animated by the belief that he alone has the knowledge to design a social blueprint that can transform society for the better. History and literature contain many such blueprints. While they sometimes look good on paper, real live human beings are a diverse lot (and not merely in affirmative action's sense of diversity). The millions of individuals in the United States include unimaginably diverse combinations and varieties of experiences, interests, desires, and talents.

Twentieth-century Austrian economists Ludwig Von Mises and Friedrich A. Hayek articulated some of the strongest critiques of social engineering. Mises commented:

> . . . a social collective has no existence and reality outside of the individual members' actions. The life of a collective is lived in the actions of the individuals constituting its body.

> . . . one may say that a social collective comes into being through the actions of individuals.[31]

Only individuals are conscious or can take action. All our experiences are with individuals, acting either on their own or with other individuals. In light of the vast numbers of individuals and the differences between them, Hayek has observed that

> it is impossible for any man to survey more than a limited field, to be aware of the urgency of more than a limited number of needs. Whether his interests center round his own physical needs, or whether he takes a warm interest in the welfare of every human being he knows, the ends about which he can be concerned will always be only an infinitesimal fraction of the needs of all men.
>
> This is the fundamental fact on which the whole philosophy of individualism is based. It does not assume, as is often asserted, that man is egoistic or selfish or ought to be. It merely starts from the indisputable fact that the limits of our powers of imagination make it impossible to include in our scales of values more than a sector of the needs of the whole society. . . .[32]

Unconstrained visions not only presuppose that human beings are impossibly altruistic, but that at least some of them have more knowledge than anyone can have. Hayek has described the socialist belief that any one person or committee of persons or government can know what is good for an entire society as a "fatal conceit."[33] No database is large enough to hold—and no human brain powerful enough to integrate—the enormous quantity of information required. Social planners inevitably use a simplistic model, often based on the needs and demands of a highly visible few. Their model cannot help but fail on any larger scale that includes the needs and interests of those outside the scope of the planners' knowledge and experience.

These limitations also apply to economic *egalitarianism*. Equality of condition as a regulative ideal is a popular doctrine among intellectuals: The majority of moral, social, and political philosophers pay homage to it. Departures from it are hedged about with careful qualifications, as in John Rawls's treatise *A Theory of*

Justice.[34] But is equality of condition possible? I conclude that it is not, because that possibility would require the truth of deterministic explanations of inequality—combined, moreover, with the possibility of an elite defying determinism in its own case—combined with the likelihood of that elite having both the will and the knowledge to abolish itself along with other elites, while perpetuating a productive society. Each of these assumptions is highly problematic on its own, and they are even more so in combination.

Equality of condition should be rejected as an impossible ideal. Moral philosophers have an adage: Ought implies can. In the case of equality of condition, we cannot; therefore, there is no "we ought." One cannot make the impossible a moral requirement. The tragic irony is that in the twentieth century, millions of people have been slaughtered and millions more enslaved, while new elites became entrenched—all in the name of eventual equality.

Genuine equal opportunity laws can assert no more than that under law all should be equally free to develop their talents and abilities as best they can and thereby rise by their own efforts. Such laws can provide no guarantes of statistical outcomes or anything else. The shift in emphasis from opportunity to results occurred because of the tacit philosophical assumption that economic equality is both a possible and a natural state. But there is no evidence whatsoever that economic equality among individuals either is or *could be* a natural state.

There are ineradicable differences in level of ability and talent between individuals in every field of endeavor. In music, there are very few Mozarts. In literature, few Dostoyevskis. In physics, few Einsteins and Hawkings. Among inventors, few Edisons. Among industrialists, few Henry Fords. Among philosophers, very few Platos and Aristotles. And among political leaders, few Thomas Jeffersons and James Madisons.

An egalitarian may insist that when all is said and done, these differences will somehow balance out. But there is little evidence for even this more modest claim, or any account of what social outcome such evidence would entail. It seems far more likely that the natural state for human beings is not equality but *in*equality— based not only on differences in innate ability, but also on enormous differences in motivation among those of similar ability. Governments may seize the fruits of the productive efforts of citizens and redistribute them, but no one has ever figured out how to redistribute either ability or motivation. If a political agenda based on such wildly unrealistic assumptions remains in place, its end result cannot possibly be anything other than a gradual undermining of freedoms in the United States, and of the autonomy of every institution it touches. Sadly, when we examine its effects on institutions of all kinds, this is exactly what we do find.

FIVE

The Insidious Spread of Social Engineering

Consequences to Alleged Beneficiaries of Preferential Treatment

Social policies that withstand sustained logical scrutiny, as well as the best tests provided by the laboratory of history and human experience—and whose underlying assumptions thereby demonstrate some probability of containing more truth than falsity—can bring great social benefits. But clinging to policies and assumptions against all reason does enormous harm.

The Philosophy of Social Engineering has failed every test of experience: The historical failure of Marxism is merely one instance of social engineering's consistent, worldwide failure. Marxists spent seventy years trying to engineer the perfect society in the Soviet Union. They produced only poverty, slavery, and misery on a scale never before seen.

Because preferential policies are rooted in the same social engineering assumptions the Soviets once held, we can expect similar negative effects if these policies are fully implemented in the United States. For social engineering does not solve real social problems. It creates problems out of whole cloth by comparing existing institutions with its ideals and finding the institutions wanting on those terms. It then infiltrates and manipulates the institutions to bring them into line. That the institutions may have been doing just fine before being manipulated—even by the lights of many members of the favored groups—does not cut any ice with social engineers. What matters is their vision, period.

Thus we can expect to find damage done to every institution and occupation they touch—damage that can only grow if contracting, hiring, and admissions according to preset ratios and group-normed criteria become the only politically acceptable ways of proceeding. In sum, what has been foisted on our institutions is a deeply incoherent, unworkable, and dangerous agenda.

In accordance with the collectivism at the heart of social engineering, affirmative action does not offer benefits to members of groups on the basis of their individual circumstances, but on the basis of their group identity. Thomas Sowell has shown in detail how this benefits only a few in targeted groups, while actually harming many others, and leaving the rest no better off than before.[1] Our findings have borne this out. In the construction industry, it is impossible even to identify those who have suffered the worst effects of past discrimination. The same is true for black students offered preferential admissions in colleges and universities.

We have seen the principal reason for this failure: No one can possibly have the case-by-case knowledge of *individuals* and their circumstances that would enable a preferential policy to benefit even the majority of those it targets. Thus it is not surprising that such policies tend to work against those who need them the most, simply by favoring those who are at least marginally qualified and who are therefore probably less harmed by past discrimination. Similarly, preferential policies work to the advantage of those who have the right connections and are good lobbyists and organizers—attributes not significantly different from those that have benefited some whites.

This explains something often observed: The primary beneficiaries of affirmative action as it has actually developed, particularly in higher education, are not poor blacks or members of other disenfranchised groups such as native Americans, but middle- and upper-class women. Reasons why affirmative action and kindred policies tend to benefit women more than blacks are not hard to find. Women are even less homogeneous a group than blacks. For all the talk about how women *on the average* earn less than men for the same amount of work, Sowell has shown that *single* women, on the average, were earning *more* than men in 1971—before affirmative action had grown into social engineering.[2] There are additional differences between women who have children and women who do not, both in terms of income and in terms of career choice. This is because many careers such as law and medicine cannot be interrupted by pregnancy and childrearing, and then simply reentered ten years later. In these rapidly changing fields, without continuous exposure or retraining, knowledge and skills quickly become obsolete.[3]

Women who make the same total career commitment that most men do earn as much as most men. But many women prefer not to define their priorities in imitation of traditional men. These factors are seldom taken into account by those who pontificate on how "women, on the average, earn 59 percent of what men earn for the same work" and indignantly demand compensatory measures.

Meanwhile, genuinely poverty-stricken members of ethnic minorities often remain beyond the reach of even the most efficient and well-intentioned affirmative action programs, if they are unable to transcend their immediate circumstances enough to come into these programs' orbits. This is especially likely if they have been led to believe they cannot do so because they have learned from their peers or others that applying oneself to one's studies, making good grades, and aiming for a higher rung on the economic ladder are "white things."

The end results of being left with unfulfilled promissory notes from the messages they were given—promises unfulfilled because they are impossible to fulfill—are disillusionment, discouragement, and a sense of betrayal. These attitudes in turn precipitate a vicious downward spiral: Discouragement and disillusionment breed lack of diligence and perseverance, which create dependence—with generous welfare "safety nets" habituating that dependence. Dependence further erodes self-respect. A sense of betrayal engenders frustration, anger, and hostility, which culminate in self-destructive behavior.

This may be why many blacks and other ethnic minorities such as native Americans seem unable to break free of a pattern of poverty, crime, teen pregnancies and broken families, chemical dependency, and the hopelessness that accompanies these. This cycle acts to reinforce rather than dissolve the very stereotypes about the "inferiority" of ethnic minorities that the civil rights movement aimed to overcome. Thus, three decades of unworkable government programs have achieved the exact *opposite* of their original aims, leaving the majority of those in targeted groups demonstrably worse off than they were before.[4]

These same consequences flow from, and are reinforced by, the psychology of victimization. Anne Wortham has recently shown how what she calls the stance of victimhood has resulted from the collectivization of the idea of a victim. An actual victim is a person who has suffered harm by a destructive agency, human or natural. However:

Unlike actual victimization, the stance of victimhood is a technique of self-presentation and impression management that involves the symbolic elaboration of actual victim status. Because symbolic elaboration is a quality of conceptualization and not of concrete reality, one need not be an actual victim to make an implicit or explicit claim to victim status. Whether he actually has experienced injustice or not, the symbolic victim presents himself as the embodiment of all the real or imagined suffering of his membership group as a whole.[5]

Shelby Steele has provided an eloquent and moving account of the harm done to both blacks and whites by the psychology of victimization. He introduces the concept of *holding* as "any self-description that serves to justify or camouflage a person's fears, weaknesses, and inadequacies."[6] *Race-holding* applies this to race:

The theory of race-holding is based on the assumption that a margin of choice is always open to blacks (even slaves had some choice). And it tries to make clear the mechanisms by which we relinquish that choice in the name of race. With the decline in racism the margin of black choice has greatly expanded, which is probably why race-holding is so much more visible today than ever before. But anything that prevents us from exploiting our new freedom to the fullest is now as serious a barrier to us as racism once was.[7]

Race-holding, Steele maintains, is a form of self-victimization.

The race-holder whines, or complains indiscriminately, not because he seeks redress but because he seeks the status of victim, a status that excuses him from what he fears. A victim is not responsible for his condition, and by claiming a victim's status the race-holder gives up the sense of personal responsibility he needs to better his condition. His unseen purpose is to hide rather than fight, so the anger and, more importantly, the energy that real racism breeds in him is squandered in self-serving complaint. The price he pays for the false comfort of his victim's status is a kind of impotence.[8]

In Steele's view, affirmative action has encouraged this frame of mind.

Another liability of affirmative action comes from the fact that it indirectly encourages blacks to exploit their own past victimization as a source of power and privilege. Victimization . . . is what justifies preference, so that to receive the benefits of preferential treatment one must, to some extent, become invested in the view of one's self as a victim. In this way, affirmative action nurtures a victim-focused identity in blacks. The obvious irony here is that we become inadvertently invested in the very condition we are trying to overcome. Racial preferences send us the message that there is more power in our past suffering than our present achievements—none of which could bring us a *preference* over others.[9]

Steele identifies the fallacy built into the demand for proportional representation:

When affirmative action escalated into social engineering, diversity became a golden word. It grants whites an egalitarian fairness (innocence) and blacks an entitlement to proportional representation (power). *Diversity* is a term that applies democratic principles to races and cultures rather than to citizens, despite the fact that there is nothing to indicate that real diversity is the same thing as proportional representation. . . .
    Racial representation is not the same thing as racial development, yet affirmative action fosters a confusion of these very different needs. Representation can be manufactured; development is always hard earned.[10]

What of those who can legitimately lay claim to having been helped by preferential treatment—those who obtained desirable positions for which, as applicants, they would probably not have been noticed without affirmative action? Certainly many blacks now in academe fall into this category. However, even these situations are often a mixed blessing for all concerned. There are short-term pluses but also minuses, both short- and long-term. Given that someone admitted to college or given a job for the sole purpose of changing the racial ratio was not admitted or hired on the basis of demonstrated merit, by the statistical laws of probability some will nevertheless turn out to have the capabilities needed to thrive in their new environment, but an embarrassingly large number will not.

Consider the situation of the black youth who is admitted to a prestigious Ivy League university not because of his high school grades and SAT scores (which were lower than those of many rejected whites and Asians), but rather to increase the percentage of blacks in the student body. His ability to do college-level work was not the central factor in his admission. Consequently, there is a better than even chance that he will find himself in over his head. Moreover, he soon realizes that to his white and Asian classmates, he has AFFIRMATIVE ACTION written all over him.

Unfortunately, affirmative action officers and diversity bureaucrats cannot prepare him for a full course load, study for him, or take his tests for him. Thus he finds himself unable to keep up—and acutely sensitive to the stereotypes. Unless he can adjust to this environment of mixed signals, he is in danger of becoming another attrition statistic, labeled a failure by both himself and others. A preferential admissions program has dealt him a psychological blow from which he may never recover. His admission benefited those concerned with ratios as ends in themselves; it did not benefit him.

Those who *do* have the ability to keep up with their new peers may still find themselves stigmatized, by others and themselves. Just about everyone on campus is aware of programs aimed exclusively at advancing the interests of minorities on campus. Thus even the most academically prepared members of groups targeted by such programs may find themselves victims of the suspicion that they obtained their admissions or other benefits because of their favored status. With the disregard of academic merit to which coercive preferential policies tend, combined with the secrecy surrounding their implementation, no one can be sure whether he or she is a direct beneficiary. Coworkers, colleagues, and fellow students of possible beneficiaries of affirmative action may regard them with a suspicion or disdain that wouldn't exist in a merit-based hiring system, and this suspicion or disdain is likely to rub off even on those who were fully qualified.

Possible direct beneficiaries may suffer a crisis of confidence on their own, coming to doubt their own abilities and achievements. Given the importance attached to having earned one's way in the world, which is still an important part of our cultural ethos, they question whether they really earned their status. This may affect their performance as students, faculty, or employees.

Faculty members who fall into affirmative action categories are likely to be objects of such suspicion on the part of skeptical students. Whenever these suspicions have a fairly obvious basis in fact—if, for instance, the person who was hired to change the racial ratio is not effective in the classroom—that person will hardly serve as an effective role model for her group. This is an obvious objection to the role model argument for affirmative action. Will a person be respected enough to serve as a role model, if his students suspect that the principal reason for his being there is affirmative action?

Some black students are rebelling against the affirmative action stigma. When the Columbia Law Review, based at the law school of Columbia University, initiated an affirmative action program, the negative response from minority students who believed they had earned their way into the system was swift.[11] In a similar vein, I have had conversations with female academic philosophers who resent the insinuation inherent in official "affirmative action for women" policies that imply their inability to advance on their own merits. Similarly, they resent the patronizing approach of radical feminists who claim to speak for them.[12]

One defender of affirmative action, philosopher Thomas Nagel, has admitted that "it comes to be widely felt that success doesn't mean the same thing for women and minorities."[13] Indeed it does not and cannot mean the same thing as long as double standards are in force and are known to be in force—and who, today, doesn't know about them? Even the most successful and meritorious members of protected groups may be seen by the nonpreferred not as achievers who earned their college admission slots or their jobs, but as passive recipients of government favors.

An increasing number of black students are dealing with this situation as best they can—by isolating themselves from the majority community. The growth of black separatism, with its own philosophy (Afrocentrism), its own music (rap), and even its own code of dress (Malcolm X hats, T-shirts, and the like) has been well documented. This separation alienates young blacks from their white peers and isolates them further from the ideas and principles they must internalize, and the actions they must take, if they are to succeed in American society—or any modern, industrialized society. Shelby Steele places the blame squarely on today's black leadership:

> Because black leadership has, itself, recomposed the doubts of its own people, it has settled on a very distorted view of their situation. By seeing only victimization, they missed the fact that in 1964, when the Civil Rights Bill was passed, we were a people with very little experience of real freedom. As many have said, this bill was more an Emancipation Proclamation than the earlier one. But, though it delivered greater freedom, it did not deliver the skills and attitudes that are required to thrive in freedom. Freedom is stressful, difficult, and frightening—a "burden," according to Sartre, because of the responsibility it carries. Oppression conditions people *away* from all the values and attitudes one needs in freedom—individual initiative, self-interested hard work, individual responsibility, delayed gratification, and so on. . . . It is not that these values have never had a presence in black life, only that they were muted and destabilized by the negative conditioning of oppression. I believe that since the mid-sixties our weakness in this area has been a far greater detriment to our advancement than any remaining racial victimization.[14]

This leads Steele to call for a new agenda.

> . . . our leadership, and black Americans in general, have woefully neglected the power and importance of these values. . . . I don't think we will have a true black leadership until there is a willingness to break through the distortion that sees victimization as the primary black problem. We need a leadership

that names our doubts and then insists on the values by which
we can defeat them.[15]

What is needed, in other words, is a body of ideas—a set of values—that will enable blacks to preserve their ethnic identity if they
choose to do so, but in ways that will not undermine their opportunities to advance economically. The contemporary intellectual
"mainstream", obsessed with a confused multiculturalism married
to a statist Philosophy of Social Engineering, has failed miserably
to provide such ideas.

Consequences for Higher Education and
Academic Research: the Ad Hominem
Response Revisited

A frequent response to such arguments is that the arguers, if white,
subscribe to covert racism, and if black, to a kind of neoslavery.
Derrick Bell insists that racism is built into the structure of liberal
democracy itself and that blacks who defend such ideas as individual freedom are like "slaves willing to mimic the masters' views,
carry out orders, and by their presence provide a perverse legitimi-
zation to the oppression they aided and approved."[16]

This response is irrational but powerful. The purveyors of hard
leftism, with their roots in the radical student movements of the late
1960s, have attained influence in top-rated universities, throughout
the legal system, and in the media. They have become the new
Establishment. With the election of Bill Clinton to the presidency,
and his appointment of Donna Shalala (who advocated quotas and
speech codes at the University of Wisconsin) as Secretary of Health
and Human Services, and of Sheldon Hackney (who instituted
similar measures at Penn State) to the helm of the National Endowment for the Humanities, the left-wing agenda is rapidly being
implemented in Washington.

One of the chief aims of the new Establishment has been the
defense of race and gender preferences. Until recently, it refused to
permit serious discussion of any negative effects of such preferences. Yet the problems have reached such a level of severity, and
have been brought to the public's attention so compellingly, that it
now has no choice.

The critique of the current generation of academic leftists was launched with Allan Bloom's *The Closing of the American Mind* in 1987,[17] followed closely by E. D. Hirsch's *Cultural Literacy*[18] and, the following year, by Charles J. Sykes's *The Hollow Men.*[19] During this time, the National Association of Scholars formed and became the only prominent organization of intellectuals actively opposing the drift toward more and more extreme forms of radicalism, relativism, and intellectual nihilism in American education.[20] Its journal, *Academic Questions,* soon become a primary source for firsthand accounts of affirmative action horror stories, confrontations between leftists and dissidents, and the effects of antischolarship on the academy. In 1990, Roger Kimball's *Tenured Radicals*[21] appeared; in 1991, Dinesh D'Souza's *Illiberal Education* blew the lid off, naming names and identifying several major colleges and universities as launching pads of political correctness.

In reaction, leftist antischolars and their supporters have dug in their heels. Two new academic organizations quickly formed: Teachers for a Democratic Culture and the Union of Democratic Intellectuals.[22] Given the enormous power the term *democracy* has always commanded for propagandistic purposes,[23] the usage of *democratic* by these organizations insinuates that the National Association of Scholars and *its* supporters do not support democracy. Yet many members of that organization joined it precisely because they see P.C. trends as dangerous to the survival of political democracy—which, in the belief of the National Association of Scholars, thrives in a cultural context that emphasizes individual rights and responsibilities along with high standards of logic and evidence in decision making.

Nevertheless, by late spring, 1991, official denials were in force: It had become the party line among the politically correct to deny that political correctness exists as anything more than a bogeyman in the minds of right wingers. For example, Catharine R. Stimpson condemns

misuse of the term "politically correct"—or P.C.—[as] a rhetorical virus that has been spreading through higher education and the media so rapidly that it is nearing comic self-parody. . . .
. . . [Conservatives'] . . . disagreement with P.C. principles

. . . has become a convenient label for developments they oppose, such as affirmative action, women's studies, black studies, ethnic studies, gay and lesbian studies and cultural studies. Like "Willie Horton," P.C. is easy to pronounce and remember.[24]

Stimpson assures us that the "new scholarship" is just the latest change in an intellectual environment whose history "is one of constant change. One change today is social and demographic, the increasing diversity of students, staff, and faculty members."

This has precipitated necessary intellectual changes: "We are thinking about and teaching new subjects with new methods— the history of women, for example." All in all, the debate over P.C., in Stimpson's words, is "obscuring the debates that are being conducted responsibly on our campuses." The responsible character of these "debates" would come as a surprise to all those faculty and students who have deliberately or inadvertently found themselves saying the wrong things and being vilified, ostracized, and sometimes suspended. Note Stimpson's use of the term *conservative* and her evocation of Willie Horton, by way of demonizing those whose viewpoints differ from her own. Stimpson's statement is restrained, however, compared to others. Some of these statements make clear the connection between affirmative action and current trends in the humanities. One syndicated columnist, speaking on behalf of the two new academic groups mentioned above, described the movement to expose antischolars and their methods as "part of an organized conservative campaign to turn back gains made by women and minority groups, especially in anxious economic times."[25]

No less powerful an organization than the American Association of University Professors weighed in with a "Statement on the 'Political Correctness' Controversy" that began:

In recent months, critics have accused American higher education of submitting to the alleged domination of exponents of "political correctness." Their assault has involved sloganeering, name-calling, the irresponsible use of anecdotes, and not infrequently the assertion that "political correctness" is the new McCarthyism that is chilling the climate of debate on campus and subjecting political dissenters to the threat of reprisal. For all its self-righteous verve, this attack has frequently been less than candid about its actual origin, which appears to lie in an only partly concealed animosity toward equal opportunity and its first effects of modestly increasing the participation of women and racial and cultural minorities on campus.[26]

Let's dissect this statement. The authors claim that critics of the new scholarship and its attendant inclinations toward censorship and other forms of coercion, have engaged in "sloganeering, name-calling, [and] the irresponsible use of anecdotes." It is not clear what is meant by "sloganeering"; perhaps this refers to the use of the term *political correctness*. However, the critics did not invent this term; they merely adopted it after noting the irony of its historical association with Leninists who toed the party line too closely. The term stuck.

As for the accusation of "name-calling," at the risk of committing a tu quoque I can only wonder what the authors would call what was done to Murray Dolfman or Alan Gribben or the many others who were tormented by radical students, colleagues, or administrators for running afoul of the new codes of speech or opposing antischolars' curricular reforms. Dissidents from P.C. have been the targets of sometimes nasty reprisals for refusing to conform; to deny this is dishonest. Does the citing of real-life examples constitute "irresponsible use of anecdotes"?

The statement's conclusion is a repetition of the insinuation that the critics are dishonorably motivated. We have noted the popularity of this ploy. When Duke University political science professor James David Barber started up a chapter of the National Association of Scholars (NAS) there, Stanley Fish opened fire in a letter to the campus newspaper stating flatly that the organization was "widely known to be racist, sexist, and homophobic" (adding that its members should not be appointed to academic committees because of their "illiberal attitudes").[27] Barber, to his credit, stood his ground.

Later, when Dinesh D'Souza challenged Fish to identify "three concrete examples of racism, sexism, or homophobia" by any leading NAS member, Fish replied:

I don't have to respond to any request for three. I can just respond to the question of what I meant by saying that, which I hereby repeat. What I did say . . . was that the organization is widely known to be racist, sexist, and homophobic and I was alerting my colleagues as to the nature of the organization they were being asked to join. What I meant by that was in reference precisely to the high-sounding materials to which you refer. These are materials which declare, "We are not against women; we are not against gays; we are not against minorities. We just wish their works to enter by neutral, objective standards." And then when the question is asked, "Where do these neutral, objective standards come from?" it turns out that they come from the very works and points of view being championed by members of this organization. So that although the assertion of no discrimination against these groups is made, a mechanism and a way of thinking is put in place that has that effect. So that on the general principle that if it walks like a duck, talks like a duck, and produces duck-like effects, it's a duck, I say again, it's racist, sexist, and homophobic.[28]

It is rare for the attack on the possibility of objective, neutral standards to be expressed so clearly (and by a deconstructionist, no less!). Fish's reply boils down to the familiar contentions that each group has its own standards, that efforts toward objectivity and neutrality are nothing but self-serving white male standards, and that any defense of universal standards is synonymous with racism, sexism, and homophobia.

Another article in the same issue of *Academe,* by Cathy N. Davidson, one of Fish's colleagues at Duke, carries the attack on critics of antischolarship further by introducing the term "PH" for "Political Hypocrisy":

Instead of simply (and honestly) proposing a conservative agenda, the new PH tactic is to claim unbiased objectivity, then to denounce the faults of the present-day academy from that ostensibly nonideological stance, and finally to demand reforms that turn out to be highly ideological and politicized (although never acknowledged as such).[29]

This reiterates the everything-is-political-and-hence-*you-too*-are-political theme. Davidson contends that members of the political "right" are merely attempting to mask their racism, sexism, and homophobia by criticizing affirmative action instead of attacking women, minorities, and homosexuals openly.[30] However, the few specifics she cites show her portrayal to be unreliable.

At one point, Davidson attacks Dinesh D'Souza for having published an interview with Klan leader David Duke in the *Dartmouth Review,* leaving the unstated insinuation that the interview was sympathetic and that D'Souza is therefore a racist.[31] Her source seems to have been a mixed review of *Illiberal Education* that appeared in *The New Yorker,* which made the same assertion and dropped the same insinuation.[32] Yet had Davidson or the reviewer for *The New Yorker* bothered to track down the relevant issue of the *Dartmouth Review* and actually read it, she would have found that the interview was hostile, not sympathetic.[33] Her article dismisses the many confrontations resulting from leftist zealotry as "the same half-dozen or so horror stories . . . endlessly recycled." Then it reaches a new low by referring to the University of Michigan student who objected to having to room with a militant homosexual and was threatened with discrimination charges as "that pathetic young man."[34]

Such dishonest ploys by P.C. defenders have become typical. Fasaha M. Traylor, of a Philadelphia-based educational foundation, describes D'Souza's criticisms of affirmative action and political correctness as "eerily similar" to nineteenth-century arguments for racial inferiority, but offers no details about what the similarities are.[35] Ad hominem arguments all the way down! Small wonder that the defenders of affirmative action, radical feminism, and multiculturalism despise the logocentric view of scholarship—the view that there really are intellectual standards to which all of us must conform to be taken seriously and that a fallacy is a fallacy is a fallacy. If they conceded the existence of rational standards governing discourse, they might feel an uncomfortable obligation to conform to such standards!

While there are undoubtedly people who are both conservative and critical of the new tendencies in academia, the agenda of the critics of political correctness is not conservative—David Barber, who began the NAS chapter at Duke, describes himself as a liberal Democrat. There are other political liberals involved in the NAS.

The critics of P.C. have never claimed to be totally unbiased or objective; what they *do* uphold is objectivity as a regulative ideal of scholarship whose validity is independent of one's group identity. This ideal is what antischolarship rejects. Such a rejection has the consequence that all modes of thought—including scholarly inquiry—are reducible to political power struggles. Yes, reforms made on the basis of upholding objectivity as a regulative ideal do have political consequences, in that antischolars accept as fact the superiority of collectivism over individualism, and socialism over capitalism. If questioning these assumptions means being ideological and political, so be it.

Given the fragility of antischolarly assumptions, certain topics and positions have to be as protected as the groups that advocate them; speech about these topics is therefore subject to taboos. Social engineering cannot achieve its goals in an intellectual environment encompassing a free flow of ideas and information. The best example of thought control in today's academy is affirmative action itself and the results that Frederick Lynch, William Beer, Roger Kimball, Dinesh D'Souza, and others have documented.

Beer examined the sociological literature on affirmative action and found it spotty, guarded, and superficial. The literature takes as given, without offering proof, that "differences between groups are primarily caused by discrimination."[36] Questioning such givens is taboo in the academy, and those who ask the wrong questions place their careers in jeopardy. Recently, Lynch reflected on his research on the topic of affirmative action:

> For me this research saga illuminated the powerful taboos which have dominated the American intellectual landscape for more than twenty years, and I learned a great deal from the experience. I would, however, never do such a thing again. My career has been badly damaged.[37]

Tight labor markets in the humanities and social sciences only worsen the danger that critics of contemporary orthodoxies will find themselves simply written out of their disciplines and deprived of their livelihoods. Aspiring academics naturally consider their options and decide not to rock the boat. They are sometimes advised by mentors to be their own censors and avoid "sensitive" subjects—otherwise they will not be offered academic positions, period. Stephan Thernstrom recently wrote that the present situation

> makes me even gloomier than before about the choices confronting young scholars who don't as yet have tenure, or tenure at a place where they wish to stay. In advising someone younger, and as of yet unestablished, who had my intellectual interests and views, I would feel compelled to inform him frankly that telling the truth as he sees it may cost him dearly, and that his professional advancement will be best served by avoiding certain subjects, however great his interest in them. If you don't have "p.c." (politically correct) views, for example, you would be out of your mind to teach in one of the University of California's now required courses in American cultures—which are designed to approach American history as a study in racial oppression. Let slip a favorable reference to Moynihan or Glazer or Sowell or Richard Rodriguez, I would bet, and your employment record will have INSENSITIVE stamped in red all over it.[38]

Even scientific research proposals have been rejected by peer review committees not because of flaws in their methodologies, but because their topics conflicted with referees' political stances. A recent study found that research proposals for investigating the effects of height and weight on hiring procedures in Fortune 500 companies had a 95 percent approval rating. But a methodologically identical research proposal for investigating the effects of reverse discrimination on white male applicants for positions in Fortune 500 companies was approved only 40 percent of the time and elicited referee comments like the following: "The findings could set Affirmative Action back twenty years if it came out that women with weaker vitae were asked to interview more often for managerial positions than men with stronger vitae."[39]

Sometimes the taboos have gone so far as to suppress concrete research findings. Gerald Lesser of Harvard was told to withhold from publication some results of comparative studies of verbal and reasoning skills for fear they "might be misinterpreted and used to foster racism."[40] A potential for violence was suggested.

Tenured philosophy professor Michael E. Levin of City College of New York was not only forced to stop teaching a required philosophy course but was the target of death threats that resulted in armed guards accompanying him to class—all for publicly criticizing affirmative action, and expressing politically unacceptable views on race and intelligence.[41]

Recently, National Institutes of Health (NIH) funding was withdrawn for an entire conference at the University of Maryland at College Park that planned to explore the possibility of a genetic basis for criminal tendencies. The topic aroused hostility on the part of those who felt that such research might yield results that could be misused by racists.[42]

In the face of such powerful forces, the vast majority of academics are "going along in order to get along." This mindset has precipitated what Roger Kimball called the "collapse of the center," a situation in which those running colleges and universities, and the majority of those inhabiting them, simply lower their eyes and cede to the radical left whatever it wants in order to keep the peace.[43] Who wants to be publicly excoriated as a racist, sexist, or homophobe? This is now the worst trio of epithets that can be hurled at someone. (The dynamic duo of *conservative* and *right-wing* runs a close second.)

The real victims of this mass capitulation are students. A recent survey funded by the Kettering Foundation shows that the prevailing mood among college students is cynicism. One professor comments:

> Cynicism prevails. More and more students have become cynical about the possibilities of democracy itself. It finally comes down to power and how to grab one's share of it. The notion that people could make alliances with each other, could come together over shared purposes seems more and more elusive, impossibly romantic to students. And that is troubling.[44]

In the face of evidence that they can be severely disciplined for saying the wrong thing, many students will simply do whatever they have to in order to get their grades, graduate, and be gone. Unfortunately, in the process they become convinced of the barrenness of the intellect, the impotence of reason, and the reduction of life to a power struggle.

Henry Louis Gates, Jr., recently predicted that the "rainbow coalition" was "ready to take control. . . . As the old guard retires, we will be in charge."[45] If purveyors of social engineering do come to control the curriculum, it is clear that academic integrity will become a thing of the past as more and more of the academy falls under the sway of increasingly brazen forms of politically motivated irrationalism.

This is already happening to early American history. As the 1992 quincentennial of Columbus's discovery of America approached, American Indian Movement leader Russell Means proclaimed that "Columbus makes Hitler look like a juvenile delinquent."[46] American archeology and physical anthropology are also under attack from Indian activists. "It's conceivable," one such activist boasted enthusiastically, "that some time in the not-so-distant future there won't be a single Indian skeleton in any museum in the country. We're going to put [the physical anthropologists] out of business."[47]

Legal studies, already breeding grounds for some of the most hard-left views in the country, will be further corrupted as "critical race theory" pushes radical critiques of American jurisprudence to new extremes.[48] An attack on economics by radical feminists is stirring.[49] As more and more subjects are subjected to the depredations of activist antischolars, intellectual substance is being replaced by political demagoguery. The humanities and social sciences no longer communicate the sense that ideas matter, much less enable students to build intellectually profound, emotionally rich, personally productive, or socially constructive perspectives on reality.

The Collapse of the Educational System?

There are no doubt many who view the picture I have painted as alarmist—perhaps even more extreme than authors I have occasionally cited, such as D'Souza, since I have singled out efforts to defend and extend affirmative action as the primary cause of campus woes. I have insisted that it is affirmative action that underlies multiculturalism, radical feminism, and other forms of antischolarship, and it is the Philosophy of Social Engineering that underlies affirmative action. If I have contributed anything original to the debate over affirmative action, it lies in identifying this set of relationships.

But I wish to conclude my remarks on the impact of these policies on American education by making an observation that is not at all new. It has been made by countless observers: *Today's students, whether in secondary school or in college, are not learning.* Indeed, our college graduates rank below those of other major powers (and in many cases, they rank below small, comparatively obscure countries) in every major subject area.

The opening gambit in the culture wars was played on April 26, 1983, when then Secretary of Education William Bennett's thirty-six page study *A Nation at Risk* was released and touched off a national debate. The study reported that American students were behind their foreign counterparts in mathematics and science and that the resulting low standards threatened to undermine American leadership in global markets, especially high-technological ones. The study noted that thirty-five states required no more than a single year of mathematics and science each for a high school diploma, while countries such as Japan require four years of math through calculus, and four years of science through physics. Though not singling out specific policies, the study concluded:

> The educational foundations of our society are presently being eroded by a rising tide of mediocrity that threatens our very future as a nation and a people. . . . If an unfriendly foreign power had attempted to impose on America the mediocre educational performance that exists today, we might well have viewed it as an act of war.[50]

Allan Bloom's *The Closing of the American Mind* was the first book to expose the negative effects of the 1960s on American education. He took the necessary first step toward blowing the whistle on what was being done to scholarship in the name of race-and-gender parity and, more generally, on what the relativistic worldview taken for granted in the humanities had done to an entire generation of students. Bloom immediately became the target of extensive and highly ad hominem attacks. E. D. Hirsch, too, was criticized for making *cultural illiteracy* a household word, and he soon attempted to recant under pressure.[51]

But what Hirsch publicized under this term is not a WASP-male myth but an objective social and educational reality which increasingly threatens the future of the United States. In early 1987, the television documentary program *60 Minutes* produced a segment entitled "Kurt Waldheim—TV Anchorman?" The segment highlighted the massive political, historical, geographical, and scientific illiteracy of a group of community college students who were interviewed on current events. They had no idea of the location of cities such as Tripoli or Beirut and couldn't name the country on our southern border. They thought Kurt Waldheim was a television anchorman and Karl Marx was one of the Marx Brothers. They had no idea of when the Cuban Missile Crisis occurred nor what was at stake. The students thought the proceedings amusing: They laughed and made fun of their *60 Minutes* interviewers. Many in the audience were not laughing.

In 1989, a set of findings released by the National Endowment for the Humanities (NEH) indicated similar levels of ignorance. The NEH study revealed that 25 percent of college seniors have no idea when Columbus discovered America, could not distinguish Winston Churchill's words from Josef Stalin's, and believe that the Marxist slogan "from each according to his ability, to each according to his need" appears in the U.S. Constitution.[52] The same year, the National Science Foundation released the results of a similar survey showing that 21 percent of its respondents could not describe the astronomical relationship between the earth and the sun. Of those who knew the earth circles the sun, 73 percent could not say how long it takes.[53]

Clearly, we have a problem. Lowered standards are not a myth invented by some right-wing conspiracy to take back the campuses. Lowered standards are objective, well-documented facts. What explains this sorry state of affairs? We should not be too hasty in assigning all the blame to one specific policy such as affirmative action. There is, for example, the overemphasis on college and university athletics, for example—especially in the south. There is also some reason to believe that American public education has been in trouble for a long time.[54] One writer has traced the problems to the Morrill Act, which created the land grant system and along with it the impression that education should be a utilitarian enterprise. This implied that subjects like philosophy and literature were in the curriculum for decorative purposes only—leaving them all but unaccountable to the larger culture.[55] From a larger perspective, affirmative action is as much effect as cause; the educational system is merely the worst casualty of social engineering, as it has spread through American culture like a cancer.

That said, the court-ordered busing of the 1960s nevertheless stands out as a major contributor to the decline of education. For as every believer in affirmative action will agree, we did have many separate but unequal schools during the years prior to the *Brown* decision. Court-ordered busing moved blacks into white schools (and vice versa) but did nothing to remedy the fact that most black children were well behind most white children educationally. Consequently, without the lowering of standards, that generation of black children was in no position to keep up.

Standards were in fact lowered. As a result, today all students—black and white—are behind, and our ability to educate our young is fading rapidly. This tragic outcome helps no one, including black students. It only offers more evidence of the disastrous practical consequences of social engineering. Unfortunately, the influence of that destructive ideology is now spreading to other institutions.

Feminists and the Military

The Philosophy of Social Engineering aspires to control not merely higher education or small business, but every institution in society. Social engineers cannot tolerate the survival of islands of institutional autonomy, for people who want to be autonomous would depart the institutions and occupations controlled by social engineers and seek out those largely unaffected.[56] Until recently, the military was such an institution. Prior to the end of the cold war, social engineers by and large left the military alone. It seemed obvious that the military was not and could not be an equal opportunity employer. To fulfill their obligations, the various military branches had no choice but to discriminate on a variety of bases from gender and age to physical ability, height, weight, and eyesight.

However, events ranging from the presence of women in Desert Storm to rising gay militancy compel us to investigate the infiltration of the military by social engineers. This situation is even more dangerous than the education debacle, for a competent military force remains necessary to the defense of our borders in an unpredictable world. First assaulted by feminists seeking gender integration of combat, the military was then targeted to remove its ban on homosexuals.

The radical feminist entry into the military began in the late 1980s when the Department of Defense, the Navy, and the Marine Corps established task forces that opened noncombat positions to women and strengthened measures for dealing with sexual harassment.[57] Representative Patricia Schroeder (D-Colo.) had already sponsored a bill toward opening combat roles to women. Her argument seems eminently reasonable, asserting that

> [When] you look at women, they have the same individual differences as men do. . . . It all depends on individual differences and I think that is what we ought to be recognizing.
>
> I honestly think that the combat exclusion can weaken the military by lowering standards and making it harder to find a larger pool of all male volunteers. I think we ought to be looking at the standards and whether or not the person complies with the standards rather than the gender.[58]

This emphasis on individual, genderblind qualifications is admirable. Unfortunately for Schroeder (if she is sincere), there is zero chance that its honest implementation would produce the result she and other feminists want: a significant increase in the number of women in all positions—including combat positions.

Public Law 102–190, enacted in December 1991, created a Presidential Commission on the Assignment of Women in the Armed Forces to study the subject. The Commission found that

> A gender-neutral standard will unfairly subject most women to standards which are unrealistic for general fitness and will not be challenging for the majority of military men. A study that investigated whether women could meet the same physical fitness standards as men addressed this question. Study findings revealed that only 21 women of 623 tested (3.4 percent) achieved a score equal to the male mean score on the Army Physical Fitness Test. Only 7 percent of women could perform 60 push-ups while 78 percent of men could achieve this score.[59]

In other words, *contrary to what Representative Schroeder implied, there are large physical differences between men and women that would result in the the exclusion of most women from many military roles (certainly from ground combat) were gender-neutral standards in force.* The Commission admitted:

> The evidence before the Commission clearly shows distinct physiological differences between men and women. Most women are shorter in stature, have less muscle mass and weigh less than men. These physiological differences place women at a distinct disadvantage when performing tasks requiring a high level of muscular strength and aerobic capacity, such as hand-to-hand fighting, digging, carrying heavy loads, lifting and other tasks central to ground combat.
>
> The Commission also heard from women of tremendous physical ability who expressed a desire to serve in the ground combat arms. There is little doubt that some women could meet the physical standards for ground combat, but the evidence shows that few women possess the necessary physical qualifications. Further, a 1992 survey of 900 Army servicewomen showed that only twelve percent of enlisted women and ten percent of the female noncommissioned officers surveyed said they would consider serving in the combat arms.[60]

The only way of meeting the political demands for women in combat is to gendernorm the military by refusing to hold women to the same standards as men. Thus women do not compete against men but only against other women, exactly as in racenorming for admission of blacks into college. For basic training standards, gendernorming was similarly recommended:

> Testimony from several experts indicated that implementing gender-neutral standards would lead to dramatic increases in rates of injury and attrition among women. For example, studies involving Army recruits indicate women are at a higher risk for exercise-induced injuries than men. Compared to men, women had a 2.23 greater risk for lower extremity injuries and a 4.71 times greater risk for stress fractures. The men sustained

99 days of limited duty due to injury while women incurred 481 days of limited duty.[61]

We must consider what such a lowering of standards would mean if we actually achieved a gendernormed military, and a war broke out that forced women to go into combat on a large scale. There can be no doubt that casualties among women would be considerably higher than among men. The politically imposed double standard would instantly become a real single standard on the battlefield, placing many women at an obvious life-threatening disadvantage.

This raises a second concern: The response of men to the possibility of women being harmed. One of Schroeder's interlocutors in the hearing referred to the "attitude of protectiveness" that is "deeply ingrained in the American male psyche."[62] In a combat situation, this could result in "male combatants hanging back to help a female combatant who may have been wounded and thus might endanger the entire unit."[63]

Other problems are not hard to identify. In fact, the Commission cites five areas where any general elimination of the rule excluding women from combat roles might create serious problems:

1. the ability of women to perform on the same level as men from the point of view of physical strength, endurance, and stamina
2. the lack of privacy and forced intimacy on the battlefield, which would include lack of separate bathing and washing facilities, latrines, etc.
3. the need to block the sense of protectiveness Western men instinctively feel toward women
4. sexual misconduct resulting from any of the above
5. pregnancy[64]

This does not include the prospects of women being captured and held as POWs. Addressing this possibility, the Commission report added that

Ground combat incurs a high risk of capture by the enemy. The Commission's review of our nation's recent wars with respect to POWs suggests that potential enemies may not accord respect for the Geneva Convention and customary rules related to protection of prisoners. . . . The Commission heard testimony from DoD representatives and POWs who indicated that the mistreatment of women taken as POWs could have a negative impact on male captives.[65]

Not to mention what would be done to the women!

David Horowitz cited William S. Lind, the former adviser to Gary Hart, who testified before the Commission:

In combat, men will act to protect the women and this will undermine the effectiveness of the unit. The male soldier's protective instinct is heightened by his knowledge of what the male enemy will do to females taken prisoner of war. This is not mere theory. The Israelis, who pioneered the introduction of women in combat during their War of Liberation, now bar women from combat. They found exactly this, that "if you put women in combat with men, the men immediately forget about their tactical objective and they move instead to protect the women."

The Israelis abandoned the practice of putting women into combat positions because it weakened their forces and exposed their fighting men to even greater risks.[66]

The Philosophy of Social Engineering maintains that it is possible to change people's thinking, and hence behavior, by changing the determinants on their thought. Some of the results are blood-chilling:

. . . under the guidance of feminist social engineers, our newly sensitized military leadership marches on. The Air Force has established a SERE program (Survival, Evasion, Resistance, and Escape), including its own "prisoner-of-war" camp in the state of Washington to desensitize its male recruits so that they won't react like men when female prisoners are tortured. In short, in their infinite wisdom, Ms. Schroeder and her feminist allies have enlisted the military in a program to brainwash men so that they won't care what happens to women. That's progress and social enlightenment, feminist style.[67]

The public discussion of women in combat has been predicated on the assumed existence of large numbers of women waiting to enter combat roles—women who are able to meet the same standards as men but are kept out solely by the exclusionary rule. There is no evidence that supports this assumption and much evidence against it. One of Schroeder's discussants asked, "Why do we need your legislation if the Army wants to put women in combat. . . . I think we have got good laws now that are working and we have good regulations. I do not think women, as far as I can tell, are screaming to get into infantry units and go into combat."[68]

Ironically, the current situation grew out of the introduction of nondiscriminatory, gender-neutral standards to measure the physical strength of recruits, and hence their preparedness for many of the responsibilities of military life. These standards provoked objections from feminists who realized that they would bar the vast majority of women from the combat roles that are crucial to career advancement. While paying lip service to individual qualifications, Schroeder and her allies are actually pushing for gendernormed qualifications.

The result was the reduction of the test to a guidance tool and the institution of the depressingly familiar "benign" double standard. This guidance tool, however, still kept women out of physical combat itself; with the Schroeder Amendment, its ability to do that is now in doubt. These efforts prompted then Secretary of Defense Richard Cheney to state that

> [I]t's important for us to remember that what we are asked to do here in the Department of Defense is defend the nation. The only reason we exist is to be prepared to fight and win wars. *We're not a social welfare agency.* . . . This is a military organization. Decisions we make have to be taken based upon those kinds of considerations and only those kinds of considerations.[69]

But as I write, the ban on women in combat continues to be lifted by the regime that has assumed control in Washington with the arrival of President Clinton.

Once again, we do not have a bona fide social problem being solved. We have a circumstance that was out of step with the feminist branch of the Philosophy of Social Engineering being "corrected." Most women are not pushing to be placed in combat; feminists are pushing for women to be placed in combat. The Commission reported testimony "that no human society has ever intentionally used female soldiers in extended combat except in cases of national survival."[70] Tragically, the first victims of our national folly will be the women who have allowed themselves to become pawns in the radical feminist struggle for political domination.

Remember one of the main tenets of radical feminism: *gender* is not a biological category but a sociopolitical one. Gender roles are socially constructed by men to oppress women, quite in accordance with the psychology of victimization. These roles are, in the long run, arbitrary. In accordance with sociocultural determinism, they can be changed by changing the determinants on men's thought and conduct. Hence the key to successful integration of women into the armed forces is not innate sex differences but the attitudes of men, to be changed by reeducation. Commander Rosemary Mariner testified:

> As with racial integration the biggest problem confronting gender integration is not men or women but bigotry. It is bigotry that is the root cause of racial and sexual harassment. From common verbal abuse to the criminal acts of a Tailhook debacle, sexual harassment will continue to be a major problem in the armed forces because the combat exclusion law and policies make women institutionally inferior.[71]

"Sensitivity training" is recommended to change these attitudes and has now become routine. Careers have been ended prematurely because of "insensitivity," particularly in the wake of Tailhook. Three-star admiral John H. Fetterman, a naval aviator with thirty-seven years of service, was virtually forced into early retirement by this scandal. He had been accused over a sexual harassment hotline of protecting an aide accused of sexual harassment. No evidence was produced. In the brave new world of sexual harassment politics, evidence is frequently not required. Men are presumed guilty until proven innocent in complete reversals of justice. The sense that no evidence is required is a good sign that an ideology, not justice, is being served.

The special role of military institutions has long been recognized. To fulfill this role, they must be kept free of political agendas imposed from outside. Putatively egalitarian social engineering is such an agenda. It has crippled higher education; it will do the same to the military.

Parity Demands: the Public Menace

Racenorming and gendernorming are inevitable responses to the realization that there really must be some objective standards for entering into occupations and for measuring performance. Such intellectually dishonest practices represent desperate attempts to shore up the egalitarian focus of social engineering in the face of hard reality. After all, in the "real world" people can either do their jobs or they cannot. An employee can either read the instructions on a piece of machinery or not. In the military, a woman either has the necessary physical strength to avoid holding back her unit, or she does not. It should be common sense that people are qualified for their positions if they can perform what those positions require, and not otherwise.

A marginal workforce will be marginal no matter what its racial composition. A marginal military will be unprepared to defend a nation's interests, regardless of its gender makeup. Whether social engineers like it or not, uniform standards are not merely social constructions or rationalizations by white men, but are rooted in accurate comprehension of the world we all share and must live in. The harm and danger to those exploited in the furthering of social agendas go far beyond inconvenience to a white man passed over in favor of a less qualified black woman.

One of the most widely publicized reverse discrimination cases, *Bakke v. the Regents of the University of California at Davis,* was fought over an admissions set-aside at a medical school. Let's imagine a successful surgeon who has acquired a variety of skills—scientific, technical, and interactional. Four years of college, plus three years of medical school followed by intensive periods of internship, have honed these skills to precision.

Some surgeons will develop high levels of specialized ability (as in brain surgery) and go on to lucrative, perhaps highly visible careers. Others will be sufficiently qualified to perform many kinds of operations successfully but will have more modest careers outside the limelight. Still others, for varying reasons, will never be more than marginal and should rightly have to explore other career options.

It should go without saying that hospital personnel boards must have the autonomy to hire the most highly skilled surgeons they can find. Demonstrated ability—not race or gender or any other nonoccupational characteristic—must be the central criterion.

Now consider what happens if a hospital is forced to adopt an affirmative action plan, having been told that it must "attempt to recruit and hire more black surgeons in order to diversify the staff" and that it will be monitored from the outside by diversity bureaucrats. The hospital's autonomy and capacity to hire on merit will be seriously compromised if it cannot find a sufficient number of highly qualified black surgeons. Obviously, if a hospital is forced to hire—on the basis of race or gender—someone who has not demonstrated the appropriate level of experience and ability, the lives of patients will be endangered in case the person does not know a given procedure at the crucial time.

The airline industry affords an even more common example— probably more of us fly than have surgery. Pilots and air traffic controllers have the lives of hundreds of people in their hands every day. Their training to meet specific criteria for employment must be correspondingly rigorous. Consider what would result if demands to increase the diversity of the workforce by preferential recruiting and hiring were acted upon throughout the airline industry. Since roughly 12 percent of the American population is black, numerical parity would require that airlines give preferential treatment to blacks until their numbers reach the 12 percent figure.

The dangers of downplaying individual qualifications are clear. I do not think even the most ardent backers of affirmative action would fly in a plane if they had doubts about the pilots' and air traffic controllers' qualifications for being there. Such doubts would not be evidence of covert racism, but merely common sense. Arguments that merit-based hiring and promotion are discriminatory should they yield results other than statistical parity, or that there aren't really any objective standards for determining whether someone is qualified to hold a given position, would receive the ridicule they deserve if they were not advanced by obviously intelligent people and defended with the utmost seriousness.

Homosexuals: the Next Affirmative Action Group?

Homophobia is defined as an irrational fear of homosexuals and homosexuality, a fear alleged to be widespread throughout "straight" society and accordingly institutionalized along with racism and sexism. The implication that homosexuals are a victim group no less than blacks and women has been accompanied by an upsurge of homosexual militancy. Groups with such names as ACT-UP and Queer Nation have led the upsurge. We have also seen the rise to prominence of the National Gay and Lesbian Task Force, along with the National Coalition of Gay Organizations. Gay and lesbian studies have appeared on campus; gay and lesbian student groups are often accorded the same privileges and protections afforded ethnic-minority and feminist student groups.

The strongest evidence that homosexuals have powerful advocates for their entrance to the world of affirmative action preferences is a bill, S.B. 574 (H.R. 1430 in the House of Representatives), sponsored by gay congressman Barney Frank. This bill amends the Civil Rights Act of 1964 to encompass broadly defined "discrimination" by sexual orientation. Bill Clinton's election and his immediate effort to lift the ban on overt homosexuals in the military are watershed events in the drive to obtain victim status for gays, whether through passage of this bill or by Executive Order.

Meanwhile, powerful efforts are afoot to persuade the public to accept homosexuality as the moral equal of heterosexuality. These efforts have been concentrated in the schools. The New York City borough of Queens school district tried to impose on very young children a "Rainbow Curriculum," which treats homosexuals as undeserving victims of blind prejudice. The exposure of first graders to books with names like *Heather Has Two Mommies, Daddy's Roommate,* and *Gloria Goes to Gay Pride* provoked a full-scale rebellion from the community, including many black and Hispanic parents.[72]

Yet in reality, homosexuals differ in crucial ways from other groups claiming victimization. These differences come under three headings:

1. the comparative invisibility of homosexuality and concomitant difficulty in discriminating against all homosexuals

2. the inclusion of many known homosexuals in the literary, scholarly, and artistic canons of Western civilization
3. the uncertainty surrounding homosexuality's possible causes

By the invisibility of homosexuality, I mean its invisibility in a physiological sense. There are obvious physiological differences between the sexes. Likewise, there are distinct physical traits that mark most individuals as black, Hispanic, native American, Caucasian, or Asian. There are, however, no visible traits that mark a given person as homosexual. Even overt behavioral traits are notoriously unreliable: An effeminate man is not necessarily gay, nor is a woman with masculine features necessarily lesbian. The only trait essential to being homosexual is something not visible at all—a sexual attraction to a person of the same sex.

This trait cannot even be determined by watching a person over a long period of time, for it may or may not be acted upon. There are presumably people with homosexual tendencies who are not sexually active. Given the invisibility of homosexuality in this sense, two facts are unsurprising: (1) There are few if any reliable assessments of the actual percentage of homosexuals in the population, and (2) It is likely that covert homosexuals exist in practically every field of endeavor, though they have tended to concentrate somewhat in the arts.

One possible inference from these realities is that homophobia is indeed irrational. But an equally valid inference is that any claim homosexuals make about historical victimization is very suspect— far more than for women, blacks, and other minorities. It is true that Western literature and philosophy, for example, give us relatively few works by authors who were female or black. In contrast, many of our most important works of literature, art, sculpture, and philosophy were produced by men who were gay.

Plato, for example, is known to have been gay. There is abundant evidence of his homosexuality in his dialogues, which are punctuated with references to the "handsomeness" of the lovers of his male characters. In fact, homosexuality was accepted during the period of Greek history during which Plato was writing. Other significant writers and artists were gay: Leonardo Da Vinci, Michelangelo, Erasmus, Marlowe, Lord Byron, Rimbaud, Verlaine,

Proust, Gide, Cocteau . . . the list goes on and on. Homosexuals cannot claim underrepresentation in the galaxy of Western cultural stars. Nor is it likely, given their lack of physiological distinctiveness, that they have been widely discriminated against by employers in general.

Nevertheless, although overt homosexuality has been largely accepted in some cultures, ours is not presently one of them. Our culture, whose basic values are rooted in the Judeo-Christian tradition, regards homosexual conduct as immoral. Many other cultures reject homosexuality even more categorically. Islamic society's treatment of homosexuals is considerably more brutal than any "gay-bashing" that occurs on the streets of America.

A deeply rooted popular ethos, then, rejects homosexuality as morally unacceptable behavior and on this basis resists the efforts of gay and lesbian activists. Examples are the measure in Oregon that openly called for discrimination against homosexuals, and a measure in Colorado that rejected all legislation offering them special treatment in the workplace. These measures, though defeated or suspended, had the support of a sizable number of citizens. Such efforts, along with the unfortunate violence occasionally directed against homosexuals, have fueled in gay activists the belief that they indeed are a victimized group deserving compensatory preferential treatment.

Yet it is significant that scientists interested in homosexuality (most of whom are themselves homosexual) do not insist that the phenomenon is a "social construction" of some kind, as do radical feminists concerning gender. Rather, they are seeking a biological basis for it. This is the implication of the gradual shift from using the term *sexual preference* (which implies that homosexuality is chosen behavior) to the term *sexual orientation* (which implies no such choice).

If a biological basis for homosexuality is ever found, it may appear to strengthen the status of homosexuals as a legitimate minority group and diffuse moral objections as well: How can you morally condemn someone for how he or she was born? As Chandler Burr recently observed, "Homosexuals have long maintained that sexual orientation . . . is something neither chosen nor changeable; heterosexuals who have made their peace with homosexuals have often done so by accepting that premise."[73]

The findings to date are worth noting. In 1990, neurobiologist

Dick Swaab claimed to have discovered a physiological difference between the brains of homosexual and heterosexual men. A cluster of cells called the suprachiasmatic nucleus is nearly twice as large in homosexuals as in heterosexuals.[74] However, it is not clear whether such a phenomenon is a cause of homosexuality or merely one of its effects. Simon LeVay, the best-known neurobiologist attempting to understand homosexuality, made this observation.[75]

LeVay has focused his research on the hypothalamus, a region of the brain intimately involved with sexual behavior. He claims to have found that the hypothalamus does contain structures that differ significantly in homosexuals. This result, as LeVay himself admits, is highly inconclusive: His sample size was small (forty-one people); the nineteen homosexual men in this group had all died of AIDS; there were no samples of brain tissue from lesbians; and, as of this writing, LeVay's research has not been reproduced by others. Chandler Burr concludes that "the notion that homosexuals and heterosexuals are in some way anatomically distinct must hold the status of tantalizing supposition."[76]

However, from none of this does it follow that a case can be made for making homosexuals the next affirmative action group. The homosexual authors and artists who have long held honored places in the Western cultural canon are not honored *because* of their homosexuality but because they created works of historical importance. Their homosexuality is incidental and irrelevant. We might call this phenomenon *historical homosexuality:* the fact that homosexuals have tended to accumulate in the arts and have made important contributions apparently have little if anything to do with their sexual orientation.

There is a lesson radical feminists and Afrocentrists can learn from the long-accepted fact that homosexuals have made important contributions to Western culture: What matters, in determining the historical importance of a work of literature or art or philosophy, is its ability to hold up over time. Radical feminism and other schools of antischolarship such as Afrocentrism deny the validity of objective criteria that enable us to affirm such value.

This should also be considered against the backdrop of a mind-set increasingly dominant among homosexuals, which I call *radical homosexualism.* The main difference between historical homosexuality and radical homosexualism is the latter's consonance with the Philosophy of Social Engineering. Many of today's homosexual artists produce works whose distinctiveness stems not from their capacity to stand the test of time but merely their attempt to celebrate the homosexual lifestyle. These works are calculated to shock and offend the straight majority. One thinks of Robert Mapplethorpe's works, many of them funded through National Endowment for the Arts (NEA) grants—in other words, funded by taxpayers, many of whom find homosexuality morally objectionable.

The influence of social engineering is evident when we consider the issue of homosexuals in the military. Homosexuals have served in the military with distinction and have been able to do so because they kept their sexual orientation private. Furthermore, many of the objections reasonably brought against women in combat do not apply to gays. This has led some writers to contend that the only reason for not lifting the military's ban on homosexuals is homophobia. Historian E. Anthony Rotundo recently summarized:

> The issue is not the military competence of homosexuals, but the fears of heterosexuals in the military. Officers fear a breakdown of morale and good order, but most of the grounds they cite are easily dismissed. They say that they fear the unpredictable effects of love affairs between soldiers (but homosexual love affairs already happen in the military); they fear the open practice of sex in the barracks (but President Clinton has reaffirmed the ban on such behavior); and they fear harassment of soldiers by gay and lesbian superiors (but experience in other settings shows that if the military had a clear, well-enforced sexual harassment policy, it could minimize such incidents. Further, in the wake of the Tailhook scandal, there are signs that the military may be getting serious about opposing sexual harassment).[77]

In other words, the solution to the problem of the acceptance of known homosexuals in the military, again, is reeducation. I think the matter is more complicated. Rotundo overlooks the distinction between historical homosexuality, which does not identify achievements as group-specific, and radical homosexualism, which (in accordance with the sociocultural determinism of the Philosophy of Social Engineering) does so identify them, and which will inevitably advocate the increase of the number of homosexuals in the military as an end in itself. The intrusion of overt homosexuality into the military will mean the rise to power not of historical homosexuality (which has never sought group power or even drawn attention to itself), but of radical homosexualism, which does both—and seeks legal mandates of protection.

Problems Rotundo cites as "easily dismissed" are not so easily dismissed. If, for example, there were homosexual love affairs among men in the military in the past, these were unquestionably covert. No one really believes that such affairs would be covert in the "new" military, under the influence of radical homosexualism. New possibilities emerge of openly gay or lesbian officers "hitting on" young recruits.

The degree to which recruits would be protected by sexual harassment policies is questionable. The primary targets of harassment policies have always been heterosexual white men. Given social engineering's track record of double standards whereby members of certain groups are protected at the expense of others, harassment policies are likely to be selectively implemented.

In the wake of an incident in North Carolina (also cited by Rotundo), it appears probable that radical homosexualism will do the homosexual community more harm than good, as group-defined policies so often bring harm to intended beneficiaries. In this incident, three Marines set upon and savagely beat a man after he came out of a gay bar, then made a political statement: Their intent was to send a message to President Clinton opposing his efforts to lift the ban on homosexuals in the military.

Tolerance of overt homosexuality cannot be engineered; it cannot be programmed into people by force. The assumption that it can illustrates the sociocultural determinist component of social engineering. The assumption that it *should* illustrates the egalitarian component. The assumption that radical homosexuals and their allies in the Clinton administration can implement effective educational techniques illustrates the elitist component.

Tolerance for overt homosexuality can only come about over a long period of time and is only forestalled by homosexuals who place themselves on display in ways that the majority of Americans, not all of them heterosexual, find offensive (as in "gay pride" rallies that feature same-sex couples doing public strip-teases and displaying affection openly). Homosexuality is rejected by the majority of Americans, at least as a moral equal of heterosexuality. Much of this rejection is rooted in traditional religious and moral beliefs.

This reality renders government-enforced preferential treatment for homosexuals considerably more problematic than for women and blacks.

Consider the following scenario, no longer hypothetical in certain parts of the country (such as California), representing a situation likely to occur were S.B. 574 to become law: A businessman who happens to be a Bible-believing Christian receives a number of applications from avowed homosexuals (who may, for all we know, be attempting a test case). He refuses to hire any of them, because he believes on Biblical grounds that homosexuality is wrong. He finds himself hauled into court and accused of discrimination on the basis of sexual orientation. We have seen what the EEOC attempted to do to Mike Welbel with far less evidence of discriminatory intent. Obviously, a discrimination suit brought by a member of a protected group can be devastating.

Christians, Moslems, and members of other religious faiths will be forced to stand by and watch their faiths being sacrificed on the altar of social engineering, as the government sees to it that the percentage of overt homosexuals in the workforce is increased in the same way it has forced businesses to preferentially hire women and blacks. Incidents like the one involving the University of Michigan student who was threatened with discrimination charges for complaining about his militantly homosexual roommate, and reports that the Cracker Barrel restaurant chain is facing legal difficulties as a result of a longstanding refusal to hire homosexual employees, suggest that we have reached this point.

With the ascendancy of radical homosexualism and its protection by our legal system, social engineering becomes a strong threat to religious liberty—which presumably includes the liberty to refuse dealings with purveyors of lifestyles the religious person considers immoral. It is the individual's right to hold and exercise her religious beliefs, however unscientific, that is at issue here. Social engineering, American style, begins to resemble the intolerance toward religious beliefs (especially toward beliefs differing from those held by the people in power) that we typically see in totalitarian societies, communist and otherwise.[78]

Of course, physical attacks against homosexuals are as unconscionable as physical attacks against any citizen (other than a physical aggressor or fleeing criminal). In a free society, homosexuals should be able to walk down the street without looking over their shoulders, or walk into a gay bar without fear of physical attack when they leave. And what consenting adults do in their own bedrooms can reasonably be considered their private affair: Many Americans have no problem with the repeal of overly stringent sodomy laws.

But do militant, overt homosexuals have the right to force everyone to affirm gay lifestyles as morally equivalent to heterosexual monogamy? How can society be organized so that the right of homosexuals to live as they see fit is protected, while simultaneously protecting the rights of other citizens who want to uphold ideals at odds with promiscuous or militantly gay lifestyles?

The answer to such questions, I believe, lies in exploring alternatives to the Philosophy of Social Engineering. Proponents of various aspects of the Philosophy of Social Engineering are now in control of the educational system; they are dominant in the arts and the media. With the admission of women to combat and overt homosexuals into the military, social engineering will have gained a firm foothold in that institution as well.

We have therefore an urgent need to develop an alternative from the ground up, an alternative that demonstrably offers blacks, women, and homosexuals *more* than does the Philosophy of Social Engineering. It is time to face reality: Preferential policies based on social-engineering assumptions have benefited principally the opportunists in favored groups, have brought harm to many other human beings of all colors and both sexes, and have done immense damage to every institution they have touched. Fortunately, a number of thoughtful social observers have given us the outlines of an alternative to social engineering. We turn now to their insights.

The Philosophy of Social Spontaneity

The Philosophy of Social Spontaneity

The Philosophy of Social Engineering and its progeny have permeated most American institutions. It thus represents the greatest threat to freedom we have yet faced, because it subverts from within. Yet we have seen that its assumptions, methods, and results are not logically, empirically, or morally strong enough to withstand serious questioning. So the determining factor will be whether the American people have sufficient will to keep asking questions—and keep refusing to accept dishonest answers—until the social, political, and cultural structures of social engineering can be dismantled.

Assuming that we as Americans will have that staying power, the question then becomes: What next? For however misguided the ideology that turned calls for equality of opportunity into demands for special favors and guaranteed outcomes, the problems addressed by the civil rights movement were and are real. Discrimination against black people is a fact of American history. Their achievements often have been invisible. The problems addressed by the early feminists were also real. Some women undoubtedly have been denied recognition and refused opportunities simply because they were women. Likewise, when gays have a factual basis to fear being physically attacked in the street, something is surely wrong.

Many people are indeed so insecure in their identities that they cannot tolerate those who obviously differ. Violent hatred of others on the basis of involuntary group characteristics should always offend our sensibilities. It is unjust, for no one chooses his group identity, leaving aside for now those borderline cases of religious affiliation and unanswered questions about the biological basis of homosexuality. The healthier side of multiculturalism recognizes this and calls attention to the evil of intolerance. (If only all the multiculturalists were sincere and consistent in advocating tolerance.) Recognizing that prejudice does create injustice, we must ask: Where *do* we go from here? Our critique of reverse discrimination in the workplace, lowered standards in education, radical feminists crippling the military, and gays imposing their values on others will ring hollow in the absence of a credible alternative. Such an alternative should show how to go beyond preferential policies while offering women, racial minorities, and gays real freedom and dignity. It should demonstrate by force of contrast that the entitlements offered by preferential policies are bogus enticements that conceal new forms of enslavement.

Such an alternative does exist: I call it the Philosophy of Social Spontaneity. In its essentials, the Philosophy of Social Spontaneity consists of the following:

1. *individualism,* as opposed to collectivism
2. *individual free agency,* as opposed to sociocultural determinism
3. *individual liberty* for all adult citizens of sound mind, to the extent they exercise the *individual responsibility* that liberty requires
4. a *minimal state* whose primary function is the protection of individual liberty under the rule of law
5. a call for revival of the *independent sector* of private institutions and voluntary associations to ameliorate social problems more effectively than the top-down approach of government

    Finally, the mortar of the Philosophy of Social Spontaneity—the concept that integrates the other components—is
6. the concept of *property rights*

Let's look at each concept in turn. Individualism contends that the most basic unit in civil society is the *individual person,* not a society or group. Only individuals have minds: Only they have the internal configurations that enable them to prioritize needs and desires, make decisions, and carry out plans. Societies, races, genders, and classes have no such properties: They are merely collections of individuals organized in a myriad of ways (to the extent they are organized at all). Institutions and collective agencies within society grow out of the cooperative actions of individuals, and their performance is ultimately reducible to the actions of the individuals who compose them. Any description of a *collective action* by such an agency is a metaphorical shorthand, for collective entities do not *act* in a real sense.[1]

The introduction of the *action* element brings us to the premise that individuals are *freely acting agents*. In accepting this, we oppose all forms of determinism applied to human beings and so transcend the "nature-nurture" debate. While necessary conditions can be given for all human actions (for example, an awake and alert, properly functioning brain and nervous system), *sufficient* conditions cannot be so given. Thus a person is always more than a product of a particular upbringing or sociocultural environment or genetic code (which is not to deny that these do *influence* what a person is and does). From this perspective, the assumption that we are living in an entirely deterministic universe is just that—an assumption, not only unproven but unprovable. It is a metaphysical, not scientific, thesis, for it cannot be inferred from any scientific findings, nor is it a hypothesis within any scientific domain. Its strangest consequence, as we have seen, is that its truth is incompatible with its own rational defense.

Let's approach the issue another way. Human beings are unique among animals in their ability to think abstractly, form judgments, identify values, set goals, outline strategies for achieving them, and so guide their actions according to principles that go beyond immediate experience. Other animals can arrange raw materials into more suitable forms, as when beavers build dams, but nothing in the animal kingdom comes close to what human beings can do. We are not invoking mysterious or "supernatural" phenomena here, but it is clear that human beings are more than *natural* phenomena in the same way that falling objects or growing plants or even animals following instinct are natural phenomena.

While animals are capable of being manipulated, only humans are capable of *discovering*—apprehending on a conceptual, cognitive level—that they are being manipulated and then taking action to disrupt that manipulation. Only humans are capable both of being coerced and of responding to coercion by formulating a strategic rejection of the coercive agency. If we look at falling objects or growing plants or dogs or horses, the category *coercion* simply doesn't apply to them in the way it applies to humans.

This means that human beings have responsibilities no other forms of life have: They must learn to take responsibility for the content of their thoughts and the direction of their actions. Indeed, if we are to survive in the world, we have no alternative but to learn and constantly improve our knowledge of the principles according to which the nonhuman world operates (physical, chemical, biological, ecological, economic, and so on). This is enshrined in Sir Francis Bacon's adage that "nature, to be commanded, must be obeyed."

Rational actions can only be taken by individuals. Collective entities do not have sense organs, brains, or nervous systems. They are even less capable than lower animals of experiencing, reasoning, or planning. It makes no sense to consider them *morally significant* entities. Since only individuals can act, individualism and free agency best describe the essence of being human.

Supporting evidence for the validity of individualism and free agency as integral to a description of the human condition comes from a historical reality no longer to be denied: Societies organized roughly in accordance with these assumptions (whether or not explicitly formulated) are capable of sustaining high levels of freedom, prosperity, and security—along with cultural excellence in the arts, the sciences, and religion—over long periods of time.

When individualism was replaced by collectivism, and the concept of free agency was eclipsed by the idea that an individual is a helpless automaton of mindless material and historical forces, cultural progress slowed and in our time has begun to reverse. An honest examination of human history leads one to conclude that individualism and free agency form the basis of the only practical framework for human social organization. Hayek has argued that human individuals are so numerous and so diverse that no person or committee or database can possibly access the knowledge that would be necessary to organize human energy and real, flesh-and-blood diversity according to a single blueprint. We need to add that individualism is a social metaphysics, not an ethical theory (human beings *are* social creatures, though not in the way and not to the degree collectivists have imagined). Individualism is therefore compatible with—but does not necessarily entail—more specific moral philosophies such as the ethical egoism advocated by philosophers like Ayn Rand, Tibor Machan, Eric Mack, and others.[2]

One may of course take it upon oneself to act to benefit others using one's own resources. Indeed, I think it likely that when human associations and interactions are voluntary, many individuals will naturally want to help those less fortunate. This was the motive force behind what Richard C. Cornuelle calls the independent sector, which provided a wide variety of welfare and philanthropic services before the rise of big government.[3] Individualism as a social philosophy leaves such decisions up to individuals and does not permit the decisions and values of any one person or government agency to become the basis of public policy.

The Philosophy of Social Spontaneity observes that people of any economic status are more likely to be harmed than helped when they are treated as helpless victims. Even the best-intentioned social engineers know too little of the actual situations of the thousands their decisions impact. This is the lesson taught by Mises and Hayek among others of the Austrian school.

The concepts of individualism and free agency lead naturally to the view that individual liberty is the most desirable state of affairs one can promote. By *liberty,* we mean a state of affairs "in which a man is not subject to coercion by the arbitrary will of another or others."[4] The Philosophy of Social Spontaneity joins the Austrian school in recognizing that not only have all forms of socialist, fascist, and welfare-statist economic planning failed, but they *had* to fail. They were attempting the impossible. Thus the Philosophy of Social Spontaneity advocates free market capitalism in the realm of economic policy alongside freedom in the realm of personal morality.

Individual liberty includes (indeed requires) the economic liberties to choose a form of employment or entrepreneurship, to trade with others on an open market, and to dispose of the fruits of one's labors as one chooses. Economic liberties—as recent experiences in eastern Europe and elsewhere around the globe so vividly testify—are necessary, though not always fully sufficient, conditions for other freedoms: of religion, of assembly, of speech, of the press, and so on. When economic liberties are protected, the conditions are established for peaceful, voluntary cooperation and general prosperity.

A corollary to the defense of economic liberty inherent in the Philosophy of Social Spontaneity is a firm rejection of claims made by some individuals on the fruits of the labors of other individuals. In a free society, one must take responsibility for one's own life, take up an occupation that permits peaceful transactions with others for mutual benefit, and avoid the temptation to live at the expense of others. Since preferential policies are built on the premise that some are today entitled to live at the expense of others because of wrongs committed against their ancestors, these policies are incompatible with the Philosophy of Social Spontaneity.

However, social spontaneity is not equivalent to anarchism. Our philosophy does not advocate the abolition of the state. It does limit the state's powers to three principal functions: (1) protecting individual liberties, (2) serving as the agent of punishment for those who infringe on the liberties of others by coercion (for example, murder, assault, or theft) or fraud (such as swindles and forgery), and (3) protecting national borders. Great parts of the common law tradition of the West are devoted to spelling out the origin, nature, and limits of our liberties, and large parts of the U.S. Constitution are devoted to distinguishing the powers of the various branches of government, ending (in the Bill of Rights) with specific limits on the powers of government over individual citizens.

It is important that the state be so limited. The Philosophy of Social Spontaneity is rooted in the same distrust of the state that motivated the founders of liberal democratic theory—men like Locke, Burke, Smith, and Paine. This distrust is not limited to the state itself but extends to those who would use the state to give themselves unearned advantages or illegitimate power over others. Racists have always instinctively recognized that the state, with its legal and bureaucratic apparatus, is the most formidable weapon they can wield against their targets. Thus it is urgent that the state *not* have the capacity to be used as an instrument for such purposes. A state that is powerful enough to coerce its citizens for benign purposes is powerful enough to coerce them for evil purposes—and sooner or later will do so.

As history too clearly shows, liberty is a very fragile state of affairs. It does not spring into being, but can be achieved only after a long struggle. Even then, it is not self-perpetuating or self-protecting: It can be corrupted by those who seek power over others or privileges at others' expense. This is just what is happening to us in the late twentieth century.

Some readers may respond: *This is all well and good for the Socially Spontaneous, but how will you overcome the legacies of discrimination and group-based hatred?* It's a legitimate question. The revival of Cornuelle's independent sector is part of the answer. In the quest for solutions to such problems as racial discrimination, the Philosophy of Social Spontaneity warns us to rely not on the manipulation of outcomes by government, but only on government's protection of the freedoms of those who encounter discrimination. What people subject to discrimination need most is the freedom to create and support a wide variety of associations and institutions of their own—familial, educational, religious, and philanthropic.

The family is a good place to begin. It is the critically important institution for the inculcation of values in children. Some of the most vicious attacks by radical feminist antischolars are directed against the family as a supposed bastion of patriarchy. It is doubtful, however, that a free society can successfully nurture its young without traditional family units and provide children with their first role models of strong and loving parents. Then, from bonds developed within extended families or between families come support networks that are crucial in times of adversity. Such networks can continue to extend outward to churches; professional, educational, and civic organizations; and other social institutions.

This paean to the independent sector will strike some readers as naive or archaic. But as Richard Cornuelle has shown, this sector contributed a great deal to American life before the rapid expansion in the size of government that began with the New Deal. Its vitality was praised by Alexis de Tocqueville in *Democracy in America* as one of American society's most remarkable traits. During its heyday, the independent sector (often acting through churches) created what became the nation's leading colleges and universities.

It also built hospitals and started a variety of what became commercial firms, particularly in the insurance industry.[5] The National Foundation for Infantile Paralysis, an independent association, almost singlehandedly raised the money that led to the eradication of polio.[6] Numerous museums, art exhibits, opera houses, and symphonies were created and funded by the independent sector.[7] Its activities have also included assisting the unskilled and underprivileged.[8] Cornuelle writes:

> The independent sector is a kaleidoscope of human action. It takes a thousand forms and works in a million ways. And a tremendous raw strength undergirds its rich variety. Welded into our national life at every level, it functions at any moment when a person or group acts directly to serve others. The independent sector is, to begin with, 190 million individuals in 50 million families who do not limit their lives to pay-earning work (the personal commercial sector) or occasional trips to the voting booth (the personal government sector). We are the richest, best educated, most ingenious people in the history of the world. Seventy-one million of us in the labor force produce goods and services worth $630 billion annually. We channel much of this wealth—plus talent and energy not counted by the GNP figures—through the independent sector.[9]

However, the independent sector eventually fell behind government in providing services. What went wrong? Cornuelle's analysis identifies three reasons for the weakening of the independent sector. For one, we never really understood it; its activities were so diverse and widely scattered that in the face of the more organized commercial and governmental sectors, we had no theories of how to nurture it. Second, in the absence of discipline, it sometimes allocated resources poorly. As Cornuelle put it, it penalized fraud, but not incompetence.[10] Third, the independent sector never learned to articulate its unique role. Its practitioners did not *talk;* they *acted.* They were not intellectuals, they were not politicians and bureaucrats; they were doers.[11]

Today, however, a resurgence of the independent sector is both possible and desirable. After the Great Depression, the independent sector retreated and government expanded. Sixty years later, we have the testimony of history that when government attempts to solve problems it not only fails but creates a host of new ones—an irony predicted by Ludwig von Mises and others. Recognizing this must be coupled with a growing understanding of the independent sector. Independent sector practitioners must recognize the need to compete with government rather than merely petition it. This will require a major attitudinal shift, for there exist innumerable private agencies representing hundreds of interests and needs. But in today's climate of dependence on government, most of these agencies—their main offices based in Washington—have been transformed into lobbying groups competing for federal, state, and local dollars, rather than relying on their own ingenuity to raise money and address problems themselves.

As we have seen, reliance on government has major dangers: Some sage once said, "With every government dollar there are strings attached." Dependence on government leads to more dependence, more bureaucracy, more talk, and less accomplishment. Eventually, once-independent organizations lose both their autonomy and their ability to address real problems effectively.

In a flourishing independent sector, private foundations and organizations are formed through the voluntary association of individuals who have recognized a need unmet by the commercial and governmental sectors. They then pool their resources or call for donations to start new productive endeavors to meet the needs. Independent organizations do not rely on the sanction of any government—federal, state, or local—nor do they thrive at the expense of others through the forced expropriation and redistribution of wealth.

The Philosophy of Social Spontaneity urges all citizens—white, black, brown, male and female, heterosexual, or homosexual—to develop and maintain a strong family unit and personal network, to obtain the best education they can for the least cost, to acquire skills, and to put them to use in constructive ways. It further urges that the resulting actions be infused with an awareness of others, tolerance of differences, and compassion for those who have suffered misfortunes for reasons beyond their control.

It should be clear that the Philosophy of Social Spontaneity does not inevitably lead to a heartless Hobbesian individualism or an every-man-woman-and-child-for-himself view of the world. That's a caricature of individualism. For although individuals are free to take whatever actions they deem fit so long as they do not interfere forcibly with others, they cannot simply disregard the interests of others. In a spontaneous society, individuals must take actions that benefit others in order to increase their own prosperity. In other words, they must answer to the marketplace.

Let us dwell for a moment on this marketplace. The *market* is not some mysterious force. It is simply the entire constellation of economic actions and transactions that occur in any society—buying and selling goods, purchasing stocks and bonds, hiring employees and paying wages, and so on. In a *free* marketplace, these activities come about as responses to expressed needs, desires, and interests of numerous consumers.

Anyone who can respond effectively to a particular need or desire can become a *producer,* and if the need or desire is widespread, the producer may become wealthy. In this way, wealth is generated through services to others within the marketplace. If an individual has an idea for a new product, he may become an entrepreneur and attempt to sell potential consumers on the idea, thus creating a new market. If he succeeds in winning over a large body of consumers, he may grow wealthy; otherwise, he will not.

In a free society, a person cannot foist an idea onto others who do not agree or are not interested. Profit in a free society is *earned:* It results from having satisfied one's customers. A *price* represents the value placed on a product or idea by the consumers to whose desires the producer must respond. A *wage* represents the value placed on the services of an employee by his employer.

This explains why the person who drops out and becomes a "starving artist" will experience a sharp decline in his standard of living and may have to content himself with living on society's margins. This, too, is the choice of some. Having plenty of money and living in comfortable surroundings are subjective values. Persons who make contrary choices ought to be tolerated so long as they are not attempting to live at the expense of others.

The concept that binds other elements of the Philosophy of Social Spontaneity together is that of *property rights.* There has been no clearer statement of this concept than the one provided by John Locke over 200 years ago:

> Though the earth and all inferior creatures be common to all men, yet every man has a property in his own person; this nobody has any right to but himself. The labour of his body and the work of his hands, we may say, are properly his. Whatsoever then he removes out of the state that nature hath provided and left it in, he hath mixed his labour with, and joined to it something that is his own, and thereby makes it his property. It being by him removed from the common state

nature hath placed it in, it hath by this labour something annexed to it that excludes the common right of other men. For this labour being the unquestionable property of the labourer, no man but he can have a right to what that is once joined to, at least where there is enough and as good left in common for others.[12]

Locke's first point may be summed up as: *Everyone is the sole owner of his own life.* One's life is one's property. Conversely, no one is the owner of any other person's life; in this simple inference is the most profound moral objection to slavery imaginable. The only way to sustain one's life without implying ownership of others is through rational action. Thus in order to make sense out of self-ownership (ownership of one's life), we must add that one owns the products of one's mind as well.

Since some of these products include actions taken on one's surroundings, having arranged them in more suitable ways, *everyone is also the sole owner of his own labor.* One's labor is one's property. No one has any claim on the labor of another. One's labors may be the physical labors of the "laborer" in the ordinary sense of that word, or they may be the more sophisticated mental labors of the entrepreneur who has an idea, who must execute it and plan its introduction to a body of potential customers. Given that the effort involved is the entrepreneur's, it will follow that the entrepreneur is the sole owner of his business.

Finally, everyone is also the sole owner of the fruits of his own labor. The fruits of one's labor are one's property. No one has any claim on the fruits of the labor of another. One may of course transact for the fruits of the labors of another in the context of an agreed-upon exchange. Through such transactions, all may sell their labors or their goods for compensation. It follows from one's ownership of the fruits of one's entrepreneurship that one may hire or not hire by whatever criteria she sees fit. If she proceeds intelligently, she will reap the rewards; if she proceeds unintelligently, she will suffer the consequences.

In civil society, this logic is encoded in *rights.* We say that one has a *right* to one's life, to one's labor, to the fruits of one's labor. Rights emerge in a social setting but apply to individuals. They are rights to take action oneself, not claims on the fruits of the actions of others. Rights are very different from *entitlements,* though entitlements are sometimes politically marketed as "rights." Rights can be exercised in civil society without interfering with others. Entitlements are claims that can only be fulfilled at the expense of others. Rights are rooted in features of the human condition that have an objective basis in the natural order; entitlements have no such basis.

In practice, entitlements are granted by government and can be fulfilled only at the expense of productive citizens through governmental redistribution of the fruits of the actions of those citizens, thus trespassing on their liberties. The more productive the citizen, the more she becomes a target of redistribution programs. This inevitably creates an increasingly strong disincentive to produce, resulting in the society's decline in prosperity. This is the principal reason socialist and interventionist programs do not work: They are simply out of touch with the conditions of human survival and prosperity on this planet.

The only satisfactory role for governmental authority is the protection of individual liberties, such as the rights of individuals to make their own choices and direct their own actions, provided these choices and actions do not interfere with the similar liberties of others. The government can best secure these individual liberties by encoding them as rights.

This view of government's proper role rules out not just affirmative action but even antidiscrimination laws. For is not the governmental proscription against discrimination essentially an interference with the entrepreneur's right to hire whom he sees fit? Is it not therefore an infringement on his property rights? I believe this is indeed the case.[13] But haven't we then made things *worse* rather than better, for minorities, women, and other groups that have suffered from discrimination? To understand that this is not necessarily the case, we need to take a look at how much damage the state historically has done to such groups by instituting and maintaining discrimination. Expecting the state to rectify injustices for which the state itself is largely responsible is like using gasoline to put out a fire.

It is time to question seriously the assumption that state action is, has been, or ever can be entirely or even mostly beneficial to women and minorities. This assumption is deeply entrenched in today's dominant intellectual and political cultures. It denies the historical reality that the problems that have plagued groups such as blacks were actually created by government—in a sense, by our failure to consistently practice the principles of individualism and limited government on which this country was founded. These problems can only be solved today by dismantling the machinery created to advance social engineering, thereby opening the way for us to practice social spontaneity.

The State and Blacks: with Friends Like This, Who Needs Enemies?

Much has been written about discrimination against blacks in American history as if it can simply be assumed that free and autonomous institutions are chiefly responsible for it. We are expected to infer from this that government intervention is the solution. But does history really support this assumption?

The proposition that government intervention is the primary historical source of harm to blacks will seem incredible to those encased in today's dominant ideology that regards the state (especially when in politically correct hands) as a major benefactor to minorities. But in historical reality, the state has seldom been a friend to black interests.

Despite grassroots opposition on both moral and economic grounds dating back to Revolutionary War times and even earlier, slavery as an institution had—and required for its survival—the full protection of the United States government, as did the view that blacks are genetically and intellectually inferior to whites. Even Abraham Lincoln took the view that blacks had no rights a white man was obligated to respect. The *Dred Scott* decision gave legal force to this view in 1857 by denying that constitutionally protected freedoms applied to "negroes." After the Thirteenth Amendment ended slavery in the South, the Fourteenth affirmed equal protection under the law to all citizens, and the Fifteenth made it clear that the Fourteenth included newly freed slaves. The mood among black leaders of the day was optimistic: Frederick Douglass wrote that blacks would soon be recognized as "a class of men noted for enterprise, industry, economy, and success," and with this recognition they would "no longer have any trouble in the matter of civil and political rights."[14] Indeed, blacks were voting, serving in the armed forces, starting businesses (including their own schools), publishing newspapers, serving on juries, and in some cases holding political office.[15]

But as the nineteenth century entered its final decades, these advances were slowed and then reversed by a spate of state and local legislation that made direct efforts to block the economic progress of blacks. These laws were being upheld by the highest court of the land, the U.S. Supreme Court. Jim Crowism came out in the open with the passage of laws in the 1860s calling for segregation in public accommodations. But more significant in actually restricting the economic activities of blacks were laws that offered special privileges to established enterprises while restricting the entry of newcomers into markets. Civil rights attorney Clint Bolick has called attention to the *Slaughter-House* Cases of 1873, which he identifies as a crucial development in the transformation of black America from a group of temporary outsiders with enormous potential to a group trapped in lower-caste status.[16] What happened was this: The state of Louisiana enacted a statute granting the equivalent of a twenty-five-year legal monopoly to a number of existing slaughterhouses in the New Orleans area. This meant the forced closing of other slaughterhouses and the prevention of new competitors from entering the market. Three separate legal challenges on both Thirteenth and Fourteenth Amendment grounds were heard in 1873 by the Supreme Court, which after bitter division upheld the statute by a 5–4 vote.

The Court's reasoning, as Bolick shows, rested on a specious distinction between civil rights derived from the states and those derived from national citizenship, applying the Fourteenth Amendment's equal protection clause only to the latter. Thus was economic liberty for outsiders effectively gutted: They were now legally blocked from competing openly with established businesses. One can immediately see how this would harm anyone with less experience, less capital, or fewer "connections." Thus it was particularly detrimental to blacks. The decision was applauded by white supremacists who feared the results of open competition with free blacks. Historically, despicable white supremacists have had no more love for free institutions than have noble social engineers.

As the Jim Crow era arrived in full force, black participation in the political arena was ended through the nullification of black voting rights, and their economic mobility was limited by vagrancy laws forbidding unemployment in conjunction with laws limiting the time a black person could spend seeking employment. Other laws sought to prevent labor recruiters from competing with one another in an open market for the services of black workers. As

Bolick concluded, these laws in combination "represented a rather transparent attempt to guarantee a stable, servile, and inexpensive supply of labor akin to slavery, relegating blacks to a separate, subordinate caste."[17]

Among black leaders in that difficult time, Booker T. Washington kept the idea of black educational and economic progress alive through a philosophy of self-reliance, stressing the need for education and gradual self-improvement through hard work. In 1881, he founded the Tuskegee Institute to further this goal. Tuskegee went on to become the most prestigious black university in the South.

Washington is harshly criticized by the current generation of black historians for his willingness to cede the political arena to the white establishment. Woodward comments that "in proposing the virtual retirement of the mass of Negroes from the political life of the South and in stressing the humble and menial role that the race was to play, he would seem unwittingly to have smoothed the path to proscription."[18]

However, in significant respects Washington's pragmatism was vindicated. Although blacks remained almost invisible politically, a growing percentage made steady educational and economic progress despite Jim Crow repression. Whites continued to compete for black labor, despite restrictions that were proving unenforceable in a society where such restrictions were attempts to create fortified islands in a sea of freedom. As a result, during their first fifty years of freedom blacks increased their per capita income by 300 percent. Black schools educated thousands of youths who went on to become newspapermen, attorneys, and doctors. Black illiteracy fell from 80 percent to 45 percent.[19]

We can see that specific government actions were the main source of black oppression and the biggest obstacle to black progress. Without a legal apparatus to manipulate, the white supremacist mentality could have done relatively little to prevent the economic advancement of blacks who were sufficiently enterprising to discover and satisfy legitimate needs, including those of other blacks.

Plessy v. Ferguson was the biggest legal setback for black economic liberties. This ruling upheld another Louisiana law maintaining separate railroad cars for blacks and whites. When the Supreme Court upheld this law, "separate but equal" facilities quickly spread to other institutions and occupations, especially educational ones. In *Berea College v. Kentucky,* the Supreme Court upheld the state's right to enforce segregation on a private school that had long admitted both blacks and whites on the basis of their individual qualifications.[20]

The most deadly aspect of *Plessy* was the clause that permitted the classification of individuals on the basis of race, with Justice Brown invoking a "reasonableness" doctrine: "So far, then, as a conflict with the Fourteenth Amendment is concerned, the case reduces itself to the question whether the statute of Louisiana is a *reasonable* regulation. . . ."[21] Justice Harlan wrote the single dissenting opinion, which could have been the rallying cry for the civil rights struggle to come:

> Our Constitution is colorblind, and neither knows nor tolerates classes among citizens. In respect of civil rights, all citizens are equal before the law. . . . The law regards man as man, and takes no account of . . . his color when his civil rights as guaranteed by the supreme law of the land are involved. It is therefore to be regretted that this high tribunal, the final expositor of the fundamental law of the land, has reached the conclusion that it is competent for a state to regulate the enjoyment by citizens of their civil rights solely upon the basis of race.[22]

Harlan's voice of racial reason lost out, and coercive laws offering legally protected privileges to some at the expense of others continued to multiply.

With Friends Like These (Continued): the Minimum Wage

Black economist Walter Williams is a leading proponent of the hypothesis that government action has been the most serious obstacle to black advancement. His book *The State against Blacks*[23] was published in 1982, and the silent treatment it received from the "civil rights" establishment was deafening. This is unfortunate, because Williams presented the alternative to collectivism, statism, and elitism with unparalleled forcefulness and clarity. Williams

identified the problem for black America this way: "severe govern-ment-imposed restraints on voluntary exchanges. Or to put it an-other way: the diminution of free markets in the United States."[24]

Williams focuses on two specific problem areas—minimum wage laws and occupational licensure. He argues that policies en-forced under these labels invariably worsen whatever conditions for discrimination already exist, by setting restrictions on *outsiders*—people who are just getting started, who are without connections or similar resources, and who are therefore economically vulnerable. This group is bound to contain a disproportionate number of ethnic minorities.

Minimum wage laws date from 1938, when Congress passed the Fair Labor Standards Act. The act has been amended several times, each time raising the minimum wage. On April 1, 1990, it went up to $4.20 per hour. Minimum wages were created under the theory that individuals should have a minimum standard of living and need to be protected from underpayment that might result from the asymmetrical power relationship between employer and employee. It and Social Security became our first entitlements during the Roosevelt era. In theory the minimum wage helps employees, espe-cially employees on the lowest rung of the economic ladder. But in practice it doesn't work out that way.

Economists have long known that minimum wage laws actually harm those on the lowest rung of the ladder. Government, by passing a minimum wage law, may dictate that *if* a commercial enterprise or other organization hires someone, it must pay that person a minimum hourly wage. What it cannot dictate is that the enterprise or organization *must* hire, period. Thus a person whose skills are deemed insufficient to be worth the minimum hourly wage is not hired. A minimum hourly wage has the effect of pricing would-be workers out of the labor market, and those priced out of the market are precisely those with the fewest skills and the least education. As Williams explains:

> If a wage of $3.35 per hour must be paid no matter who is hired, what kind of worker does it pay to hire? Clearly the answer, in terms of economic efficiency, is to hire workers whose productivity is closest to $3.35 per hour. If such workers are available, it does not pay the firm to hire workers whose

output is, say, $2 per hour. Even if the employer were willing
to train such a worker, the fact that the worker must be paid
a wage higher than the market value of his output plus the
training cost makes on-the-job training an unattractive proposition.[25]

If the minimum wage is $4.20 per hour, all would-be employees
whose skills are worth less than $4.20 per hour to employers will be
unable to find employment. Since blacks are disproportionally represented in this group, minimum wage laws do them more harm
than good, with the greatest harm done to the poorest and most
vulnerable members of the black community—uneducated black
teenagers trapped in the cycle of urban poverty. In addition, employers who cannot maintain a sufficiently large workforce at minimum wage costs are forced out of business, condemning even more
people to unemployment and depriving customers of whatever
goods or services those businesses had to offer.

That minimum wage laws cause unemployment has long been
maintained by economists of the Austrian school, such as Ludwig
von Mises.[26] Today even mainstream economists have come to
realize and admit that minimum wage laws aggravate unemployment and keep unemployed individuals dependent on government,
for no one can increase the market value of a person's skills by
legislative fiat.

People who, as a result of being priced out of the labor market,
are unable to gain employment cannot obtain the experience that
would enable them eventually to command higher wages. Hence
they are caught in a downward spiral. The ranks of the unemployed
and dependent in our society are much larger under a minimum
wage regime than they would be if employers were permitted to hire
them at wages their services are capable of commanding on an open
market.[27]

Williams adds that the interference with market processes created by minimum wage laws is likely to contribute to, rather than
reduce, whatever tendency to discriminate already exists. Such interference encourages discriminatory practices by introducing
noneconomic considerations into the hiring process. Suppose an
employer is a racist who would prefer a workforce consisting exclusively of whites. He has several job openings, and an applicant pool

with a ratio of blacks to whites roughly proportionate to their ratio in the local population. The employer must pay at least the minimum wage to whomever he hires. So there is no economic disincentive to counterbalance his (racist) noneconomic incentive to limit his hiring to whites.

But suppose there was no minimum wage, and blacks were willing to work for a dollar an hour less than the whites who had been hired. That this could happen will, of course, horrify egalitarians. But the employer now has a powerful economic disincentive to refuse employment to blacks so long as they are willing to do the same work as whites and do it equally well. His disincentive is the opportunity to have a workforce equal in productivity at less cost to him, plus the realization that those he turns away might end up working for the competitor down the street.

As for the injustice of wage disparity, in a healthy economy there will always be competition for the services of anyone who can build a reputation for responsibility and hard work. Blacks will be no exception and in time will bid up their ability to command higher pay. To entice blacks, a competitor may offer them significantly higher wages; their current employer will have to improve their wages and benefits or risk losing them. Thus the market is an avenue not only to higher levels of black employment but also to progressively less discriminatory wages.

Williams notes that during the "unenlightened times" shortly after the turn of the century when there was no minimum wage, black unemployment was not only lower than today, it was lower than *white* unemployment. In 1910, 71 percent of blacks over the age of nine had some kind of employment, as opposed to 51 percent of whites.[28]

But how, some ask, can blacks (or anyone else) afford to live at the wages that might result from an elimination of minimum wage laws? The first thing to remember is that a "starvation wage" is superior to unemployment (assuming that welfarist disincentives to work have also been eliminated). In addition, the market supplies an avenue to better wages for individuals who are willing to work at improving their skills. Finally, the competitive mechanisms of a free economy lower the prices of consumer goods, so that even comparatively low wages can buy more.

In any discussion of wages, it is important to recall basic truths of economics. "We cannot distribute more wealth than is created,"

Henry Hazlitt pointed out in his classic *Economics in One Lesson.* "We cannot in the long run pay labor as a whole more than it produces."[29] Consequently, government decrees that force up wages in the absence of corresponding increases in productivity ultimately bring harm to the economically vulnerable—including many black people. Once priced out of the labor market and offered welfare disincentives to reenter it, they remain unemployed, unskilled, and dependent. This is indeed the condition of many in today's inner cities.

A Further Restriction on Black Enterprise: Occupational Licensure

Another way in which government interference with economic liberties works to the disadvantage of black Americans and other vulnerable groups is through occupational licensure. Occupational licensure is the government-sanctioned practice of controlling entry into markets through the requirement of officially approved licenses. Typical government agencies involved in occupational licensure include the Federal Trade Commission, the Federal Communications Commission, and the Interstate Commerce Commission.

At first glance, occupational licensure seems justified, because there are occupations (such as medicine) where the public needs to be protected from unsafe or unscrupulous practitioners. The way to institute such protection would seem to be through the introduction of licensing procedures requiring that practitioners have met a set of rigid entry standards. These normally include completion of appropriate levels of schooling, passing oral or written examinations, and going through appropriate internships. But two questions arise with regard to occupational licensure: What are the unintended side effects? Are the underlying assumptions justified?

One evident side effect of occupational licensing is that it results in a smaller group of practitioners in any given occupation than would exist in an uncontrolled market. The "chosen few" can then exercise considerable control over their trade, leading to higher-than-market prices for their services. This may seem a small price to pay for insuring the safety and honesty of practitioners.

But four things must be noted. First, the requirement to obtain a license imposes additional expense on would-be entrants;

attaining the stipulated level of schooling entails whatever costs (such as tuition) are involved in admission to approved schools, as opposed to the lesser expense that would be involved in, say, a private apprenticeship. Second, those experts who set the requirements, administer the examinations, and issue the licenses, charge fees that add further to the costs to would-be entrants. Third, oversight activities take time away from the experts' own practices and create bureaucratic overhead.

Fourth, this group of insiders can wield enormous power over who can enter the profession. Such power is suspect for two reasons: (1) Licensing laws tend to come about not as the result of consumer complaints about inferior products or services, but rather as the result of lobbying by established practitioners, and (2) These practitioners often write "grandfather" clauses into licensure laws that exempt themselves from the criteria they place on newer entrants.[30]

Believers in affirmative action should examine occupational licensure closely. They claim that one of the reasons we need affirmative action for blacks is to counter longstanding preferential treatment for whites. Advocates of affirmative action have long railed against an unfortunate tendency within many occupations, to wit, that desirable positions often go not to the most qualified applicants, but rather to those better positioned to exploit the "old boy" system through personal contacts, as in the old saw "It's not *what* you know but *who* you know."

Such insider networks rarely include blacks and tend to work against them not only because they are black but because they are vulnerable newcomers (such practices will obviously work against poorly connected whites as well). But such networks of elites can remain intact primarily because they have created artificial, legally protected barriers to market entry.

This raises the question: Is the quality control of some good or service better served by an open market with a free flow of information available to all consumers responsible enough to make use of it, or by a network of insiders who have lobbied successfully for government protection? Stringent medical licensing, for example, has not prevented large numbers of successful malpractice suits in which it was shown that the doctor was incompetent or dishonest. It has never been established that licensing requirements protect the public from unsafe or unscrupulous practitioners.

It is unlikely that all who have the ability to practice safely and competently can afford the costs of licensing requirements. On average, blacks have less capital to spend on license-obtaining procedures than do whites. Hence entry into many occupations is priced out of their reach, unless they are willing to practice on the wrong side of the law. The tendency to form personal networks will increase, not decrease, as white men attempt to position themselves in ways that get around affirmative action. People after all will usually try to protect themselves from outside interference, no matter what their skin color or circumstances. "Who you know" will become more, not less, important as government presence in the market increases.[31]

Let's take a concrete example—the taxicab industry. Driving a taxi is an occupation that under free market conditions would be within the means of most citizens, including poor urban blacks. What would it take for someone to go into business for himself as a taxicab operator? In principle there are just two conditions: (1) a reliable automobile, and (2) a solid knowledge of the city. Virtually anyone who can read a map could learn enough to meet the second condition. The first condition seems harder, but the automobile need not be owned; it could be rented or even borrowed. Hence, becoming an independent taxi operator would seem a good means by which an enterprising black person could earn a good living through supplying a much-needed service.

But virtually all American cities impose restrictions on entry into this business by licensing regulations, some of them quite expensive—in effect creating a government-sponsored monopoly. The New York City taxicab industry has been under a "medallion" system since 1937, when the Haas Act was passed. Under the Haas Act, those operating taxicabs were sold medallions for ten dollars each. 13,566 such medallions were originally issued. During World War II, 1,794 were returned by those entering the armed forces, leaving 11,772 (the 1,794 were never reissued).

The selling price for a medallion had risen to $60,000 for independent taxicab drivers by the time Williams wrote *The State against Blacks* in 1982.[32] By 1991, it had risen to over $120,000![33] Such an astronomical price creates a virtually uncrossable barrier to legal entry into this market for everyone who does not have $120,000 to spend. Very few of us, white or black, can afford that; it certainly excludes most urban blacks.

Other cities have equal or greater barriers to entry into the taxicab industry. In Philadelphia, the Pennsylvania Public Utility Commission is the government agency controlling the industry. This commission will issue a certificate of "public convenience and necessity" to applicants who can prove themselves fit for $20. But there is a catch: Applicants are subject to review by existing taxicab owners, who can use legal means to reject the application. The insiders retain attorneys whose only purpose is to discourage new entrants by keeping them tied up in litigation, so that their potential competitors will eventually run out of funds and be forced to give up, or simply quit out of frustration.

In such cases, we have not free markets but economic enclaves controlled by individuals who are not actually protecting consumers but merely erecting barriers against outsiders.[34] Such practices exclude the majority of blacks, not because of their skin pigmentation per se but because of their situation as outsiders. These are not the only practices sanctioned by government that have tended to hamper black advancement. One thinks also of zoning ordinances that prevent people from starting businesses out of their own apartments and laws preventing people from selling goods on sidewalks.

There are many such laws and regulations on the books, and their existence reinforces our starting point: What is holding back blacks is not merely discrimination but the absence of freedom of opportunity. The primary barrier to freedom of opportunity in American society is government, the very agency that contemporary black leaders look to for support. Historically and worldwide, government has proved itself only rarely and fitfully the ally of the weak or oppressed and far more often contributes to their oppression—even in democratic societies.

The Present Situation of Black Americans

These realities militate against the assumption that government is a reliable friend to black interests. Historically, blacks have been harmed far more by government than they have been helped. Furthermore, after three decades of legislation and court decisions ostensibly aimed at helping black people, this pattern continues. In most respects, the majority of blacks are no better off than they were in 1964 when the Civil Rights Act became law, and many are demonstrably worse off.

Depressingly well-known statistics show that being young, black, and male can be very hazardous to one's health, particularly in inner cities. Roughly one out of every four young black men is in prison, on parole, or has a police record—more than are in college despite years of preferential admissions. The leading cause of death among young black men is murder, with the murderers usually being other black men. The deadly confrontation may arise out of anything from drugs to a fight over an athletic jacket or even a pair of tennis shoes—so greatly has individual life been devalued.

Drug dealers roam many black neighborhoods almost at will, terrorizing communities to the point where even police are afraid to patrol at night. Black teenagers quickly learn to emulate the drug dealers and pimps, having learned that they can make far more money, much faster, by selling drugs to other teenagers (and sometimes even preteens) than by staying in school and learning traditional skills. They too often end up dead or in prison where they learn the trade of the career criminal.

The ethos of multiculturalism, with its neosegregationist tendencies, and its inclination to identify escape from such conditions up the economic ladder as a "white thing," has to a great extent *encouraged* this tragic cycle. The role model it has inculcated in many black teens is that of the "cool" drug dealer or rap musician, wearing gold chains, shades, and having an "attitude," expressing himself with clothing and language selected for their ability to shock and intimidate. To do well in school and strive for economic success, on the other hand, is to "act white"; black teens have been beaten up and sometimes even murdered on school playgrounds for refusing to conform to this new and deadly self-stereotype.[35]

This situation has come about in large part because the urban black family has been almost destroyed. Large numbers of black youth are now born out of wedlock and grow up without a stable male role model at home. Welfare mothers, often teenagers themselves, usually lack marketable skills and hence remain poor and dependent. Current laws in most localities offer them few incentives to change their situation. Such an environment can hardly be anything other than a breeding ground for the downward spiral. Given such conditions and their actual if unintentional encouragement by the left-liberal, white intelligentsia and conformist government bureaucrats, it would be surprising if the condition of black America were other than it is.

Racial tensions are worse than at any time in recent memory. New York City, Miami, Virginia Beach, Milwaukee, and Los Angeles have experienced serious confrontations in recent years. In some cases, threats of mass violence have been made. During a *60 Minutes* interview, Milwaukee's radical black alderman Michael McGee threatened a race war within five years if his demands for black entitlements, including large transfers of wealth from the white to the black community, are not met.

In Los Angeles, racial violence on a large scale broke out in response to the initial acquittal of four white police officers accused of beating Rodney King, a convicted felon, following a high-speed car chase. During ensuing riots, an innocent white man, Reginald Denny, was dragged from his truck by a group of blacks, beaten unconscious, and left for dead.

Such confrontations do not always involve whites. Longstanding tensions exist between blacks and Cuban Americans in Miami, between blacks and Jews in New York City, and between blacks and Korean Americans on the West Coast (Koreans and Hispanics probably suffered more losses from the Rodney King riots than whites). These tensions seem to be born of resentment against the successful outsider, given that Koreans and other Asians have only recently settled in this country and soared ahead.

But there is no mystery about the successes Asian Americans have achieved: They are hard workers who believe in education and a strong family unit. To succeed, they pool their resources and help one another, relying on their own independent sector. In contrast, black Americans (as Shelby Steele and others have noted) have adopted as positive values the very stereotypes the civil rights movement attempted to overthrow. Attempts to advance on the basis of effort are scorned as evidence of an "Uncle Tom" mentality that supposedly mimics the "dominant group". Thus an irrational but powerful mindset discourages adoption of the values necessary to improve one's status in any free society.

This is the sorriest possible commentary on almost four decades of government efforts to help blacks, and on the ideology that has rationalized such help. But we shouldn't be surprised. A growing literature shows that no matter how noble the intentions, top-down government efforts usually compound the problems they set out to solve, whether they be education, homelessness, drug abuse, or racism.[36]

It is time to face the fact that neither relativism nor statism offers viable solutions to the problems faced by minorities in America. In fact, they have largely intensified the problems. There really is just one alternative: Abandoning the contemporary theology of the state and returning to the *classical* liberal thought on which this country was founded. The Philosophy of Social Spontaneity represents an effort to do this. But what does it offer black people in particular?

Social Spontaneity and Black Self-empowerment: the Case of Mr. Johnson

Government is no friend to genuine black interests, particularly if among those interests we count intellectual and economic independence and advancement. The Philosophy of Social Spontaneity regards black people—and white people—not as statistical ciphers who derive their identity from their race, but as flesh-and-blood human beings capable of crafting their own identities and raising themselves by their own efforts. It affirms their capacity and responsibility for taking control of their own lives. It repudiates costly restrictions on the economic initiatives and activities of those not "in the club." Above all, the Philosophy of Social Spontaneity means repudiating the psychology of victimization, along with the entire vaguely Marxist view of the world that divides us up into "oppressors" and "victims." I do not think we can stress enough how this view degrades and destroys human beings of any ethnic heritage.

Black people will then be freed to rediscover the philosophies of self-help and self-reliance expounded in different ways by their ancestors Frederick Douglass and Booker T. Washington, and expounded today by a range of so-called black conservatives including Thomas Sowell, Walter Williams, Shelby Steele, Glenn C. Loury, and Justice Clarence Thomas.[37] We must also repudiate the sociocultural determinism that gives the victim mindset its major impetus. We must affirm the possibility of free choice and hence of transcending one's immediate circumstances. This allows the recovery of individual responsibility, which must be the starting point for the recovery of all other values that are prerequisite to successful participation in a free society.

As a starting point, there are brilliant success stories in black history that offer a gold mine of insights. There are too many such stories to do justice to them all, but I wish to present for the reader's consideration the case of John H. Johnson, who rose from poverty and welfare to found the magazines *Negro Digest* and, later, *Ebony* and *Jet,* along with other ventures.[38] Along the way, he became one of the wealthiest black individuals in the country.

Johnson was born in 1918 in Arkansas City, Arkansas, in (very poor) Desha County along the banks of the Mississippi. As a youth he moved with his mother to Chicago and there obtained a job with the black-owned Supreme Life Insurance Company. The break that would lead him into the magazine world was his assignment to Supreme Life's monthly newspaper *The Guardian,* of which he quickly became the editor. Since Supreme Life was for all practical purposes the economic center of black life in Chicago, Johnson was able to observe and learn from the most important economic and political figures on the scene.

In 1942, with a $500 loan he started the magazine *Negro Digest* and its parent organization, the Negro Digest Publishing Company. A number of shrewd moves, including soliciting an article from then first lady Eleanor Roosevelt, assured that the venture would make money, and by the end of 1943 Johnson bought his own building for $4,000.

Johnson's potentially biggest setback came from the federal government. In 1943 there was a war going on; the government had placed restrictions on the use of many goods, including paper. Regulation L-244 restricted the use of paper according to what Johnson calls a nothing-keeps-nothing formula. This meant that if a business used a certain amount of paper in its first year of operation, it was restricted to that amount in subsequent years. Since Johnson had used 7.43 tons of paper to print *Negro Digest* in its first year, he would have to restrict his paper usage to 7.43 tons *even though his circulation had climbed from a few thousand to over 100,000.* This would destroy his business. Johnson went to Washington without an attorney, pled his case by pointing out that due to racial exclusion he was not a member of any publishers' association and had no "direct access" to the regulations, and won his appeal. He went on to found *Ebony* the following year. *Ebony* became the first successful publication portraying the full range of black culture published by a black man, full of information and articles written by and for black people. In 1951, Johnson began publishing the newsmagazine *Jet*. The rest, as they say, is history. Johnson's autobiography is packed with insights of value to us all. To cite some examples:

> There's an advantage in every disadvantage, and a gift in every problem. . . .
> . . . This is how we changed our fate and made a ladder out of a wall.
> The first step . . . was to redefine the situation so we would have the initiative and would understand clearly what we had to do. This meant that we had to study the battleground and understand the strength and weaknesses of the opposing forces. We knew—how could we help knowing?—that all the high ground and money and weapons were in the hands of our adversaries. But it was worse than useless in that day to grind our teeth and curse racism. The question, the only question, was what were we going to do with what we had in order to make things better for ourselves.
> If I had to identify the most important step in a strategy of success, I would pick that question. For the basic problem for a young man or a young woman is not what other people are going to do but what *you* are going to do.[39]

Johnson observes that racism restricts the economic freedom of whites as well as blacks:

> Racism was a double-edged sword that cut both ways. It cut deeply into my profits and made it impossible for me to cross the economic equator of race. It also cut deeply into his profits and made it impossible for him and other White distributors to maximize their profits in the inner city. For racial divisions kept White distributors from penetrating into the secret nooks and crannies of the close-knit Black community.[40]

For Johnson, a partial solution to the problem of racism is

> to eliminate the artificial barriers that keep Black, ethnic, and female entrepreneurs from developing their own bases and moving from those foundations to parity and participation in the common market.

The road to the future, in other words, depends on ethnic entrepreneurs doing their own thing instead of depending on external banks and financiers who will, out of necessity, force them to do their thing.

. . . I believe Black entrepreneurs must participate at every level in all economic institutions. There is a danger, however, in undue reliance on external investors. Today, as in the heyday of great ethnic entrepreneurs, Black, Oriental, Jewish, Italian, and Irish, the commonsense approach is to build from your own base and assimilate instead of being assimilated.[41]

Blacks and members of other ethnic minorities must become society's participants instead of its pawns. Johnson's recommendations exemplify the Philosophy of Social Spontaneity at its best. He insists there are certain values and principles that work for everyone:

I was born into a strong family and reared in a strong community where every Black adult was charged with the responsibility of monitoring and supervising every Black child. I was reared in a community where every Black adult was authorized to whip me, if I needed whipping, and to send me home for a second whipping from my mother, whether I needed it or not.

Sixty years later, I attended a meeting of the Advisory Board of the First Commercial Bank of Little Rock with, among others, Sam Moore Walton, the richest man in America. We discovered with surprise and delight that we had six things in common. We were nonsmokers and nondrinkers who were born into poverty. We grew up in small southern towns and were reared by strong and loving parents who spared neither hugs nor rods.

Is there a message in this?

Yes. The message is that we've strayed in Black America—and in White America—from the values of family, community, and hard work. And we've got to go back to that future. We've got to go back to the time when being an adult was a dangerous vocation that required a total commitment to the community and every child in it.[42]

Listen to his description of the no-nonsense principal of the tiny school he attended as a boy:

Professor Johnson, like most of the pioneer Black teachers, taught everything: reading, writing, arithmetic, manners. He inspected our clothes in the morning to make sure we were neat and clean. And he insisted on polished shoes and correct behavior. He was, in fact, an extension of the home. Like my mother, like almost all Arkansas City parents, he carried a big stick and used it.

Although the four-room school was somewhat primitive by modern standards, it stressed excellence and brought better results than most contemporary schools. There was no nonsense in this building. We knew that education for us was a matter of life and death, and that certain graduates of this school, including my half sister, Beulah, and my cousin, Willie, had climbed out of their dungeons on a ladder of words.

Always, everywhere, by word, by example, by the carrot and stick, Professor Johnson pressed this message: What they did, you can and *must* do, too, or go to the wall.[43]

John Johnson draws our attention to the unsung, unknown black America that lived by these rules even through the Jim Crow era.

Like almost all Blacks and Whites, I'd assumed that Black entrepreneurs had been confined to the side streets of American commerce because of a lack of experience. Imagine my surprise when I discovered that Blacks had operated in the mainstream of money from the beginning of the American drama and had sold goods and services to both Black and White consumers.

. . . By the American Revolution, there were scores of prominent Black business people, including Samuel Fraunces, the owner of New York's Fraunces' Tavern, the favorite watering hole of George Washington, and James Forten, who employed forty workers, Black and White, in his Philadelphia sail factory.

Later, in the nineteenth century, Blacks were prominent in the fashion and clothing fields, the coal and lumber industry, and retail and wholesale trade.

They operated foundries, tanneries, and factories. They made rope, shoes, cigars, furniture, and machinery. They operated major inns and hotels in southern and northern cities and were in some cities the Hyatts and the Hiltons of their day. In addition to all this, they held virtual monopolies in the catering, barbering, and hairdressing fields.[44]

Johnson observes that "history, money, and all the forces of the universe are on the side of the man or woman who sets a goal and works night and day to achieve it."[45] He points out:

There are so many twists and turns in a life that you never know where a job, however small, will lead you. It's in your best interest, then, to do every task assigned you well, for you never know when these skills can be utilized later.[46]

Also: "Never burn your bridges behind you. And leave every job and every situation so you can come back, if you want to or need to."[47] Finally:

I didn't start a business to get rich—I started a business to provide a service and to improve myself economically. I think it's a mistake to set out to get rich. You can't get rich trying to get rich. What you need to do is to dream small dreams, because very often when you try to see things in their largest form, you get discouraged, and you feel that it's impossible. But if you can somehow think and dream of success in small steps, every time you make a step, every time you accomplished a small goal, it gives you confidence to go on from there.[48]

Johnson does not condemn welfare or government job programs outright.

There's been a lot of criticism of the welfare system from people who know little or nothing about poverty or welfare. Unlike most of the critics, I've been there, and I have no hesitancy in saying that I'm in favor of welfare for those who need it. I certainly don't condemn it. When we were on welfare, we needed it.[49]

But he does repudiate welfare *dependence* and sees government as the employer of last resort.

> The problem, I think, is the purpose of welfare and the organization of the welfare system. The goal must always be to *get off* welfare, and we got off as soon as we could.
>
> That's one of the reasons I believe the government must play a role as the employer of last resort, when all else fails. We got off the welfare rolls two years later when my stepfather got a [Works Progress Administration] job, and I got a job with a division of the National Youth Administration headed by Mary McLeod Bethune.
>
> We moved on from these government jobs to better times and better jobs. But the WPA-NYA ladder was a necessary first step that let us keep our dignity and hope until the private economy could provide alternatives.
>
> As the only former welfare recipient in my tax bracket, I have earned the right to say that this experience is relevant to the economic crisis of the eighties. When you look at the armies of misdirected youths roaming urban streets, it becomes obvious that we could create taxpayers and perhaps millionaires by organizing modern equivalents of the alphabets of the thirties—the WPA and NYA projects and [Civilian Conservation Corps] camps—that saved the American economic system. We need to think deeply about this opportunity. . . .
>
> Because we received help at a critical moment in our lives and because we never lost the will to end dependence on welfare, we broke free and began the slow rise to that economic emancipation without which political emancipation is a mere mockery.[50]

None of us could ask for a better role model than John Johnson. His story is awe-inspiring, particularly when we realize that he started not just from a situation of poverty but within a legal framework enforcing discrimination. Yet many such role models exist, and their stories are told in his publications (among others). Young blacks do not lack role models in American society. What they lack is a sufficient number of highly visible advocates who will acknowledge these role models and the implications of their success.

The time has come for a new civil rights strategy that repudiates preferential treatment, the psychology of victimization, and the entire baggage of social engineering—working instead toward using the independent sector to empower blacks from within communities. A civil rights movement based on the Philosophy of Social Spontaneity would send to members of minorities this message: Your legitimate rights as individuals and citizens will no longer be violated by government bureaucrats with their restrictive regulations, special interest groups with their self-serving agendas, or social planners who impose such agendas with no regard to the actual situations of individual members of your community.

As a result, you will be able to identify or create opportunities. You will be legally and practically able to take whatever actions you need to take. You will reap the rewards of life in a society in which the role of government is limited to protecting your right to your life and the fruits of your labor.

The Philosophy of Social Spontaneity is not a magic wand that will solve minority problems with one wave. It rejects the view that there are magic wands for social problems. The Philosophy of Social Spontaneity will work only if certain values are widely practiced both by the white majority and by the minorities who would benefit most from a refocused civil rights movement. John Johnson's life and many black Americans' lives exemplify such values. Like many black Americans, Johnson probably supports some forms of affirmative action. But I believe the time is rapidly approaching when more and more prominent black people will endorse the need for a civil rights movement that eschews statism and affirms the personal and social values that have proven successful in so many times and places for all races.

For our society to implement the Philosophy of Social Spontaneity on a grand scale will be a challenging and exciting enterprise, requiring energy, determination, and patience.

Racists will still exist but will be socially and economically marginal. Racially motivated hatred and discrimination are profoundly wrong. Although a free society would not legally prohibit any employer from hiring exclusively whites if he wanted—or exclusively blacks, or exclusively Hispanics—such practices should be morally condemned. When they occur on a broad scale, everyone loses. Johnson recalls:

> I've talked to scores of Black millionaires who say, almost to
> a man or woman, that they made money not because of race
> but in spite of race. I know what they mean, for if I hadn't
> operated with the handicap of racial barriers, I could have
> made billions instead of millions.[51]

The solution is education based on respect for individual rights, responsibilities, and achievements. When we learn to see people of different races as individuals who share many of the same fears and aspirations as we do, who are in their essentials not that different from us, we will find ourselves less inclined to hate them or dismiss them or fear them. This message should be conveyed by all educational organizations and civil institutions.

It suggests that we learn to get along not (as the multiculturalists would have us do) by *focusing obsessively on group differences* but by emphasizing *similarities:* Our common problems in a world we share, under laws that are the same for all, and in which we all have a better chance of advancing our interests through peaceful cooperation.

I do not believe that government-imposed machinations are effective in changing prejudicial attitudes, righting the historical wrongs that grow from them, or preventing their occasional cropping up. An entrepreneurial spirit of cooperation and marketplace incentives offer more effective, less coercive disincentives for racism. In a free marketplace, discrimination on any arbitrary basis is economically counterproductive. A white business owner who refuses to hire qualified black individuals simply because of their skin color, or insists on hiring a poorly qualified white kid because he and the kid's father graduated together, does himself economic harm.

Consider two competing business enterprises operating under free market conditions: We will call them B and C. B's management refuses to employ black people at any level other than unskilled labor, such as janitorial service. It does not permit them to rise to any level of corporate responsibility. B doesn't have a black clientele of any significance, for its board of directors prefers not to deal with blacks.

C, on the other hand, has a policy of hiring and promotion on the basis of merit alone. As a result, C employs in positions of responsibility a number of highly qualified and motivated black individuals who were unable to obtain employment with B (for under free market conditions, they cannot call down government force to obtain employment with B; under free market conditions no one is *entitled* to a position with any particular firm).

C attracts the patronage of both black and white clienteles and does business with black-owned firms shunned by B. Clearly, B's racially biased policy can only hurt it in a free society. In such a society, B cannot claim privilege or request legal protection from competition with C. Hence C is in a position to begin outperforming B all across the board. B may eventually be forced out of business.

In a free society, racism will be a liability, not an asset. Racist enterprises will almost automatically end up at a disadvantage. Since the targets of racism can always take their goods and services to the competition, racists will end up hurting themselves more than the objects of their hate.

Will a free market eventually end discrimination and racism? Probably not. There will always be those who cannot learn from experience, who cling to familiar beliefs at any cost. In a free society, they will simply have to live with the social and financial consequences of their actions. But free markets and discriminatory preferences are in the final analysis at odds with each other, whether the preferences be those of old-fashioned racism, which offered special privileges to whites, or affirmative action, which offers special privileges to blacks.

Our illustration will work just as well if we remove the traditional-racist component from B's policies and replace it with a strong affirmative action program that gives positions of responsibility to unqualified black individuals. Any preferential program undermines individual incentives and thus corporate effectiveness. In a free market, a firm must seek out the best available employees or contractors; otherwise, it will lose them to competitors. If it refuses to deal with individuals because of arbitrary biases, those individuals will take their money or services elsewhere. So while a free market may permit private racist sentiments to survive, business consideration will render such sentiments impotent.

The Philosophy of Social Spontaneity is our best hope for increasing economic empowerment of minorities. Their problem is not too much capitalism but too little. The problems facing black people result not from too little government help but from too much interference, both in the form of "help" packages that keep black Americans dependent, and in the form of the psychology of victimization that keeps them discouraged and resentful—attitudes hardly conducive to self-betterment.

In a free-market society, there will be no legal machinery to prevent enterprising black individuals from entering markets previously controlled by whites. In a free market in which most occupations are not controlled by networks of insiders, markets will be more accessible to outsiders such as blacks.

Once black people penetrate a few more highly visible markets (without government favors) and outpace many of the whites already there, as blacks have already done in the fields of sports, music, and entertainment, whites will not be able to complain of reverse discrimination. Racial stereotypes will be terminally weakened. Widespread implementation of the Philosophy of Social Spontaneity will bring the *Dred Scott* mentality crashing to earth faster than any form of government-mandated preferential policy ever could. We will be in the best possible position to achieve what early civil rights advocates hoped for: A colorblind society in which individuals are indeed judged, in Martin Luther King, Jr.'s memorable words, by the content of their character.

Conclusion

Our society, like most societies, has a legacy of poor treatment of minorities and others who lack power. Many whites have behaved badly and stupidly in the past; some still do. Thus we should support *voluntary* efforts on the part of employers to seek out qualified minorities and women who for various reasons might not apply for a desirable position, despite being able to do the job. The same goes for *privately funded* minority scholarships for qualified black students who might not otherwise be motivated to go to college. The desirability of improving the situations of nonwhite Americans is not in question.

Rather, the debate concerns what assumptions—and what kind of public policy based on them—will take us from today's rapidly deteriorating situation to a situation in which the civil rights of all citizens are genuinely protected, and in which everyone who makes a sincere, sustained effort to provide a needed service has a real chance to succeed. This is what the American Dream is about.

The path we have taken for the past twenty years is one we must abandon. It is the path of trying to rectify past injustice with present, different injustice, and of assigning immense power to government in the name of civil rights. Preferential policies are simply not an appropriate response to discrimination. They benefit not those most in need of help, but rather the most skillful and well-situated opportunists.

Preferential policies also do immense harm to institutions and occupations with their assumption that we can legislate qualifications ex nihilo. These policies have created enormous, unwieldy but nevertheless power-hungry networks of bureaucrats and federal judges accountable to neither the American people nor the U.S. Constitution. Compliance with their autocratic orders has lowered standards for student admissions and created racial tension on many college campuses. This has led in turn to growing resentment, intolerance, racial polarization, and the self-segregation of black students.

Among faculty, preferential favors have bent teaching and scholarship in the direction of those who are willing to rationalize these favors, leading inevitably to the additional intolerance and restrictions on academic freedom characteristic of political correctness, along with abandoning the ideals of objectivity and intellectual truth. Finally, preferential policies saddle their "beneficiaries" with a stigma that many thoughtful members of targeted groups are beginning to recognize and oppose.

Most dangerously of all, these policies ask us to place our faith in the state as an institution capable of rectifying injustices on a grand scale. Armed with this kind of master plan, however, social engineers invent problems out of whole cloth (for example, lack of "racial balance" in public schools) and "solve" them by subjecting us all to machinations that conflict openly with rights of free adult citizens to make their own choices. This faith in the state is as misplaced now as it has been every time in human history that it has prevailed (and brought disaster).

Affirmative action has been compared to "social policy by steamroller," now out of control and threatening to flatten everything in its path.[1] The steamroller has led to demands for equal outcomes, proportional representation, "racial balance," and "gender equality" as ends in themselves. Institutions are deeply undermined as autonomous entities and dissenting voices face severe reprisals.

Can this chain of events be slowed, the structures dismantled, and the ideological impulses behind them reversed? It's hard to be optimistic. The legal machinery that protects and extends affirmative action is not only still in place, but also has been strengthened by recent legislation such as the Americans with Disabilities Act of 1990 and the Civil Rights Act of 1991. These laws extend existing forms of government interference with the property rights of entrepreneurs. The Civil Rights Act of 1991 reaffirmed the *Griggs* "disparate impact" doctrine, which originally opened the door to legal demands for numerical parity and quotas.

Thus it is possible that no legal strategy short of a new amendment to the Constitution will put an end to preferential treatment. Such an amendment could read simply: *Congress shall pass no laws requiring any government agency, any employer, or any contractor, public or private, to give preferential treatment to any citizen on the basis of race, ethnicity, gender, religion, physical handicap, or sexual orientation.*

This amendment's legal foundation would be straightforward: Preferential treatment violates the equal protection clause in the Fourteenth Amendment. The moral foundation would be equally straightforward: Such policies violate individuals' basic right (*not* entitlement) to their own lives and the fruits of their labors, including the right to carry out economic transactions as they see fit.

Unfortunately, significant numbers of those in favored groups along with large numbers of white male bureaucrats, lobbyists, and lawyers now owe their livelihoods to the continuance and extension of preferential policies. Career bureaucrats, lawyers, and activists are not going to relinquish a massive apparatus such as the one erected by affirmative action and set-asides; they will do whatever they must to keep it in place, whether it helps women and minorities or not. Bureaucracies invariably tend to expand rather than contract; their success is measured not by the problems they solve, but by the power they exert—even if it actually exacerbates the problems. As a result, ever more groups are being brought under the *protected group* umbrella, with the disabled and homosexuals the latest additions (as of this writing!). People who can be classified as victims by current legal definition now approach 70 percent of the population.

The belief that social problems can be solved in a top-down fashion and that government is the tool to use exercises a degree of influence throughout the intellectual and political communities that would have dismayed our nation's founders. James Madison, Alexander Hamilton, and John Jay, who jointly crafted the *Federalist Papers,* disagreed on many things but were united in their realization that government is the most dangerous institution on the planet. This realization produced their ruthless, honest eloquence and their consequent preoccupation with checks and balances (on a level of sophistication that no political theorist of today approaches).

Most contemporary thought ignores their insights or attempts to discredit them as expressing the "class interest" of privileged white males. Belief in government as the solution to every social problem (real and imagined) pervades the dominant intellectual, political, and media cultures. The most visible blacks such as Jesse Jackson and visible feminists such as Patricia Schroeder, Patricia Ireland, and Molly Yard conform to this ideology. Dissident blacks (such as Thomas Sowell, Walter Williams, and Shelby Steele) and dissenting women (such as Christina Sommers and Anne Wortham) have produced a steady stream of articles, newspaper columns, and books. Yet their side of the story never receives more than token attention by the major media.

When George Bush nominated one of these dissident voices to the Supreme Court, the public was treated to an exhibition of the lengths to which "liberals" were willing to go in order to destroy someone they perceived as a threat. To this day, they insist that Clarence Thomas sexually harassed Anita Hill, though neither she nor anyone else has produced a shred of evidence to back up the claim, and there is a great deal of evidence to the contrary.[2]

The sense of self-evidence that now motivates the sexual harassment lobby—the sense that when a male is accused of sexual harassment, factual evidence is not even relevant, much less required—indicates the level of zealotry permeating the radical feminist movement, as well as the larger culture of hypersensitivity that has spread outward from the academy. This culture now routinely threatens careers on the basis of offenses no more substantial than telling off-color jokes.

The assumption that affirmative action significantly helps black Americans is also an article of faith in many circles, despite a dearth of supporting evidence and an avalanche of countering evidence. Given the depth of entrenchment of these beliefs, were affirmative action to be suddenly repealed, the nation would probably be caught up in race riots almost immediately.

Thus we cannot dismantle affirmative action without an ambitious campaign of public education, one expressing (in language any high school student can understand with some effort) the basic principles of political and economic freedom. Such a campaign must include the historical evidence that blacks *have* prospered without government assistance despite discrimination, before the affirmative action era. They did so whenever and wherever federal, state, and local governments simply left in place naturally existing incentives and opportunities for black Americans to participate freely in the marketplace. Today, what people on the lower social and economic rungs need most is for government to get out of their way.

I hope my analysis will be taken in good faith as a significant contribution to one of the most important dialogues of our time— significant in having identified the fundamental problem as *philosophical,* isolating the mistaken premises that presently guide public policy, and presenting a viable alternative. I hope others will take up where I have left off. What matters is that we reverse our drift toward the forced collectivization of our economy, the consolidation of power and privilege in the name of equality, and the balkanization of our body politic. We must recover the sense that individuals are responsible for their own actions (or inaction). If we do not, *all* of us—white and black, male and female, heterosexual and homosexual—will wake up one morning to find we no longer have a free society.

Despite their belligerent protests to the contrary, the defenders and extenders of social engineering are in the driver's seat. Tenured radicals have attained decisive influence in the country's most prestigious universities, and their foot soldiers have spent years redesigning higher education to accommodate collectivist ideologies, while carefully excluding individualist ones. Collectivists such as Marx and Engels are required reading in many courses in philosophy, history, sociology, anthropology, and economics. However, one can graduate from college without ever having heard of Ludwig Von Mises, Friedrich A. Hayek, Henry Hazlitt, or Thomas Sowell. Conservative, libertarian, or other individualist scholars who speak out are often smeared with vicious epithets: *Racist! Sexist! Homophobe! Right-winger!*

The old guard of faculty and administrators who began their careers before the affirmative action era is gradually retiring. The old guard was comparatively moderate and responsible—most of its members believed that truth could be discovered and a just society created—but as idealists they had little inkling of the mentality that had emerged in the late 1960s and gradually assumed power in the academy.

Unfortunately, many members of the old guard were possessed

by more than their share of moral uncertainty and—let's face it—cowardice. They capitulated to nearly every radical demand. This generation is thus partly responsible for the intransigence of the newly tenured radicals.[3] Now, with the ascendancy of the Clinton regime, the "long march through the institutions" has arrived at the highest centers of power.

Yet we must not despair. Despite the vicious slurs those who question the status quo must endure, the issues surrounding affirmative action, quotas, multiculturalism, radical feminism, and political correctness are more and more being discussed openly. The discussion is no longer limited to the "margins": It is occurring in major academic journals, in books brought out by mainstream presses, and in some of the country's most widely disseminated newsmagazines. Dissident scholars such as Dinesh D'Souza and Christina Sommers are willing to go over the heads of academic "experts" and take their cases directly to the public.

The National Association of Scholars continues to gain members; many are political liberals as horrified by the growth of anti-intellectualism and antischolarship in the academy as are conservatives, neoconservatives, and libertarians. Students of all races and both sexes continue to ask questions and challenge political correctitude on campus despite the risk to their personal and future professional lives. Individualist think tanks such as the Institute for Humane Studies and the Ludwig von Mises Institute draw dozens, sometimes hundreds, of students to their seminars despite the near-blackout on individualist ideas in the academy. Some of these students will pursue intellectual careers issuing direct challenges to the authority of the tenured left.

With the Clintons, the public may get to see the full fruits of the collectivist, redistributionist, and other statist ideas that lie at the root of affirmative action. If history is any guide, the public will not like what it sees. Thus there would seem to be room for guarded optimism that taboos can be broken, ideological glass houses shattered, and reason applied to matters of race, ethnicity, gender, and class.

However, we're in for a rough ride: The radicals now running the show, particularly in the universities, are so used to using pressure tactics to get what they want that dissent is literally a new experience to them. Not being believers in reasoned discourse, their standard procedure continues to be the ad hominem attack, sometimes culminating in thinly veiled calls for censorship.[4] Purveyors of affirmative action, multiculturalism, and the various forms of antischolarship will not relinquish their power without a nasty fight, possibly lasting well into the next century. By that time, higher education could lie in ruins.

Though my discussion has canvassed the effects of social engineering on a wide range of institutions, I (like Bloom and D'Souza) keep returning to the educational system. I do so because the assault on scholarship poses a greater danger to the future of this country than does any other current application of social engineering. If affirmative action and antischolarship go unchecked, we will see the end of the university as we have known it, and its replacement will be a politically controlled, racially balkanized institution.

Such an institution will churn out culturally divided and mutually hostile illiterates, rather than free and responsible adults capable of competing in a global economy and carrying our nation into the next century. The destruction of academic standards will result in failure to impart any real skills. Thus the consequences of academia's present direction, carried forth in the name of a specious egalitarianism, will be the decline of everyone's standard of living until our nation approaches the third world conditions naively idolized by many leftist academics.

Justifying multiculturalism on the basis that the United States is becoming an increasingly diverse and multiethnic society is ludicrous because a workforce without the skills necessary for survival in a highly technological global marketplace will be a noncompetitive workforce, regardless of its ethnic and gender composition. The skills required for life in a free society include not only reading, writing, and computer literacy along with scientific, technical, and mathematical skills, but also adequate, accurate knowledge of American culture, its history and institutions, the structure of its government, and the philosophy behind its founding principles. Nothing less will prepare young people to be responsible participants in a representative democracy.

There is a deep-seated totalitarian impulse behind affirmative action and antischolarship. This impulse must be seen for what it is. It manifests itself in the desire to control people and institutions—to continue court-ordered busing, for instance, despite the well-known fact that busing is supported by neither black nor white parents, who for years now have expressed their preference for neighborhood schools. It manifests itself in efforts to muzzle faculty and students who display "insensitivity" on matters of race, ethnicity, gender, and sexual orientation. Even more ominously, it manifests itself in the growing entrenchment of unaccountable power in our judicial system, as when a single federal judge in Yonkers was able to threaten an entire city with bankruptcy for "noncompliance" with a court-ordered desegregation plan.[5] This exemplifies the dictatorial mindset we are dealing with here.

There is also, I would argue, a nihilistic impulse behind this mindset—an impulse that, at bottom, hates individual human achievement and seeks to level it. This nihilistic mindset also needs to be seen for what it is. It manifests itself in the rationalizations for creeping egalitarianism, and in policies that systematically attack the prosperous and successful ("the rich").

The nihilist mindset also manifests itself in the prevailing politically correct view that "everything is political." This view rejects the search for truth and reasoned discourse in favor of ever more extreme forms of relativism and irrationalism—which sometimes merely deny that human cognition is capable of achieving unbiased knowledge of truth, and sometimes even deny that any truth exists to be known. Such denials can be used to justify rejection of neutral standards for student admissions or faculty hiring; ad hominem attacks on critics of affirmative action and "multiculturalism"; suppression of research findings that might conceivably have "adverse impact" on left-wing policy preferences; and verbal, even physical, abuse of speakers with unpopular views.

These two impulses—the totalitarian and the nihilist—unite in their implication that might makes right and that those who shout the loudest and the longest, or who use the most muscle in the least inhibited ways, deserve to win. A systematic response—both intellectual and political—is clearly called for if we are to reverse our jettisoning of intellectual, political, and economic freedoms. Such a response must answer the enemies of freedom point by point and develop an alternative that, unlike the demand for dependence concealed in social engineering, offers genuine opportunity to those groups social engineers claim to represent. My Philosophy of Social Spontaneity is one more contribution to the ongoing debate—a contribution that brings to bear the analytic skills of a trained philosopher and sketches the outlines of a comprehensive alternative philosophy.

Few would deny that some minorities—and to a lesser extent women—have suffered from unjust discrimination. Our history is checkered. But the prevailing responses are far more so. There is an adage sometimes used to justify reverse discrimination: "You can't make an omelet without breaking a few eggs." Aside from the moral revulsion such sentiments should inspire with their open advocacy of what amounts to human sacrifice, preferential policies and ideologies are not producing many omelets.

Another adage might be more appropriate: "You can't unscramble an egg." Past discrimination was a terrible mistake we must learn to live with in the sense that we must not continue it, but neither can we fully correct it. Preferential policies cannot alleviate the suffering of those now dead, nor punish the perpetrators. A perfect "balancing of the books" is an unattainable utopia. In Shelby Steele's words, the logic of affirmative action

> overlooks a much harder and less digestible reality, that it is impossible to repay blacks living today for the historic suffering of the race. If all blacks were given a million dollars tomorrow morning it would not amount to a dime on the dollar of three centuries of oppression, nor would it obviate the residues of that oppression that we still carry today. The concept of historic reparation grows out of man's need to impose a degree of justice on the world that simply does not exist. Suffering can be endured and overcome, it cannot be repaid. Blacks cannot be repaid for the injustice done to the race, but we can be corrupted by society's guilty gestures of repayment.[6]

We must learn from the past but look to the future: This means looking to the past to find out what works and what doesn't, and then applying this knowledge in the present to build a prosperous future. Our abandonment of the individualist-liberal tradition is a mistake we should undo as fast as we can.

Fifty years ago Friedrich A. Hayek destroyed the Philosophy of Social Engineering in *The Road to Serfdom*[7] (if Mises had not already done so in *Economic Planning in the Socialist Commonwealth*[8] and *Socialism*[9]). Once a socialist himself, Hayek spent the rest of his life trying to show that large-scale social planning inevitably erodes freedom and starts a drift toward totalitarianism. Even then, the plan cannot succeed: The society must either accept ever-decreasing prosperity, or plunder its neighbors amid the false prosperity of a permanent war economy. Hitler's Germany was one of Hayek's two models; the other, of course, was Stalin's Soviet Union.

Nicholas Capaldi has argued that affirmative action, if pressed to its logical conclusion, would nurture a kind of homegrown fascism in which leaders of organizations are nominally in charge and the economy is nominally private, but the real power lies in the hands of a massive state apparatus run by politicians, unelected federal judges, and bureaucrats.[10] Affirmative action, set-asides, "multiculturalism," militant feminism, and antischolarship share far too many intellectual premises with those totalitarian governments that have visited poverty, slavery, and misery on over a third of the world's populations. Statist ideologies are increasingly rejected everywhere in the world—except in Western college and university humanities and social science departments.

The large-scale planning that affirmative action entails can no longer be considered a live option. Our only hope is to check our premises before we've gone the rest of the way down the road to serfdom and found out, too late, that the society we have created is one that incubates not only continued injustice but deteriorating economic conditions and worsening interethnic hostility. It's not too late to reinstate the celebration of individual rights and responsibilities. That celebration made this a country to which the poor and oppressed of the world flocked—and where, for the most part, they prospered.

It's time to bring everyone under the umbrella of that philosophy. Social spontaneity has not failed Americans of the female sex or of minority origins. It has yet to be consistently implemented by many of them—or by our current political and cultural establishment.

Appendix A

Fellowships, Job Fairs, and "Vita Banks" Aimed Exclusively at Women and Minorities

The following excerpted language appeared in the "Bulletin Board" section of *The Chronicle of Higher Education* between January 1, 1990, and the present. These advertisements constitute no more than a small sampling from issues selected almost at random. I offer them as hard evidence of the extensive efforts on behalf of women and minorities throughout higher education today, as well as evidence that white males are systematically discriminated against by these efforts. It is clear that similar efforts exist in other occupations as well.

Open Access to Equal Access.   The Diversity Recruitment Department of the California Community College System Registry states, "In the next decade or so, the world's sixth largest economy will have the most ethnically diverse population in the world. To maintain our position in a global economy, California must have the best trained workforce available. Only a faculty dedicated to quality and excellence and able to communicate with a diverse student population can make this happen." The advertisement continues, "The California Community College Registry has been developed to find the nation's best faculty members and put them in direct contact with the more than 18,000 job openings. The Registry is now accepting applications which will be placed on a community college faculty computer network linking all 107 community college personnel offices to use in their faculty recruitment programs. . . . The Registry is particularly interested in underrepresented group members including the handicapped, ethnic/racial minorities, women, and veterans."

Graduate Fellowships for Minority Teacher Preparation.   Teachers College of Columbia University explains its Mellon Fellowships for minority teachers "aim to attract the best and brightest minority liberal arts graduates to secondary school teaching."

Gaius Charles Bolin Fellowships for Minority Graduate Students. Williams College in Massachusetts established fellowships in 1985 to "underline the importance of encouraging able minority graduate students to pursue careers in college teaching. The Bolin Fellowships enable two minority graduate students to devote the bulk of their time during the academic year to the completion of dissertation work." The advertisement goes on to explain that the Bolin Fellowship was named in honor of the first black graduate of Williams College, and is to be awarded to "minority students who are working toward the Ph.D. in the humanities or in the natural, social or behavioral sciences."

Affirmative Action Job Fairs.   Advertisements for Affirmative Action Job Fairs are posted by a number of secondary institutions—sponsors included the ACCCA (California Community College Affirmative Action Coalition).

Minority Faculty Registry.   Numerous advertisements invite vitas from minority candidates who wish to be considered for faculty teaching positions. One such registry in Southwestern University in Texas is accessed by over two hundred colleges and universities. Frostburg State University of Maryland and Northampton Community College of Pennsylvania both solicit minority resumes for their internal job banks.

Appendix B

Job Descriptions for Faculty and Top Administrative Positions Aimed Exclusively at Women and Minorities

The following job descriptions also appeared in the "Bulletin Board" section of *The Chronicle of Higher Education* between January 1, 1990, and the present. Again, these excerpts make up no more than a small sampling from issues selected almost at random. Without a doubt, support for affirmative action, multiculturalism, "educating for diversity," etc., is being incorporated directly into the "qualifications" for academic positions; critics of these issues are thereby automatically "disqualified" from further consideration.

Faculty Positions/Faculty Diversity Program. California State University at Fresno is "seeking to enhance its ability to serve a large and ethnically diverse region and student body by facilitating the application and appointment of qualified, underrepresented minority and women faculty in all academic disciplines." The copy adds that the Faculty Diversity Program and the positions for it supplement the university's normal searches and affirmative action commitments.

Associate Vice President for Diversity and Faculty Development. The University of Utah solicits applications in this advertisement for an associate vice president for diversity and faculty development. The responsibilities include "promoting and supporting diverse points of view and enhancing racial/ethnic, cultural, and gender diversity at the University of Utah." The associate vice president "reviews and approves affirmative action faculty hiring and encourages and promotes affirmative action among those who review, approve, and process faculty appointments and promotions." One of the basic qualifications for the position is "familiarity with current issues in affirmative action and faculty development in higher education."

Equal Opportunity/Diversity Issues and University Policy Development.   This advertisement for an assistant to the president at Southeastern Missouri State University details the duties of the position to include "responsibility for supervision, coordination, and active development of practices designed to enhance the university community's appreciation for cultural diversity, its climate of tolerance and respect for the rights of all persons, and its adherence to affirmative action and equal opportunity statutes, regulations, and policies." Qualifications for the position include: "a comprehensive understanding of the culture of higher education and the complex issues related to affirmative action and equal opportunity within that culture; experience with affirmative action law, practice, and administration; and a demonstrated commitment to affirmative action and the promotion of cultural diversity."

College President.   York College and Bronx College, of the City University of New York, offer a position that "serves as the chief academic and administrative officer of the institution." Among other things, leading candidates for the position will possess a "demonstrated commitment to equal employment opportunity, affirmative action, and the promotion of cultural pluralism."

Vice President for Student Services.   Texas A&M University begins the list of its preferred qualifications for the position of vice president with "a sustained record of a clear commitment to diversity and multicultural issues."

College President.   This advertisement from Mountain View College in Dallas, Texas, states that candidates for the position must possess a "demonstrated commitment to affirmative action and meeting the educational needs of students in a diverse community college environment."

Dean—College of Business Administration.   The University of Tulsa lists one qualification for application to this position as, "commitment to equal opportunity and affirmative action employment guidelines, practices, and outcomes."

Associate Provost and Affirmative Action Officer.   According to this advertisement, the associate provost at Princeton University in New Jersey will carry out the following duties: "advocate fair practices on behalf of those groups which have faced discrimination and help determine whether the needs of those groups have been met; conduct assessments of the effectiveness of campus efforts to achieve understanding and tolerance of diversity; and report periodically to the President and Provost on the progress of affirmative action and diversity efforts." The list of qualifications continues, requiring "experience and success in leading organizational efforts to attain diversity."

Head of the Division of Education.   Applications and nominations are solicited in this advertisement for the head of the Division of Education at Wayne State College in Nebraska. One of the listed qualifications for the position is a "demonstrated commitment to enhancing cultural diversity within the student body and the faculty."

Dean of the College of Education.   The Search and Screening Committee of Utah State University states a preferred qualification for the position of dean of the College of Education as "commitment to enhancing and supporting cultural gender and individual diversity."

Distinguished Professorship of Cultural Diversity.   This advertisement from the University of Wisconsin—Eau Claire begins, "The Distinguished Professorship of Cultural Diversity (primarily but not exclusively Race and Ethnicity) is a newly created position to enhance the University's commitment to cultural diversity." Among other things, the person appointed to this position will "aid departments in the infusion of cultural diversity into the curriculum." One of the qualifications for the post is a "demonstrated interest in cultural diversity including the development of curriculum and community initiatives."

Lectureships for Minorities and Women.   Weber State College in Ogden, Utah, advertises "flexible-term lectureship positions open to qualified women and minorities who are interested in pursuing a career in college teaching." The college offers "minority and women lectureship appointments" available for up to three quarters.

Assistant to the Chancellor for Affirmative Action and Minority Concerns.   This University of North Carolina at Asheville position will "provide several essential University functions including management and administration of affirmative action policies and programs, . . . investigation of discrimination and harassment complaints, fostering of campus environment which encourages and promotes the fullest participation of women and individuals from diverse racial and ethnic groups." The position will also serve as an "advocate for minority individuals, minority groups, and for women on campus." The candidate "must be familiar with appropriate state and federal regulations and have demonstrated success in the development and administration of programs addressing the concerns of women and minorities."

Notes

The Long Road to a Colorblind Legal System

1. "Executive Order 10925 Establishing the President's Committee on Equal Employment Opportunity" (Washington, D.C.: Government Printing Office, 1963), pt. 3, subpart A, section 301.

2. H. R. 7152—Public Law 88–352, Title VII, Section 705(g) (*Congressional Quarterly*, July 1964).

3. Ibid., Section 703(j).

4. 401 U.S. 424 (1971). All italics mine.

5. From John J. Ross, *Equal Employment Opportunities Compliance, 2d ed.* (New York: Practising Law Institute, 1973).

6. Nathan Glazer, *Affirmative Discrimination* (New York: Basic Books, 1975), p. 4.

7. Walter Williams, *The State against Blacks* (New York: McGraw-Hill, 1982).

8. For a good survey of dissenting black intellectuals, see Joseph G. Conti and Brad Stetson, *Challenging the Civil Rights Establishment: Profiles of a New Black Vanguard* (Westport, Conn.: Praeger Publishers, 1993).

Chapter One

1. See his *Reflections of an Affirmative Action Baby* (New York: Basic Books, 1991).

2. Frederick R. Lynch, *Invisible Victims: White Males and the Crisis of Affirmative Action* (Westport, Conn.: Greenwood Press, 1989), chap. 2.

3. Diane Bast, Mayer Freed, Daniel Polsby, and Thomas Ulen, *Disadvantaged Business Set-Aside Programs: An Evaluation* (Chicago: Heartland Institute Policy Study no. 26, June 29, 1989), p. 1.

4. Ibid., p. 46, n. 1.

5. "Discriminatory Impact of Racist and Other Special Preference Programs: A Report to the U.S. Congress" (Washington, D.C.: The Associated General Contractors of America, 1984), p. i.

6. Testimony of Gerald Buesing on behalf of Associated Builders and Contractors, Inc., before the Transportation Subcommittee, Senate Environment and Public Works Committee, U.S. Senate, November 19, 1985, on the Disadvantaged Business Enterprise Program and the 1982 Surface Transportation Act, Section 105F (Washington, D.C.: Associated Builders and Contractors, Inc., 1985), p. 2.

7. Public Law 97-424, Section 105(f) (Washington, D.C.: Government Printing Office, January 6, 1983).

8. Bast et al., (*Disadvantaged Business Set-Aside Programs,* note 3), p. 7.

9. Remarks of John C. Vande Velde, presented to the Subcommittee on Transportation, U.S. Senate Committee on Public Works, November 19, 1985, p. 2.

10. Ibid., p. 6.

11. In *Selected Affirmative Action Topics in Employment and Business Set-Asides*, vol. 1, Washington D.C.: Government Printing Office, 1985, p. 131.

12. Ibid., p. 132.

13. Ibid.

14. Ibid.

15. Ibid., p. 133.

16. Testimony of Gerald Buesing, pp. 5-6.

17. In *Selected Affirmative Action Topics in Employment and Business Set-Asides*, p. 133.

18. Quoted in "Stop Legalized Discrimination: The Case against Section 105(f) of the 1983 Surface Transportation Assistance Act" (Washington, D.C.: The Associated General Contractors of America, 1985), p. 4.

19. Ibid., p. 5.

20. Ibid., p. 6.

21. Ibid., p. 7.

22. Ibid., p. 8.

23. Ibid., p. 7.

24. Ibid.

25. Ibid.

26. Ibid., p. 9.

27. Ibid.

28. Ibid.

29. Ibid., p. 6.

30. Ibid., p. 7.

31. Remarks of John C. Vande Velde, pp. 3-4. Emphasis mine.

32. Ibid., pp. 2-3.

33. See Thomas Sowell, *Preferential Policies: An International Perspective* (New York: Morrow, 1989).

34. Remarks of John C. Vande Velde, p. 7.

35. In *Selected Affirmative Action Topics in Employment and Business Set-Asides*, p. 133. Emphasis mine.

36. Bast et al., *Disadvantaged Business Set-Aside Programs*, pp. 14–15. Sources are: "Wedtech: The Bombshells Keep Dropping," *Business Week*, June 22, 1987, p. 45; "A Tale of Urban Greed," *Time*, April 20, 1987, p. 30; Jean Davidson, "McCormick Lawsuit Hits 'Phony' Bills," *Chicago Tribune*, June 17, 1988; Maurice Possley and Ray Gibson, "Robinson Enigma Still Growing," *Chicago Tribune*, June 12, 1988; John Gorman, "U.S. Drops 3 Medley Allegations," *Chicago Tribune*, November 22, 1988; Roger Worthington, "Indians Fear Focus of Probe Is on Tribes, Not Abuse Claims," *Chicago Tribune*, February 6, 1989; The Better Government Association, "Opportunities Denied: An Examination of Minority and Business Enterprise Programs in Chicago," May 1989.

37. Remarks of John C. Vande Velde, pp. 5–6; also cited in Bast et al., *Disadvantaged Business Set-Aside Programs*, p. 13.

38. In *Selected Affirmative Action Topics in Employment and Business Set-Asides*, p. 134.

39. Ibid., p. 136.

40. Ibid., p. 135.

41. Quoted in "Stop Legalized Discrimination," p. 6.

42. Remarks of John C. Vande Velde, p. 6.

43. Bast et al., *Disadvantaged Business Set-Aside Programs*, pp. 13–14.

44. Quoted in "Stop Legalized Discrimination," p. 5.

45. In *Selected Affirmative Action Topics in Employment and Business Set-Asides*, p. 136.

46. Testimony of Gerald Buesing, pp. 3–4.

47. See, for example, "Constitutional Scholars' Statement on Affirmative Action after *City of Richmond v. J. A. Croson Co.*, *Yale Law Journal* 98 (1989), pp. 1711–16. Compare also most of the articles in *Yale Law and Public Policy Review* 8, no. 2 (1990). These are just two examples of the *sturm und drang* these Supreme Court decisions provoked in the legal community, and the relative speed of their publication is a further indication of the sudden angst felt by liberals who feared that their agenda might finally be unravelling.

48. "The Numbers Game," aired March 24, 1991, on *60 Minutes*, CBS. Compare also Mike Royko, "Where Good Sense Is in the Minority," *Chicago Tribune*, October 1990, and *"60 Minutes* Stuns Civil Rights Supporters," *Human Events*, April 6, 1991.

49. 60 MINUTES "The Numbers Game"—broadcast over the CBS Television Network, March 24, 1991. © CBS Inc. 1991. Used by permission.

50. Ibid., pp. 10–11.

51. *60 Minutes* rebroadcast of "The Numbers Game," August 24, 1991.

Chapter Two

1. This and the above cases were described in Dinesh D'Souza, *Illiberal Education* (New York: The Free Press, 1991), p. 125, 132; compare the citations noted there.

2. Joseph Berger, "Campus Strains Show Two Perspectives on Inequality," *New York Times*, May 22, 1989.

3. William Damon, "Learning How to Deal with the New American Dilemma: We Must Teach Our Students about Morality and Racism," *The Chronicle of Higher Education*, May 3, 1989.

4. In Brief, "Students March in Protest of Hate Mail on Campus," *The Chronicle of Higher Education*, November 15, 1989.

5. In Brief, "Two Fraternities Suspended after Racial Incidents," *The Chronicle of Higher Education*, April 25, 1990.

6. Denise K. Magner, "Racial Tensions Continue to Erupt on Campuses Despite Efforts to Promote Cultural Diversity," *The Chronicle of Higher Education*, June 6, 1990.

7. In Brief, "Bias Incidents Not Staged, Say Lawyers for Student," *The Chronicle of Higher Education*, May 16, 1990.

8. Julie L. Nicklin, "Brown U. Expels Student Who Yelled Racial Epithets," *The Chronicle of Higher Education*, February 20, 1991.

9. In Brief, "Students Face Discipline in Blackface Incident," *The Chronicle of Higher Education*, April 24, 1991.

10. In Brief, "Students, Faculty Members March to Protest Sorority Party," *The Chronicle of Higher Education*, November 6, 1991.

11. In Brief, "Campus Holds Service after Cross Burning," *The Chronicle of Higher Education*, March 18, 1992.

12. In Brief, "Black Students Leave College after Brawl," *The Chronicle of Higher Education*, April 15, 1992.

13. In Brief, "Olivet College President Says He Will Resign," *The Chronicle of Higher Education*, May 13, 1992.

14. In Brief, "Police Use Tear Gas on Students at Iowa State U.," *The Chronicle of Higher Education*, May 13, 1992.

15. Robin Wilson, "White Student Unions on Some Campuses Are Sparking Outrage and Worry," *The Chronicle of Higher Education*, April 18, 1990.

16. In Brief, "Clash at U. of Minn. over White-Student Group," *The Chronicle of Higher Education*, October 30, 1991.

17. Quoted in D'Souza, *Illiberal Education,* p. 269, n. 108.

18. In Brief, "Vassar Students Protest Senator's Alleged Remark," *The Chronicle of Higher Education*, February 21, 1990.

19. In Brief, "Berkeley Investigating Classroom Disruption," *The Chronicle of Higher Education*, December 12, 1990.

20. In Brief, "Fraternity's Old South Parade Riles Students at Auburn U.," *The Chronicle of Higher Education*, May 6, 1992.

21. Magner, "Racial Tensions."

22. In Brief, "56 Protesters Arrested at Berkeley Sit-In," *The Chronicle of Higher Education*, March 28, 1990.

23. In Brief, "Harvard Law Students Disrupt Commencement," *The Chronicle of Higher Education*, June 17, 1992.

24. In Brief, *The Chronicle of Higher Education*, February 12, 1992.

25. D'Souza, *Illiberal Education,* p. 11.

26. See Christopher Shea, "At Penn, Blacks Vent Anger at Student Paper,

Triggering Debate over Free Expression," *The Chronicle of Higher Education*, April 28, 1993; "Resolution of Racial Harassment Case at U. of Penn Leaves Everyone Dissatisfied," *The Chronicle of Higher Education*, June 2, 1993; Stephen Burd, "Clinton Names U. of Pennsylvania Chief to Take Over Humanities Endowment," *The Chronicle of Higher Education*, April 21, 1993.

27. Magner, "Racial Tensions."

28. Ibid. This figure was current as of 1990; the total number of racial incidents of one sort or another on college campuses is now considerably higher.

29. See Christopher Shea, "Protests Centering on Racial Issues Erupt on Many Campuses This Fall," *The Chronicle of Higher Education*, November 25, 1992.

30. D'Souza, *Illiberal Education*, p. 136.

31. Damon, "The New American Dilemma."

32. Robert Detlefsen, *Civil Rights under Reagan* (San Francisco: ICS Press, 1991).

33. Berger, "Campus Strains."

34. For example, such initiatives were lauded by New Mexico Governor Garrey E. Carruthers, a Republican. See Mary Crystal Cage, "Government Officials Urged to Create Incentives for Colleges to Increase Minority Enrollment," *The Chronicle of Higher Education*, December 12, 1990.

35. Thomas DeLoughry, "At Penn State Polarization of Campus Persists amid Struggles to Ease Tensions," *The Chronicle of Higher Education*, April 26, 1989.

36. Katherine S. Mangan, "A President's Personal Approach to Recruiting Minority Students," *The Chronicle of Higher Education*, February 7, 1990.

37. Abigail Thernstrom, "On the Scarcity of Black Professors," *Commentary* 90 (July 1990), pp. 23–24.

38. For some details see Walter Williams, "Campus Racism," *National Review*, May 5, 1989, pp. 36–38.

39. See Jan H. Blits, "Equality or Lasting Inequality?" *Society* (March/April 1990); and "Employment Testing and Job Performance," *The Public Interest* (Winter 1990).

40. In Brief, "Georgetown Law Student Disciplined, Will Graduate," *The Chronicle of Higher Education*, May 29, 1991. For Maguire's own account see his article "My Bout with Affirmative Action," *Commentary* (April 1992), pp. 50–52.

41. Reported by *The National Law Journal*, June 10, 1991.

42. See Thomas Sowell, *Preferential Policies: An International Perspective* (New York: Morrow, 1989).

43. Stephen D. Johnson, "Reverse Discrimination and Aggressive Behavior," *Journal of Psychology* 104 (1980): 11–19.

44. See for example Thomas Nagel, "A Defense of Affirmative Action," testimony before the Subcommittee on the Constitution of the Senate Judiciary Committee, June 18, 1981; reprinted in *Ethical Theory and Business*, 3rd. ed., eds. Tom L. Beauchamp and Norman E. Bowie (Englewood Cliffs, N.J.: Prentice-Hall, 1988), pp. 345–48.

45. Richard Wasserstrom was among the first to develop this core of the "multiculturalist" argument; see his "The University and the Case for Preferential

Treatment," in *Social Justice and Preferential Treatment*, eds. William T. Blackstone and Robert D. Heslep (Athens, Ga.: University of Georgia Press, 1977), pp. 16–32; compare also his "A Defense of Programs of Preferential Treatment," reprinted in *Ethical Issues in Business*, 3rd. ed., eds. Thomas Donaldson and Patricia H. Werhane (Englewood Cliffs, N.J.: Prentice-Hall, 1988), pp. 339–44.

46. For some specifics see Williams, "Campus Racism."

47. Dana Y. Takagi, "From Discrimination to Affirmative Action: Facts in the Asian-American Admissions Controversy," *Social Problems* 37 (1990), pp. 579–80. Compare also John Bunzel and Jeffrey Au, "Diversity or Discrimination: Asian-Americans in College," *The Public Interest* (Spring 1987), where similar results are documented for Princeton, Harvard, Stanford, and Brown Universities.

48. Bunzel and Au, ibid., pp. 50–51.

49. Ibid., p. 580.

50. Ibid., p. 582.

51. Ira Michael Heyman, "Don't Regress to Educational Apartheid," Letter to the Editor, *The Wall Street Journal*, July 19, 1989.

52. See: ". . . each segment of California public higher education shall strive to approximate by the year 2000 the general ethnic, sexual and economic composition of the recent high school graduates, both in first year classes and subsequent college and university graduating classes." Joint Committee for Review of the Master Plan for Higher Education, California State Legislature, reprinted in *California Faces California's Future* (Sacramento: State of California, 1988), p. 19; quoted in D'Souza, *Illiberal Education,* p. 262, n. 6.

53. Heyman, "Don't Regress."

54. For the specifics see John Bunzel, "Affirmative Action: How It Works at UC-Berkeley," *The Public Interest* (Fall 1988), pp. 111–29.

55. Takagi, "From Discrimination to Affirmative Action," p. 585.

56. Quoted in John H. Bunzel, "Minority Faculty Hiring: Problems and Prospects," *American Scholar* 59 (1990), p. 39. Bunzel adds, drily, that "Presumably HEW did not care if the members of the department voted by secret ballot or a show of hands when they bestowed the honor of 'least qualified' on one of their faculty colleagues."

57. Nicholas Capaldi, *Out of Order: Affirmative Action and the Crisis of Doctrinaire Liberalism* (Buffalo, N.Y.: Prometheus, 1985), p. 51.

58. Quoted in Nathan Glazer, *Affirmative Discrimination* (New York: Basic Books, 1975).

59. Quoted in ibid. Emphasis mine.

60. Quoted in ibid., p. 61.

61. AB 1725, signed into law on September 19, 1988, contains the following passage:

There is hereby created in the State Treasury a fund which shall be known as the Faculty and Staff Diversity Fund. The money in the fund shall be available to the board of governors [of the California Community College system] upon appropriation by the Legislature for the purpose of enabling the California Community Colleges as a system to address the goal that *by the year 2005 the system's work force will reflect proportionately the adult population of the state.* For the purpose of administering this fund, the board of governors shall develop and apply availability data and factors for measuring district progress in contributing to this goal for the system. Also for the purpose of administering this fund, it is the intent of the Legislature that the board of governors take the steps which are necessary to reach the goal that *by fiscal year 1992–93, 30 percent of all new hires in the California Community Colleges as a system will be ethnic minorities.* (Emphasis added.)

62. David Mertes, "An Open Letter from David Mertes," undated, refers directly to the law just mentioned. Mertes was chancellor of the California Community Colleges system when his letter, addressed "Dear Potential Faculty Member," was written. Specifically, it states:

Our goal, *set by law,* is to achieve proportional representation of California population [sic] by the year 2005. It's an ambitious goal, and we intend to meet it. Also, by 1992, *this same law requires that at least 30 percent of all new hires be ethnic minorities.*

The California Community Colleges *Faculty and Staff Diversity Registry* was created to maintain a large-scale computerized registry of the names, address, and qualifications of professionals like you who could contribute to the diversity of our faculty and staff. (Emphasis added.)

63. The University of Wisconsin Madison Plan (Madison, Wisc.: Office of the Chancellor, University of Wisconsin-Madison, February 9, 1988), pp. 11–13.

64. The Madison Plan One Year Later (Madison, Wisc.: Office of the Chancellor, University of Wisconsin-Madison, February 1989), p. 14.

65. The Madison Plan Two Years Later (Summary Report)(Madison, Wisc.: Office of the Chancellor, University of Wisconsin-Madison, February 1990), p. 3.

66. See Denise K. Magner, "Duke U. Struggles to Make Good on Pledge to Hire Black Professors," *The Chronicle of Higher Education,* March 24, 1993.

67. Thernstrom, "On the Scarcity of Black Professors," p. 22. See Appendix A for examples of these advertisements.

68. For some examples of these advertisements see Appendix A.

69. Denise K. Magner, "Law Professor Goes on Leave until Harvard Hires a 'Woman of Color,' " *The Chronicle of Higher Education,* May 2, 1990.

70. In Brief, "Harvard Law Professor Loses His Post," *The Chronicle of Higher Education,* July 8, 1992.

71. Thernstrom, "On the Scarcity of Black Professors," p. 23.

72. Ibid.

73. Ibid., p. 24.

74. Frederick R. Lynch and William Beer, "You Ain't the Right Color, Pal," *Policy Review,* Winter 1990, p. 65.

75. For examples see Appendix A.

76. Reported by John Bunzel, "Minority Faculty Hiring," pp. 41–42.

77. "G. Kindrow," "The Candidate," *Lingua/Franca* (April 1990), pp. 21–25. This article, predictably, provoked a heated discussion in ensuing issues.

78. Minority Update, *The Chronicle of Higher Education,* February 6, 1991.

79. Denise K. Magner, "Nomadic Scholar of Black Studies Puts Harvard in

the Spotlight," *The Chronicle of Higher Education*, July 15, 1992. Compare also Denise K. Magner, "The Courting of Black and Ethnic Scholars: Bidding War or Just a Few New Entrants into the Academic Star System?" *The Chronicle of Higher Education*, October 3, 1989. See the next chapter for some observations on the decline of scholarship and the rise of "superstardom" in the light of affirmative action in the academy.

80. Frederick R. Lynch, *Invisible Victims: White Males and the Crisis of Affirmative Action* (Westport, Conn.: Greenwood Press, 1989).

81. See ibid., pp. 109–18, 123–29 for details.

82. Ibid., p. 5.

83. For examples of advertisements which incorporate such commitments into the "qualifications" see Appendix B.

84. Quoted in Lynch, *Invisible Victims,* p. 123.

85. Ibid., p. 124; compare Lee Nisbet, "Affirmative Action—A Liberal Program?" in Barry Gross, ed., *Reverse Discrimination* (Buffalo, N.Y.: Prometheus Books, 1977), pp. 50–53.

86. Exchange quoted in D'Souza, *Illiberal Education,* p. 164.

87. Randall Kennedy, "Persuasion and Distrust: A Comment on the Affirmative Action Debate," *Harvard Law Review* 99 (April 1986), pp. 1327–46. Actually, Kennedy's statement is rather surprising, since his views are considered fairly moderate—to the point that he has been accused of "thinking white" by the Derrick Bells of the academic world (see Thernstrom, "On the Scarcity of Black Professors," p. 22).

88. Ibid., p. 1345.

89. In Brief, "President Steps Down amid Accreditation Delay," *The Chronicle of Higher Education*, April 11, 1990.

90. Stuart Nolan, "Promoting Uniformity: 'Diversity' Standards in Accreditation," *Organizational Trends*, September 1992.

91. Ibid., p. 2.

92. Courtney Leatherman, "Baruch College Wins Renewal of Its Accreditation after Planning to Improve Minority Programs," *The Chronicle of Higher Education*, July 11, 1990.

93. Nolan, "Promoting Uniformity," p. 3.

94. Courtney Leatherman, "2 of 6 Regional Accrediting Agencies Take Steps to Prod Colleges on Racial, Ethnic Diversity," *The Chronicle of Higher Education*, August 15, 1990.

95. Compare also William R. Beer, "Accreditation by Quota," *Academic Questions* 3 (Fall 1990), pp. 48–49.

96. Nolan, "Promoting Uniformity," pp. 3–4.

97. Courtney Leatherman, "Accrediting Agencies Take Steps."

98. Ibid.

99. Ibid. Compare again Beer, "Accreditation by Quota," pp. 47–48.

100. Carol Iannone, "God, Man, and Middle States: An Interview with Samuel T. Logan," *Academic Questions* 4 (Fall, 1992), pp. 51–52.

101. Nolan, "Promoting Uniformity," pp. 6, 8.

102. Iannone, "God, Man, and Middle States," p. 61.

103. Stephen S. Weiner, "Accrediting Bodies Must Require a Commitment to Diversity When Measuring a College's Quality," *The Chronicle of Higher Education*, October 10, 1990.

104. Ibid.

105. Ibid.

106. Beer, "Accreditation by Quota," p. 49.

107. Weiner, "Accrediting Bodies Must Require a Commitment to Diversity."

Chapter Three

1. See for example Scott Heller, "Colleges Becoming Havens of 'Political Correctness,' Some Scholars Say," *The Chronicle of Higher Education*, November 21, 1990; John Taylor, "Are You Politically Correct?" *New York Magazine*, January 21, 1991; "Race and Sex on Campus," *The New Republic*, February 18, 1991, entire issue; "Upside Down in the Groves of Academe," *Time*, April 1, 1991; "The Silencers," *Macleans*, May 27, 1991; "All Opinions Welcome—Except the Wrong Ones," *Insight*, April 22, 1991; Marc Wortman, "Fighting Words," *Yale Alumni Magazine*, October, 1991. This is just a sampling. For two representative collections of essays representing both sides of the political correctness debate see Paul Berman, ed., *Debating P.C.* (New York: Dell, 1992), and Francis J. Beckwith and Michael E. Bauman, *Are You Politically Correct?* (Buffalo, N.Y.: Prometheus Books, 1993).

2. Henry Louis Gates, Jr., "Whose Canon Is It, Anyway?" in *Debating P.C.*, p. 190.

3. For an early account that precedes the P.C. debates see Stephen H. Balch and Herbert I. London, "The Tenured Left," *Commentary* 83 (October 1988), pp. 41–51.

4. Barbara Smith, *Contingencies of Value* (Cambridge, Mass.: Harvard University Press, 1988).

5. Eve Sedgwick, *Between Men* (New York: Columbia University Press, 1985).

6. Paula Rothenberg, *Racism and Sexism: An Integrated Study* (New York: St. Martin's Press, 1988).

7. Jay Parini, "Academic Conservatives Who Decry Politicization Show Staggering Naivete about Their Own Biases," *The Chronicle of Higher Education*, December 7, 1988.

8. Elizabeth Ellsworth, "Why Doesn't This Feel Empowering? Working through the Repressive Myths of Critical Pedagogy," *Harvard Educational Review* (August 1989), pp. 301, 319; quoted in *Telling the Truth: A Report on the State of the Humanities* (Washington, D.C.: National Endowment for the Humanities, September 1992), p. 12.

9. Donald Lazere, "Back to Basics: A Force for Oppression or Liberation?" *College English* (January 1992), pp. 18–19; quoted in ibid., pp. 12–13.

10. Quoted in Anne Matthews, "Deciphering Victorian Underwear and Other Seminars," *New York Times Magazine* (February 10, 1991); in ibid., p. 13.

11. Charles Paine, "Relativism, Radical Pedagogy, and the Ideology of Paralysis," *College English* (October 1989), p. 563; in ibid.

12. The most extensive account of Thernstrom's and the other cases can be found in Dinesh D'Souza, *Illiberal Education* (New York: The Free Press, 1991), pp. 194–97; for Gribben's encounters see Katherine S. Mangan, "Battle Rages over Plan to Focus on Race and Gender in U. of Texas Course," *The Chronicle of Higher Education*, November 21, 1990; compare also Maxine C. Hairston, "Required Writing Courses Should Not Focus on Politically Charged Social Issues," *The Chronicle of Higher Education*, January 23, 1991; for a good retrospective on Gribben's case see Peter Collier, "Incorrect English: The Case of Alan Gribben," *Heterodoxy* 1 (May, 1992), pp. 8–10.

13. D'Souza, p. 145.

14. Ibid., pp. 202–03.

15. Ibid., pp. 8–9.

16. *Telling the Truth*, p. 14.

17. Ibid., pp. 14–15.

18. Benno C. Schmidt, Jr., "The University and Freedom," speech presented at 92nd Street Y (New York: March 6, 1991), pp. 1, 3; quoted in *Telling the Truth*, p. 5.

19. Derek Bok, "Worrying about the Future," *Harvard Magazine* (May–June 1991), p. 41; quoted in ibid., pp. 5–6.

20. Peter Shaw, *The War against the Intellect* (Iowa City, Iowa: University of Iowa Press, 1989).

21. See Roger Kimball, *Tenured Radicals* (New York: Harper and Row, 1990); D'Souza, *Illiberal Education*.

22. See, for example, Henry Beard and Christopher Cerf, *The Official Politically Correct Dictionary and Handbook* (New York: Villiard Books, 1992). While marketed as humor, it is notable that this book has been carefully researched, and the majority of the strange terms in the lexicon of political correctness are referenced.

23. Diane Ravitch, "Multiculturalism," *American Scholar* 59 (Summer 1990), p. 341.

24. D'Souza, *Illiberal Education*, p. 162.

25. Steven Yates, "Multiculturalism and Epistemology," *Public Affairs Quarterly* 6 (1992), p. 441.

26. Hilary Putnam, *Reason, Truth and History* (Cambridge: Cambridge University Press, 1981), pp. 49f. I hasten to add that Putnam would never countenance the use of his idea by our antischolars. One of antischolarship's most striking features is how its purveyors frequently borrow terms from previous (and far more original) writers such as Putnam, Thomas S. Kuhn, or Richard Rorty, without discussing these earlier usages in detail or otherwise providing a context. Sometimes no credit is given at all. Articles in radical feminist journals, for example, frequently cite only other radical feminists even when using ideas and terminology clearly traceable to nonfeminist writers.

27. To my mind the best efforts to describe deconstructionism clearly and expose its faults are John M. Ellis, *Against Deconstruction* (Princeton: Princeton University Press, 1989), and David Lehman, *Signs of the Times: Deconstruction and the Fall of Paul De Man* (New York: Poseidon Press, 1991). For good short summaries and criticisms see Joel Schwartz, "Antihumanism in the Humanities," *The Public Interest* 99 (1990), pp. 29–44, and Ward Parks, "Deconstruction, the New Nihilism," *The World and I* (April 1992), pp. 547–61. What follows is based primarily on Schwartz's and Parks's articles.

28. Quoted in Schwartz, ibid., p. 34.

29. Ibid., p. 31.

30. Quoted in D'Souza, *Illiberal Education*, p. 173.

31. Ibid., p. 174.

32. Stanley Fish, *Doing What Comes Naturally: Change, Rhetoric, and the Practice of Theory in Literary and Legal Studies* (Durham, N.C.: Duke University Press, 1989), pp. 10–11.

33. D'Souza, *Illiberal Education*, p. 175.

34. Fred Siegel, "The Cult of Multiculturalism," *The New Republic*, February 8, 1991, p. 40.

35. Denis Donoghue and Charles Griswald, "Deconstruction, the Nazis, and Paul De Man," an exchange, *New York Review of Books*, October 12, 1989, p. 69.

36. Friedrich Nietzsche, *Beyond Good and Evil: Prelude to a Philosophy of the Future*, trans. Walter Kaufmann ([1886] New York: Vintage Books, 1966), p. 21.

37. The term *different voice* is Carol Gilligan's; see her *In a Different Voice* (Cambridge, Mass.: Harvard University Press, 1982).

38. Christine Di Stefano, "Dilemmas of Difference: Feminism, Modernity, and Postmodernism," in *Feminism/Postmodernism*, ed. Linda J. Nicholson (London: Routledge, 1990), p. 64.

39. Sandra Harding, *The Science Question in Feminism* (Ithaca, N.Y.: Cornell University Press, 1986), p. 57.

40. Mary E. Hawkesworth, "Knowers, Knowing, Known: Feminist Theory and Claims of Truth," *Signs: Journal of Women in Culture and Society* 14 (1989), p. 536. Emphasis mine.

41. Harding, *The Science Question in Feminism*, pp. 78, 111.

42. Ibid., p. 29. Emphasis mine.

43. Ibid., p. 114.

44. Ibid., p. 113. Emphasis hers.

45. Alison Jaggar, *Feminist Politics and Human Nature* (Totowa, N.J.: Rowman and Allanheld, 1983), p. 132.

46. For details see Christina Sommers, "Philosophers against the Family," in Hugh LaFollette and George Graham, eds., *Person to Person* (Philadelphia: Temple University Press), pp. 82–105. Or see the literature Sommers cites: Virginia Held, "The Obligation of Mothers and Fathers," in *Mothering Essays in Feminist Theory*, ed. Joyce Trebilcot (Totowa, N.J.: Rowman and Allanheld, 1983), pp. 7–20; Ann Ferguson, "Androgyny as an Ideal for Human Development," in *Feminism and Philosophy*, eds. M. Vetterling-Braggin, F. Elliston and J. English

(Totowa, N.J.: Rowman and Littlefield, 1977), pp. 45–69; Carol Gould, "Private Rights and Public Virtues: Woman, the Family and Democracy," in *Beyond Domination*, ed. Carol Gould (Totowa, N.J.: Rowman and Allanheld, 1983), pp. 3–18; and especially Alison Jaggar, ibid.

47. Jaggar, ibid., p. 149.

48. Alison Jaggar, "Prostitution," in *Women and Values: Readings in Recent Feminist Philosophy*, ed. Marilyn Pearsell (Belmont, Calif.: Wadsworth, 1986), pp. 117, 119, respectively.

49. Catharine MacKinnon, *Feminism Unmodified: Discourses on Life and Law* (Cambridge, Mass.: Harvard University Press, 1989), p. 5.

50. Ibid., pp. 87–88.

51. Catharine MacKinnon, *Toward a Feminist Theory of the State* (Cambridge, Mass.: Harvard University Press, 1989), p. 174. All emphasis mine.

52. Ibid., pp. 172–73.

53. Quoted in Michael Weiss, "Crimes of the Head," *Reason* (January 1992), p. 32.

54. Quoted in Christina Sommers, "The Feminist Revelation," *Social Philosophy and Policy* 22 (1990), p. 150. Emphasis mine.

55. For a guided tour through some of these horror stories see again D'Souza, *Illiberal Education*.

56. Molefi Kete Asante, *The Afrocentric Ideal* (Philadelphia: Temple University Press, 1987), p. 6.

57. Ibid., p. 9.

58. Ibid., p. 165.

59. Quoted in Taylor, "Are You Politically Correct?" p. 39. This idea seems to have originated with George G.M. James's *Stolen Legacy* [originally published in 1954] (Trenton, N.J.: Africa World Press, 1992).

60. Martin Bernal, *The Fabrication of Ancient Greece. Black Athena: The Afroasiatic Roots of Classical Civilization. 1785–1985*, (New Brunswick, N.J.: Rutgers University Press, 1991).

61. Ibid., p. 73.

62. George Ghevarughese Joseph, "Foundations of Eurocentrism in Mathematics," *Race and Class* 28 (1987), pp. 13–29; the two attributions are on p. 26 and p. 16 respectively. Compare also George Ghevarughese Joseph, Vasu Reddy, and Mary Searle-Chatterjee, "Eurocentrism in the Social Sciences," *Race and Class* 31 (1990), pp. 1–26.

63. See Carolyn J. Mooney, "N. Y. City College Panel to Weigh Academic Freedom, Inflammatory Racial Views of Two Faculty Members," *The Chronicle of Higher Education*, May 23, 1990.

64. Quoted in Taylor, "Are You Politically Correct?" pp. 39–40. To my knowledge, Jeffries has never published his views in his own words but only delivered them orally.

65. Sandra Harding, *Whose Science? Whose Knowledge?* (Ithaca, N.Y.: Cornell University Press, 1991), p. 191.

66. Ibid., pp. 51–52.

67. Quoted in D'Souza, *Illiberal Education*, pp. 175–76.

68. Ibid., p. 176.

69. Originally appeared in Alan Kors, "It's Speech, Not Sex, the Dean Bans Now," *The Wall Street Journal*, October 12, 1989.

70. Smith, Lentricchia, and Gillis quoted in D'Souza, *Illiberal Education*, pp. 159, 161. If the truth be known, the "superstars" at Duke are not nearly as original as they have deluded themselves into believing they are. Virtually all of Stanley Fish's views apart from his specific defenses of affirmative action were anticipated in Paul Feyerabend's *Against Method: Outline of an Anarchistic Theory of Knowledge* (London: New Left Books, 1975), where they were better argued (and better written), and therefore harder to refute. Many of the same ideas have been presented in less extreme forms in tracts such as Richard Rorty's *Philosophy and the Mirror of Nature* (Princeton: Princeton University Press, 1979), perhaps the book most responsible for the spread of "postmodernism" in philosophy; similar ideas regarding the historical nature of science appeared in Thomas S. Kuhn's *The Structure of Scientific Revolutions* (Chicago: University of Chicago Press, 1962), and earlier still in Paul Schrenker's *Work and History* (Princeton: Princeton University Press, 1948). Whether Feyerabend would classify Fish, MacKinnon, and Jeffries among his intellectual stepchildren is anyone's guess; Rorty has, on at least one occasion, spoke well of MacKinnon's ideas (see his essay "Feminism and Pragmatism," *Radical Philosophy* 59 (1991), pp. 3–14). Kuhn, who has spent the past quarter century seriously grappling with the consequences of the views originally presented in *Structure* and trying to avoid intellectual relativism, most certainly would not!

71. See Weiss, "Crimes of the Head."

72. Quoted in D'Souza, *Illiberal Education*, p. 174.

73. An immediate qualifying remark is in order. I hasten to add that I have listened to and collected "alternative music" (as well as many other kinds of ethnic-influenced rock, folk, and "new age") for over fifteen years—even to the point of having once written for an alternative music tabloid when I was a graduate student living in Athens, Georgia—and having also seen experimental and performance art by students, I for one find these products a good bit more interesting, compelling, thought-provoking, and above all, intellectually honest, than anything the tenured professors we have been considering here have been doing the past ten years.

74. The first prominent usage of the term *incommensurable* in this context was in Thomas S. Kuhn's *The Structure of Scientific Revolutions*, arguably the most influential work of history, philosophy, and sociology of science written this century, and the one "mainstream" work frequently cited by antischolars—most of whom, it is important to add, do not understand it. Antischolars' occasional usage of Kuhn's concept of incommensurability illustrates their misconceptions well. Their usage is considerably more sweeping and radical than anything Kuhn proposed or would endorse today. Kuhn has stressed that incommensurability is a *local* phenomenon. He has spent years laboring to show how theories whose central concepts he claims are incommensurable can be rationally compared, never doubting for a moment that comparison is possible and the cognitive superiority of some theories over others capable of being established (see his

"Commensurability, Comparability, Communicability," in *PSA 1982*, vol. 2, eds. Peter Asquith and Thomas Nickles [East Lansing, Mich.: Philosophy of Science Association, 1983], pp. 669–88). One of the implications of Kuhn's views is that political struggles within a scientific community must be taken into consideration *among other, more "traditional" factors* when analyzing scientific changes. Unlike Kuhn, though, antischolars see what they examine in terms of power and political struggle exclusively—including the contention that some theories in science are cognitively superior to others.

75. Indeed, when a young Belgian scholar, Ortwin de Graef, revealed back in 1987 that De Man had written blatantly anti-Semitic articles for the pro-Nazi newspaper *Le Soir* prior to the outbreak of World War II, the result was a furor! De Man's army of followers immediately began to cook up tortured rationalizations whose end result, given the usual deconstructionist twisting of language, was that to criticize a politically correct hero like De Man was itself a sign of latent Nazi tendencies. See Kimball, *Tenured Radicals*, chap. 4, "The Case of Paul De Man," or Lehman, *Signs of the Times*.

76. For example, MacKinnon, *Toward a Feminist Theory of the State*, Part One; or Harding, *The Science Question in Feminism*, or Jaggar, *Feminist Politics and Human Nature*. For specifics see my "Gender Feminism, Incoherence, and the Scholarship Question," in Ellen Klein and David Fenner, eds., *Feminist Philosophy: Criticisms*, under consideration for publication.

77. Harding, *The Science Question in Feminism*, p. 26.

78. Hawkesworth, "Feminist Theory and Claims of Truth," p. 534.

79. Harding, "The Science Question in Feminism," p. 28.

80. Naomi Zack, *Race and Mixed Race* (Philadelphia: Temple University Press, 1993).

81. These, I would argue, are very good candidates for values that transcend race, gender, and class; I would qualify this only by noting that tolerance, for example, is an excellent value to uphold when one is dealing with people who are tolerant and a very dangerous one to maintain dogmatically when one is dealing with people who for one reason or another are intolerant.

82. Yates, "Multiculturalism and Epistemology," p. 440.

83. For a good exposé of the factual inadequacies of at least one Afrocentrist position that disputes this point, Martin Bernal's, see David Gress, "The Case against Martin Bernal," *The New Criterion* 8 (December 1989), pp. 36–43.

84. Cathy Young, *Equal Cultures or Equality for Women? Why Feminism and Multiculturalism Don't Mix* (Washington, D.C.: The Heritage Lectures no. 387, 1992), p. 1.

85. Ibid.

86. Ibid.

87. Ibid., p. 4.

Chapter Four

1. Thomas Sowell, *A Conflict of Visions: Ideological Origins of Political Struggles* (New York: Morrow, 1987), pp. 18–25.

2. See Nicholas Maxwell, "Science, Reason, Knowledge, and Wisdom: A Critique of Specialism," *Inquiry* 23 (1980), pp. 19–81.

3. John Rawls, "The Independence of Moral Theory," *Proceedings and Addresses of the American Philosophical Association* 48 (November 1975), pp. 5–22.

4. The most obvious examples here are Ayn Rand and Mortimer Adler. Though otherwise quite different in many of their assumptions and conclusions, both have pursued philosophy in the "grand tradition" that attempts to construct a comprehensive view of the universe and our place in it as moral beings. Both have been ignored or dismissed out of hand by all but a very few professional philosophers.

5. See his article "The Recovery of Practical Philosophy," *The American Scholar* 57 (1988), pp. 337–52.

6. For some interesting insights along these lines see Robert Schaeffer, *Resentment against Achievement: Understanding the Assault upon Ability* (Buffalo, N.Y.: Prometheus Books, 1988).

7. Plato, *The Republic,* 420b–420c, trans. G. M. A. Grube (Indianapolis, Ind.: Hackett, 1974).

8. Jean-Jacques Rousseau, *Euvres completes*, Bibliotheque de la Pleiade, Paris, 1959–65, vol. 3, p. 164.

9. Jean-Jacques Rousseau, *The Social Contract*, trans. Maurice Cranston (New York: Penguin Books, 1968), pp. 63–64. Italics mine.

10. See John O. Nelson, "The Two Opposed Theories of Freedom of Our Philosophical Inheritance," in *The Libertarian Alternative*, ed. Tibor R. Machan (Chicago: Nelson-Hall, 1974), pp. 38–55.

11. G. W. F. Hegel, *Philosophy of Right*, trans. T. M. Knox (London: Oxford University Press, 1977), p. 126.

12. See Stephen Pepper, *World Hypotheses* (Los Angeles, Calif.: University of California Press, 1942).

13. See Friedrich A. Hayek, *The Counter-Revolution of Science: Studies on the Abuse of Reason* (Glencoe, Ill.: The Free Press, 1952; 2d ed. Indianapolis, Ind.: Liberty Press, 1979).

14. It need not be cashed out in terms of primitive reductionism, of course. One philosophy of social science (which some call *functionalism*) focuses on empirically discoverable trends that act as sufficient conditions for certain kinds of institutional goal-directed behavior. In this view, though, individuals are not only still not autonomous agents but have no standing whatever apart from an institutional setting. Thus the basic premise—that necessary and sufficient conditions can in principle be given for every action on the part of every individual—remains intact; the difference is over the details. See Nicholas Capaldi, *Out of Order: Affirmative Action and the Crisis of Doctrine Liberalism* (Buffalo, N.Y.: Prometheus, 1985), pp. 65–70, for a brief but lucid explanation. I would take issue with Capaldi only in his apparent unwillingness to consider functionalism in this sense a form of determinism.

15. A good recent survey of this literature, along with a fairly good bibliography (though curiously, James N. Jordan's "The Dilemma of Determinism," *Review of Metaphysics* 23 (1969), pp. 48–66, is absent), can be found in Harald

Ofstad, "Recent Work on the Free-Will Problem," in *Recent Work in Philosophy*, eds. Kenneth R. Lucey and Tibor R. Machan (Totowa, N.J.: Rowman and Littlefield, 1983), pp. 39–84.

16. Capaldi, *Out of Order*, p. 2.

17. William Ryan, *Blaming the Victim* (New York: Random House, 1972).

18. Capaldi, *Out of Order*, p. 2.

19. George Sher, "Groups and Justice," in *Moral Rights in the Workplace*, ed. Gertrude Ezorsky (Albany, N.Y.: SUNY Press, 1987), p. 254.

20. Ibid.

21. Ibid., p. 255.

22. See Peter French, "The Corporation as a Moral Person," *American Philosophical Quarterly* 3 (1979), pp. 207–15.

23. For a definitive statement of methodological individualism see Ludwig Von Mises, *Human Action*, 3rd rev. ed. (Chicago: Henry Regnery, 1966), pp. 41–44.

24. Tibor R. Machan, *Individuals and Their Rights* (LaSalle, Ill.: Open Court, 1989), p. 16.

25. Mary Midgley, *Wisdom, Information and Wonder: What Is Knowledge For?* (London: Routledge, 1989), p. 5.

26. Thomas Sowell, *Compassion Versus Guilt and Other Essays* (New York: Morrow, 1987), p. 15.

27. Thomas Sowell, *Education: Assumptions vs. History* (Stanford, Calif.: Hoover Institution Press, 1986), especially chap. 2, "Patterns of Black Excellence," pp. 7–38.

28. For an example of a very clear argument to this effect, along with numerous supporting examples, see Nicholas Maxwell, "The Rationality of Scientific Discovery," *Philosophy of Science* 41 (1974), pp. 123–53, 247–95. Most history and philosophy of science since Kuhn's 1962 tract, and even before, makes one form or another of the same kind of claim, to wit, that at any given time there are various nonempirical constraints on the formulation and testing of scientific hypotheses.

29. For a detailed look at such statements see Frederic B. Fitch, "Self Reference in Philosophy," *Mind* 55 (1946), pp. 64–73; or see my "Self-Referential Arguments in Philosophy," *Reason Papers* 16 (1991), pp. 133–64.

30. For an extended account and defense of this kind of argument see J. M. Boyle, G. Grisez, and O. Tollefsen, *Free Choice: A Self-Referential Argument* (Notre Dame, Ind.: Notre Dame University Press, 1976). These philosophers also do an admirable job of organizing the relevant literature.

31. Mises, "Human Action," pp. 42–43.

32. Friedrich A. Hayek, *The Road to Serfdom* (Chicago: University of Chicago Press, 1944), p. 59.

33. See Friedrich A. Hayek, *The Fatal Conceit: The Errors of Socialism*, ed. W. W. Bartley (Chicago: University of Chicago Press, 1988).

34. John Rawls, *A Theory of Justice* (Cambridge, Mass.: Harvard University Press, 1971).

Chapter 5

1. Thomas Sowell, *Preferential Policies: An International Perspective* (New York: Morrow, 1989).

2. Thomas Sowell, *Civil Rights: Rhetoric or Reality?* (New York: Morrow, 1984), pp. 92–93.

3. Ibid., pp. 94–95.

4. For an extended treatment of some of these issues see Anne Wortham, *The Other Side of Racism* (Columbus, Ohio: Ohio State University Press, 1987).

5. Anne Wortham, "Black Victimhood," *The World and I* (April 1993), p. 370.

6. Shelby Steele, *The Content of Our Character* (New York: St. Martin's Press, 1990), p. 26.

7. Ibid., p. 27.

8. Ibid., p. 33.

9. Ibid., p. 118.

10. Ibid., p. 115–16.

11. See "Burden Is Increased" and "Shows Insensitivity," letters by Reginald Bullock and Kathleen McGarvey respectively, *The New York Times,* May 19, 1989. Compare also Stephen Labaton, "Law Review's Anti-Bias Program Revives Dispute," *The New York Times,"* May 3, 1989, and an unsigned editorial, "Brave New World at Columbia," *New York Post,* May 6, 1989.

12. See Christina Sommers, "Feminist Philosophers Are Oddly Unsympathetic to the Women They Claim to Represent," *The Chronicle of Higher Education,* October 11, 1989.

13. Thomas Nagel, "A Defense of Affirmative Action." Testimony before the Subcommittee on the Constitution of the Senate Judiciary Committee, June 18, 1981. Reprinted in *Ethical Theory and Business,* 3rd ed., eds. Tom L. Beauchamp and Norman E. Bowie (Englewood Cliffs, N.J.: Prentice-Hall, 1988), p. 346.

14. Steele, *The Content of Our Character,* pp. 68–69.

15. Ibid., pp. 69–70.

16. Derrick Bell, *Faces at the Bottom of the Well: The Permanence of Racism* (New York: Basic Books, 1992); quoted by Wortham, "Black Victimhood," p. 382. For a recent detailed examination of Bell's views see James Traub, "For Whom Bell Tolls," *The New Republic,* March 1, 1993, pp. 17–21.

17. Allan Bloom, *The Closing of the American Mind* (New York: Simon and Schuster, 1987).

18. E. D. Hirsch, *Cultural Literacy* (New York: Houghton-Mifflin, 1987).

19. Charles J. Sykers, *The Hollow Men* (Washington, D.C.: Regnery-Gateway, 1990).

20. For one account see Carolyn J. Mooney, "Academic Group Fighting the 'Politically Correct Left' Gains Momentum," *The Chronicle of Higher Education,* December 12, 1990.

21. Roger Kimball, *Tenured Radicals* (New York: Harper and Row, 1990).

22. Scott Heller, "Scholars Form Group to Combat 'Malicious Distortions'

by Conservatives," *The Chronicle of Higher Education*, September 18, 1991; compare Heller's follow up report, "Two New Groups Hope to Organize the Academic Left against Conservative Scholars and the NEH," *The Chronicle of Higher Education*, April 22, 1992.

23. This was essentially the same kind of propagandistic move the Christian Right used, after all, by calling one of its most vocal mouthpieces of the 1980s the Moral *Majority*.

24. Catharine R. Stimpson, "New 'Politically Correct' Metaphors Insult History and Our Campuses," *The Chronicle of Higher Education*, May 29, 1991.

25. Scott Heller, "'Frame-Up' of Multicultural Movement Dissected by Scholars and Journalists," *The Chronicle of Higher Education*, November 27, 1991.

26. Mary G. Gray et al., "Statement on the 'Political Correctness' Controversy," *Academe* (September–October, 1991), p. 48.

27. Mooney, "Academic Group Fighting the 'Politically Correct Left.'"

28. Quoted in *NAS Update* 2 (Fall 1991), p. 5.

29. Cathy N. Davidson, "'PH' Stands for 'Political Hypocrisy," *Academe* (September–October, 1991), p. 10.

30. Ibid., pp. 9–10.

31. Ibid., p. 11.

32. Louis Menand, "Illiberalisms," *The New Yorker*, May 20, 1991.

33. Anthony Desir's interview with Duke, which originally appeared in the November 23, 1981, issue of the *Dartmouth Review*, was reprinted (March 1, 1989) against the backdrop of Duke's grassroots popularity among working class whites in Louisiana. An editorial in a still more recent issue of the *Review* (March 4, 1992) also contains another unsympathetic interview further condemning Duke. It is interesting that between them, these two articles contain more straightforward evidence of Duke's racism than anything the "mainstream" press has produced.

34. Davidson, "'PH' Stands for Political Hypocrisy," p. 11

35. Fasaha M. Traylor, "Controversy on Campus," *Philadelphia Inquirer*, June 30, 1991; again, no specific arguments made by alleged proponents of racial inferiority are cited. These and a number of other attacks on D'Souza's character are documented in Heather McDonald, "D'Souza's Critics: PC Fights Back," *Academic Questions* 5 (Summer 1992), p. 10.

36. William Beer, "Sociology and the Effects of Affirmative Action: A Case of Neglect," *The American Sociologist* 19 (1988), pp. 218–31.

37. Frederick R. Lynch, "Surviving Affirmative Action (More or Less)," *Commentary* 90 (August 1990), p. 44.

38. Stephan Thernstrom, "McCarthyism Then and Now," *Academic Questions* 4 (Winter 1991), p. 16.

39. Stephen J. Ceci et al., "Human Subject Review, Personal Values, and the Regulation of Social Science Research," *American Psychologist* 40 (1985), pp. 994–1002 (quote is from p. 1000).

40. Nicholas Capaldi, *Out of Order: Affirmative Action and the Crisis of Doctrinaire Liberalism* (Buffalo, N.Y.: Prometheus, 1985), p. 95.

41. See Daniel Seligman, "The Case of Michael Levin," *National Review*, May 5, 1989.

42. See David L. Wheeler, "U. of Md. Conference That Critics Charge Might

Foster Racism Loses NIH Support," *The Chronicle of Higher Education,* September 2, 1992; "Meeting on Possible Links between Genes and Crime Canceled after Bitter Exchange," *The Chronicle of Higher Education,* September 16, 1992. Compare also David Wasserman, "In Defense of a Conference on Genetics and Crime: Assessing the Social Impact of a Public Debate," *The Chronicle of Higher Education,* September 23, 1992.

43. See Kimball, *Tenured Radicals,* chap. 7, "The Real Crisis in the Humanities," especially the rather depressing conclusion, pp. 184–89.

44. See David Mathews, "A Symposium on Freedom and Ideology: The Debate about Political Correctness," *Civic Arts Review* (Winter 1992), p. 4; Jean Elshtain, "Education beyond Politics," *Partisan Review* (Summer 1992), pp. 407–08; both quoted in *Telling the Truth: A Report on the State of the Humanities in Higher Education,* (Washington, D.C.: National Endowment for the Humanities, September 1992), p. 17.

45. Quoted in Dinesh D'Souza, *Illiberal Education* (New York: The Free Press, 1991), p. 172.

46. Quoted in Robert Royal, *1492 and All That: Political Manipulations of History* (Washington, D.C.: Ethics and Public Policy Center, 1992), p. 19.

47. See Clement W. Meighan, "The Burial of American Archeology," *Academic Questions* 6 (Summer 1993), pp. 9–19; quote is from a statement by Three Affiliated Tribes attorney Christopher Quayle, p. 9.

48. See Peter Monaghan, "'Critical Race Theory' Questions Role of Legal Doctrine in Racial Inequity," *The Chronicle of Higher Education,* June 23, 1993.

49. See Ellen K. Coughlin, "Feminist Economists vs. 'Economic Man': Questioning a Field's Bedrock Concepts," *The Chronicle of Higher Education,* June 30, 1993.

50. William Bennett et al., *A Nation at Risk* (Washington, D.C.: National Commission on Excellence in Education, 1983), p. 35.

51. See the account in Kimball, *Tenured Radicals,* pp. 7–8, 172–74, 185.

52. The Gallup Organization for the National Endowment for the Humanities, *A Survey of College Seniors: Knowledge of History and Literature* (Washington, D.C.: National Endowment for the Humanities, 1989).

53. The Public Opinion Laboratory at Northern Illinois University for the National Science Foundation, Washington, D.C., 1989.

54. See Mortimer Adler, "The Prewar Generation (1940)," reprinted in *Reforming Education: The Opening of the American Mind* (New York: Macmillan, 1988), pp. 3–10.

55. See Frank R. Harrison, "Plucking Minerva's Owl," *Modern Age* 21 (Spring 1977), pp. 173–83.

56. On this point see Ludwig Von Mises, *Planning for Freedom,* 4th ed. (South Holland, Ill.: Libertarian Press, 1980), p. 23. Mises' topic is government price controls; the same argument, however, can be applied to Social Engineering of whatever sort.

57. House Armed Services Committee No. 101-63, *Women in the Military,* Hearing Before the Military Personnel and Compensation Subcommittee of the Committee on Armed Services, March 20, 1990 (Washington, D.C.: Government Printing Office, 1990), p. 1.

58. Ibid., p. 3.

59. *The Presidential Commission on the Assignment of Women in the Armed Forces,* Report to the President, November 15, 1992 (Washington, D.C.: Government Printing Office, 1992), p. 5.

60. Ibid., p. 24.

61. Ibid., p. 9.

62. House Armed Services Committee No. 101-63, *Women in the Military,* p. 10.

63. Ibid.

64. Ibid., p. 25.

65. Ibid.

66. David Horowitz, *The Feminist Assault on the Military* (Studio City, Calif.: The Center for the Study of Popular Culture, 1992), pp. 24–25.

67. Ibid., p. 26.

68. House Armed Services Committee No. 101-63, *Women in the Military,* p. 9.

69. *The Presidential Commission Report to the President,* p. 43.

70. Ibid., p. 23.

71. Quoted in Horowitz, *The Feminist Assault,* p. 14.

72. See Midge Decter, "Homosexuality and the Schools," *Commentary* 95 (March 1993), pp. 19–25.

73. Chandler Burr, "Homosexuality and Biology," *The Atlantic Monthly* (March 1993), p. 48.

74. Ibid., p. 52.

75. Ibid., p. 55.

76. Ibid., p. 55.

77. E. Anthony Rotundo, "Where the Military's Antipathy to Homosexuals Came From," *The Chronicle of Higher Education,* March 31, 1993.

78. For a detailed development of this point see my "Civil Wrongs and Religious Liberty," *Journal of Interdisciplinary Studies* 6 (1994), forthcoming.

Chapter 6

1. See Ludwig von Mises, *Human Action,* 3d rev. ed. (Chicago: Henry Regnery, 1966), pp. 41–44, for the classic discussion of methodological individualism.

2. The following are representative: Ayn Rand, *The Virtue of Selfishness* (New York: New American Library, 1961), especially the essay "The Objectivist Ethics," pp. 13–35; Tibor R. Machan, *Individuals and Their Rights* (LaSalle, Ill.: Open Court, 1989); Eric Mack, "How to Derive Ethical Egoism," *The Personalist* 52 (1971), pp. 735–43, and "Individualism, Rights, and the Open Society," in *The Libertarian Alternative,* ed. Tibor R. Machan (Chicago: Nelson-Hall, 1974), pp. 21–37. For related views of David Norton, *Personal Destinies* (Princeton: Princeton University Press, 1976), Loren Lomasky, *Persons, Rights, and the Moral Community* (Oxford: Oxford University Press, 1987), and Jan Narveson, *The Libertarian Idea* (Philadelphia: Temple University Press, 1988).

3. See Richard C. Cornuelle, *Reclaiming the American Dream: The Role of Private Individuals and Voluntary Associations* (orig. pub. New York: Random House, 1965; 2d ed., New Brunswick, N.J.: Transaction Publishers, 1993). For more on the "independent sector" see below.

4. Friedrich A. Hayek, *The Constitution of Liberty* (Chicago: University of Chicago Press, 1960), p. 11.

5. Cornuelle, *Reclaiming the Dream*, p. 22.

6. Ibid., pp. 36 and 42.

7. Ibid., pp. 36–37.

8. Ibid., p. 39.

9. Ibid., p. 38.

10. Ibid., p. 50.

11. See ibid., p. 104, where Cornuelle writes:

> The people who do the country's work keep busy at it. Others talk to Congress about what they could do with more money and more power. Some people like to work; other people like to talk. Neither group is good at what they other does well. So it isn't natural for the independent sector to crow about what it does, to sell itself. Its institutions are scattered. They speak with no single voice.

In a footnote he adds:

> In any field in which you can get ahead with talk rather than results, you can observe the differing habits of the workers and the talkers. The worker hates committee meetings; the talker would rather meet than eat. The worker doesn't like to talk about how he gets his work done; the talker talks constantly about techniques he rarely practices. The worker hardly ever complains of overwork; the talker is always over his head in "work." I don't know why exactly, but the worker tends to speak plain English, while the talker speaks a kind of baroque and redundant prose. The worker is modest about what he'll get done; the talker is completely immodest about what he'll do tomorrow.

12. John Locke, *The Second Treatise of Civil Government* [1690](New York: Hafner, 1969), p. 134.

13. For a book-length argument in defense of this point see Richard A. Epstein, *Forbidden Grounds: The Case against Employment Anti-Discrimination Laws* (Cambridge, Mass.: Harvard University Press, 1993).

14. Quoted in James McPherson, *The Abolitionist Legacy* (Princeton: Princeton University Press, 1975), p. 72.

15. Thomas Sowell, *Markets and Minorities* (London: Basil Blackwell, 1981), p. 105. For a detailed discussion of the progress blacks were beginning to make in the post–Civil War era see Thomas Sowell, *Race and Economics* (New York: David McCay, 1975), chap. 2. For a brief discussion of blacks serving on juries see C. Vann Woodward, *The Strange Career of Jim Crow* (New York: Oxford University Press, 1974), p. 26.

16. Clint Bolick, *Changing Course: Civil Rights at the Crossroads* (New

Brunswick, N.J.: Transaction Publishers, 1988), chap. 2; compare also his *Unfinished Business: A Civil Rights Strategy for America's Third Century* (San Francisco: Pacific Research Institute, 1990), pt. 2.

17. Bolick, *Changing Course,* p. 33. For the full story see Woodward, *The Strange Career of Jim Crow.*

18. Woodward, *The Strange Career of Jim Crow,* p. 82.

19. Bolick, *Changing Course,* p. 35. For an account of the results of a number of black schools see Thomas Sowell, "Patterns of Black Excellence," *in Education: Assumptions vs. History* (Stanford: Hoover Press, 1986), pp. 10–32.

20. Bolick, *Changing Course,* p. 37.

21. Quoted in ibid., p. 36.

22. Quoted in ibid., p. 37.

23. Walter Williams, *The State against Blacks* (New York: McGraw-Hill, 1982).

24. Ibid., p. 32.

25. Ibid., p. 34.

26. See Mises's discussion in Ludwig Von Mises, *Planning for Freedom,* 4th ed. (South Holland, Ill.: Libertarian Press, 1980), 18–28; this essay also contains an illuminating discussion of price controls and their negative effects.

27. See Jacob Mincer, "Unemployment Effects of Minimum Wages," *Journal of Political Economy* 84 (1976), pp. 87–105, whom Williams cites as a source; also Peter Linneman, "The Economic Impacts of Minimum Wage Laws: A New Look at an Old Question," *Journal of Political Economy* 90 (1982), pp. 443–69.

28. Williams, *The State against Blacks,* p. 43; Williams's source here is the U. S. Census Bureau.

29. Henry Hazlitt, *Economics in One Lesson* (New York: Manor Books, 1962 ed.), p. 141.

30. A good short discussion, with a wide range of examples, can be found in S. David Young, *The Rule of Experts: Occupational Licensing in America* (Washington, D.C.: The Cato Institute, 1987).

31. See Richard Freeman, "The Effect of Occupational Licensing on Black Occupational Attainment," in Simon Rottenberg, ed., *Occupational Licensing and Regulation* (Washington, D.C.: American Enterprise Institute, 1980), pp. 165–79; see also Stuart Dorsey, "Occupational Licensing and Minorities," *Law and Human Behavior* 7 (1983), pp. 171–82.

32. All data are from Williams, *The State against Blacks,* p. 76.

33. Personal communication from Walter Williams to Diane Bast, September 1991.

34. Williams, *The State against Blacks,* pp. 80–81. In 1979 the commission voted to award operating rights to a taxi association that had formerly been excluded; the action was contested by the established United and Yellow Cab Companies (p. 81).

35. One thinks here of leading Afro-American antischolar Houston Baker's spirited defense of the rap groups Public Enemy and N.W.A. (Niggas with Attitude). These groups' lyrics are filled with expletives and references to violence against whites. The controversy over the song "Cop Killer" by the black heavy metal/rap crossover group Body Count, fronted by rapper Ice-T, should also be

mentioned in this context, as this song, too, has been defended by leading Afro-American antischolars.

36. For education see John E. Chubb and Terry M. Moe, *Politics, Markets, and America's Schools* (Washington, D.C.: The Brookings Institute, 1990), Myron Lieberman, *Privatization and Educational Choice* (New York: St. Martin's Press, 1989), and Joseph and Diane Bast, eds., *Rebuilding America's Schools* (Chicago: The Heartland Institute, 1991); for homelessness see William Tucker, *The Excluded Americans* (Washington, D.C.: Regnery-Gateway, 1989); for the drug crisis see David Boaz, ed., *The Crisis in Drug Prohibition* (Washington, D.C.: The Cato Institute, 1990) and Mark Thornton, *The Economics of Prohibition* (Salt Lake City, Utah: University of Utah Press, 1991). These can be added to our remarks about minimum wage laws and government-mandated occupational licensure laws as means by which government actions harm minorities.

37. Compare Glenn C. Loury, *Achieving the Dream: A Challenge to Liberals and Conservatives in the Spirit of Martin Luther King, Jr.* (Washington, D.C.: The Heritage Foundation, 1990); Clarence Thomas, *Why Black Americans Should Look to Conservative Policies* (Washington, D.C.: The Heritage Foundation, 1987). Compare again Shelby Steele, *The Content of Our Character* (New York: St. Martin's Press, 1990).

38. Johnson tells his own story in his recent book *Succeeding against the Odds: The Autobiography of a Great American Businessman* (New York: Amistad Press, 1989). The information in the following paragraphs comes straight out of this book.

39. Ibid., pp. 49–51.

40. Ibid., p. 126.

41. Ibid., p. 90.

42. Ibid., pp. 37–38.

43. Ibid., pp. 46–47.

44. Ibid., pp. 88–89.

45. Ibid., p. 95.

46. Ibid., p. 116.

47. Ibid., p. 139.

48. Ibid., p. 140.

49. Ibid., p. 75.

50. Ibid., pp. 75–76.

51. Ibid., pp. 89–90.

Conclusion

1. See Frederick R. Lynch, *Invisible Victims: White Males and the Crisis of Affirmative Action,* (Westport, Conn.: Greenwood Press, 1989) chap. 1.

2. See Edith Efron, "Native Son," *Reason* (February 1992), pp. 22–32, for evidence of the extent to which the Senate Judiciary Committee failed to understand, much less appreciate, Justice Thomas's beliefs and intellectual roots; or see Arch Puddington, "Clarence Thomas and the Blacks," *Commentary* (February 1992), pp. 28–33, for an account of how Thomas had already earned the emnity

of the "official" civil rights leadership simply by asserting intellectual independence instead of following the party line on such issues as affirmative action and quotas. Finally, and most importantly, see David Brock, "The Real Anita Hill," *The American Spectator* (March 1992), pp. 18–30, for a very detailed and ultimately devastating account of the inconsistencies and sometimes downright absurdities in Hill's testimony that Thomas sexually harassed her while she was working under his authority at the EEOC. It should come as no surprise that this article has received an official blackout by media and government elites. Brock, undaunted, expanded his account into a full-length book, *The Real Anita Hill* (New York: The Free Press, 1993). This book, too, has met with either the silent treatment or official denunciation.

3. See David Horowitz and Peter Collier, *Destructive Generation: Second Thoughts about the '60s* (New York: Summit Books, 1989), for some commentary on this period made all the more pithy by the fact that these two authors, as ex-radicals, were participants in the movements that shaped that decade. See also Allan Bloom, *The Closing of the American Mind,* (New York: Simon and Schuster, 1987), which remains the most trenchant commentary on how the universities caved in to the demands of student radicals and have been going downhill ever since.

4. Anyone doubting this should review the history of the spat between philosopher Christina Sommers and the discipline's feminist Establishment which began in December of 1987 at the major Eastern Division Meeting of the American Philosophical Association, the largest association of professional academic philosophers in the country. Sommers presented a paper entitled "The Philosophers' War against the Family." The immediate response, some of which I observed, consisted of gasps and hisses that soon evolved into catcalls. Neither the other panel participants nor anyone else made any serious effort to maintain order, and the meeting degenerated into chaos. The fact that such an event was unprecedented in the history of the organization ought to cast doubt, to reasonable people at least, on the claim of its perpetrators to the label *scholar* and expose the intellectual hollowness of the "postmodernist" blurring of scholarship and political activity.

Jeane Kirkpatrick is probably the most prominent speaker who can offer first-hand reports of similar encounters with academic and student radicals; see her "My Experience with Academic Intolerance," *Academic Questions* 3 (Fall 1989), pp. 21–29. But one of the most blatant and inexcusable cases occurred back in 1985 when left extremist Barbara Foley, leader of a group that called itself InCAR (International Committee Against Racism) led the disruption of an appearance at Northwestern University by Nicaraguan rebel leader Adolfo Calero, a disruption which included what amounted to a physical assault during which red liquid was hurled on him to symbolize the "blood on his hands." See the reprinted "Decision in the Matter of Professor Barbara Foley," *Academic Questions* 1 (Winter 1987–88).

I witnessed one of these events back in 1981 at the campus where I was then beginning my graduate studies in philosophy, when a visiting Nicaraguan leader of the Contras was shouted down and finally hounded from his podium by the local radical contingent in Athens, Georgia. I had very little sympathy with the "Reagan Revolution" that was then going on; nevertheless, this event led me to doubts about the motives of those who refused to let a speaker with whom they disagreed have his say years before the idea of investigating affirmative action and its foundations ever entered my mind.

5. For the specifics of this case see Lena Williams, "Judge Sets Deadline for Yonkers to Submit Plan for Desegregation," *New York Times,* December 19, 1985; Arnold H. Lubasch, "Ruling Is Upheld on Yonkers Bias: Federal Court Affirms Order for School Desegregation," *New York Times,* December 29, 1987; Elizabeth Kolbert, "Crisis in Yonkers: Applying Pressure; Many Are Trying to Steer Clear of the Controversy," *New York Times,* August 11, 1988; James Feron, "Yonkers Council Balks at Shift in Housing Plan," *New York Times,* September 29, 1988; et al.

6. Shelby Steele, *The Content of Our Character,* (New York: St. Martin's Press, 1990), p. 119.

7. Friedrich A. Hayek, *The Road to Serfdom* (Chicago: University of Chicago Press, 1994).

8. Originally published as "Die Wirtschaftsnechnung in sozialistischen Gemeinwesen," in *Archiv fur Sozialnissenschaften* 42 (1920). The first English-language version appeared in Friedrich A. Hayek, ed., *Collectivist Economic Planning* (London: George Routledge and Sons, 1935); long out of print, it was recently republished by the Mises Institute (1990).

9. Originally *Die Gemeinwirtschaft: Untersuchungen über den Sozialismus* (Jena: Gustav Fischer, 1922). The first English translation as *Socialism: An Economic and Sociological Analysis,* trans. J. Kahane (London: Jonathan Cape, 1936), soon went out of print. By this time Mises was an emigré struggling on the margins of academe in New York University's business school; his work was republished by Yale University Press in the early 1950s and again was allowed to go out of print. *Socialism* was finally republished (Indianapolis: Liberty *Classics,* 1981). This seminal work convinced Hayek to abandon collectivism.

10. Nicholas Capaldi, *Out of Order: Affirmative Action and the Crisis of Doctrine Liberalism,* (Buffalo, N.Y.: Prometheus, 1985) pp. 141, 151, 153–66, and elsewhere.

Index